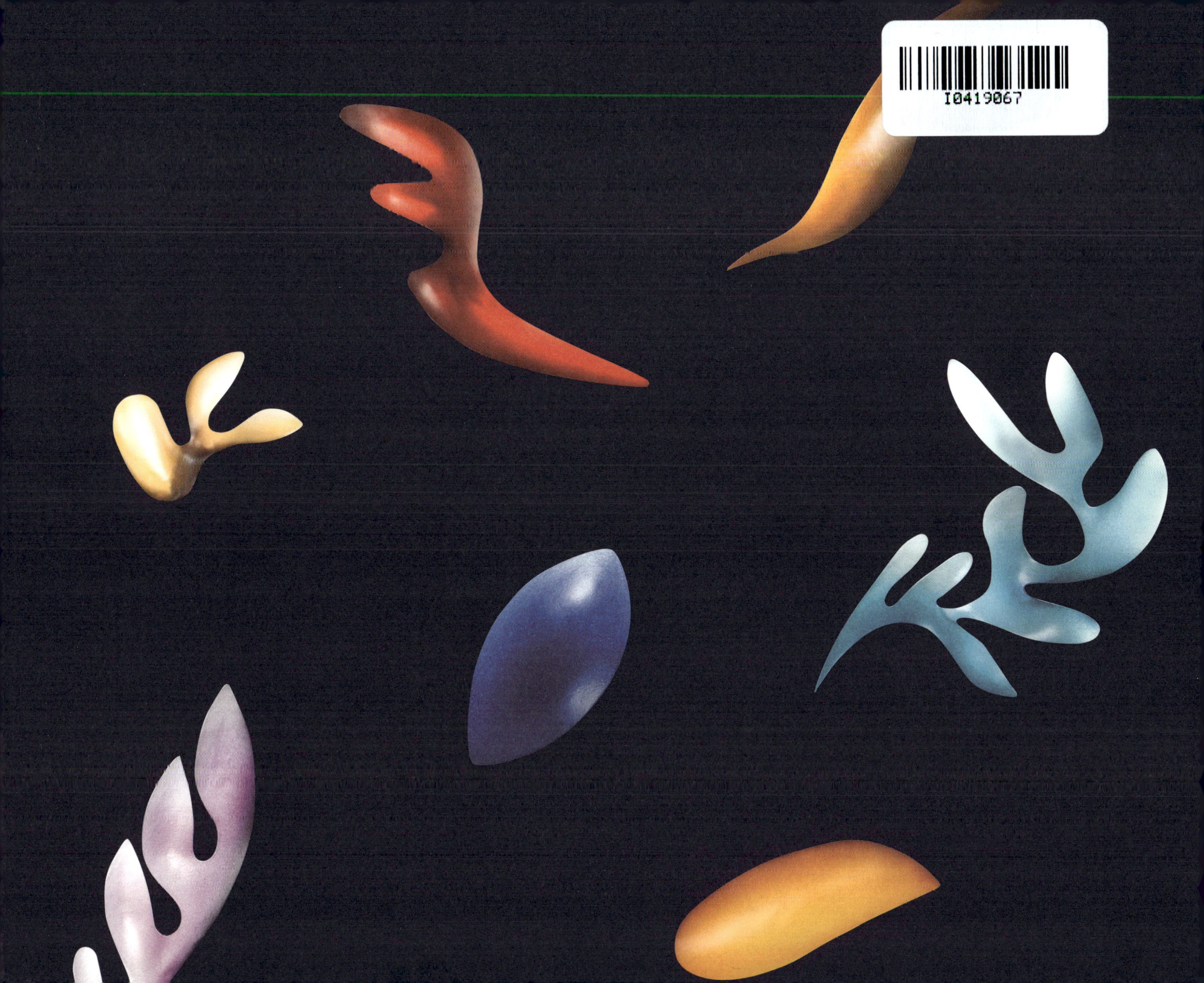

ODE TO JOY

THE ART OF
MARK DAVIS

Essay by Jeanne V. Koles

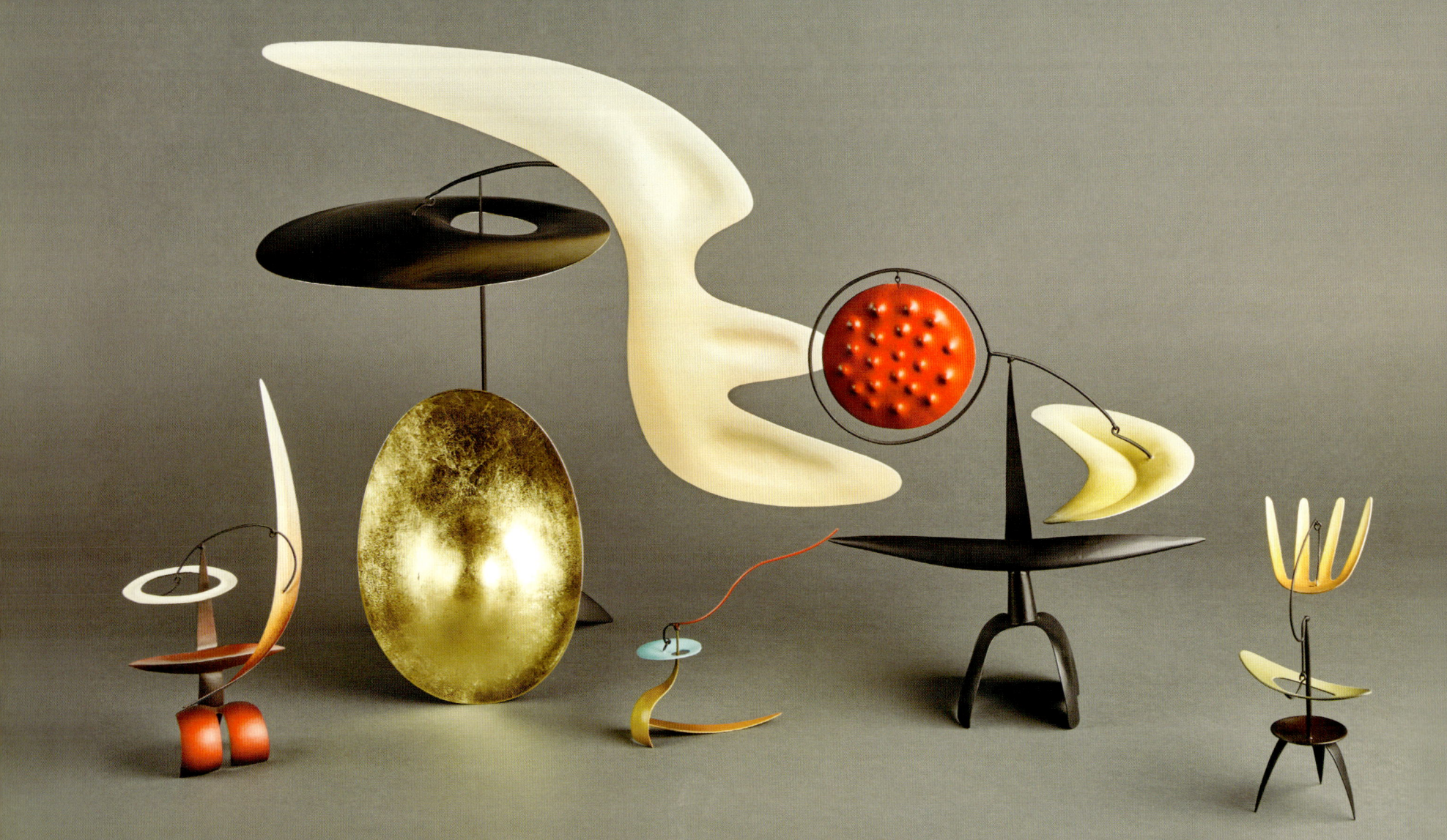

ODE TO JOY

THE ART OF
MARK DAVIS

Essay by Jeanne V. Koles

Pucker Art Publications

ODE TO JOY

THE ART OF
MARK DAVIS

Essay by Jeanne V. Koles

Library of Congress Control Number: 2015959644
Library of Congress
US Programs, Law, and Literature Division
Cataloging in Publication Program
101 Independence Avenue, S.E.
Washington, DC 20540-4283

ISBN Number: 9781879985315

Design: Leslie Anne Feagley
Editors: Destiny M. Barletta and Aubrey Catrone

Published by Pucker Art Publications
Boston, MA 02116

Distributed by Syracuse University Press
Syracuse, NY 13244

Printed in China by Toppan Leefung Printing Limited
Hong Kong

Cover:
BELLE EPOQUE
Wall-mounted mobile in brass and aluminum with steel wires, and oil and acrylic colors
24 x 61 x 11"
MD687

Back cover:
GLORY BOUND, 2015
Standing mobile in brass and aluminum, with steel wires, oil and acrylic colors, and 23K gold leaf
19 x 21 x 11"
MD712

Frontispiece (left to right):

LITTLE SOLDIER	GLORY BOUND	GOING AHEAD	A NEW GENTLE FORCE	MODERN MOVEMENT
Standing mobile in brass and aluminum with steel wires, and oil and acrylic colors	Standing mobile in brass and aluminum with steel wires, oil and acrylic colors, and 23K gold leaf	Standing mobile in brass with steel wires, and oil and acrylic colors	Standing mobile in brass and aluminum with steel wires, and oil and acrylic colors	Standing mobile in brass and aluminum with steel wires, and oil and acrylic colors
10 x 9 x 5"	19 x 21 x 11"	7 x 9 x 2.25"	13.5 x 12 x 10"	8 x 4.5 x 4"
MD703	MD712	MD715	MD705	MD674

TABLE OF CONTENTS

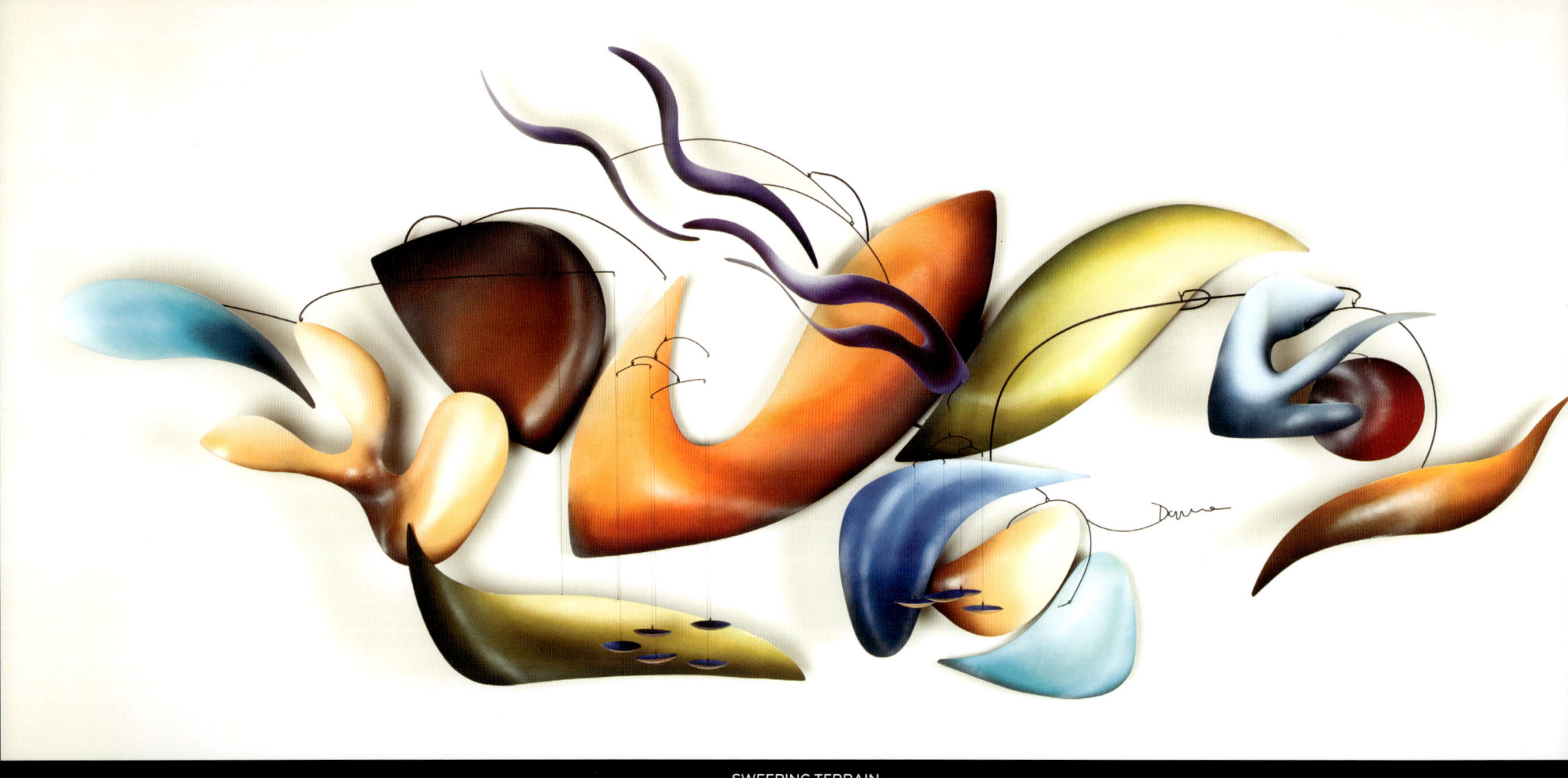

SWEEPING TERRAIN
Wall-mounted mobile in brass and aluminum with steel wires, and oil and acrylic colors
44 x 98 x 17"
MD669

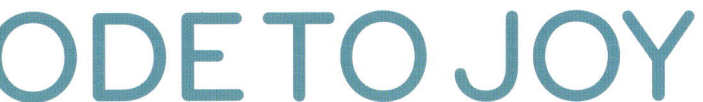

ODE TO JOY

The Art of Mark Davis

by JEANNE V. KOLES

When Mark Davis entered the world of mobiles, the genre had a notable art historical pedigree but few accomplished contemporary practitioners. The term "mobile" was coined by Dadaist Marcel Duchamp (1887–1968) in 1931 to describe Alexander Calder's (1898–1976) earliest moving creations. Calder's aesthetic was very much *du jour*, an active and dimensional take on the abstract paintings of artists like Piet Mondrian (1872–1942) and the Surrealist paintings and sculptures of Joan Miró (1893–1983). Kinetic art reached a crescendo of popularity post-World War II, when the Bauhaus philosophy of design catalyzed an international exploration of the style. In 1955, French gallerist Denise René (1913-2012), staged the watershed exhibit *Le Mouvement,* featuring artists such as Duchamp, Calder, Victor Vasarely (1906-1997), Yaacov Agam (b. 1928), and Jean Tinguely (1925-1991), among others. Published during the exhibition, Vasarely's "Yellow Manifesto" served as a founding document for the movement, announcing the death of easel painting and proclaiming that art should bring joy and beauty to human beings and create peace and harmony. By the 1960s, kinetic art came stateside with numerous exhibitions at the Howard Wise Gallery and *The Magic Theater* exhibitions organized by The Nelson Atkins Museum in 1968. Kinetic art had developed from Calder's manual engineering to a more technologically-driven approach.

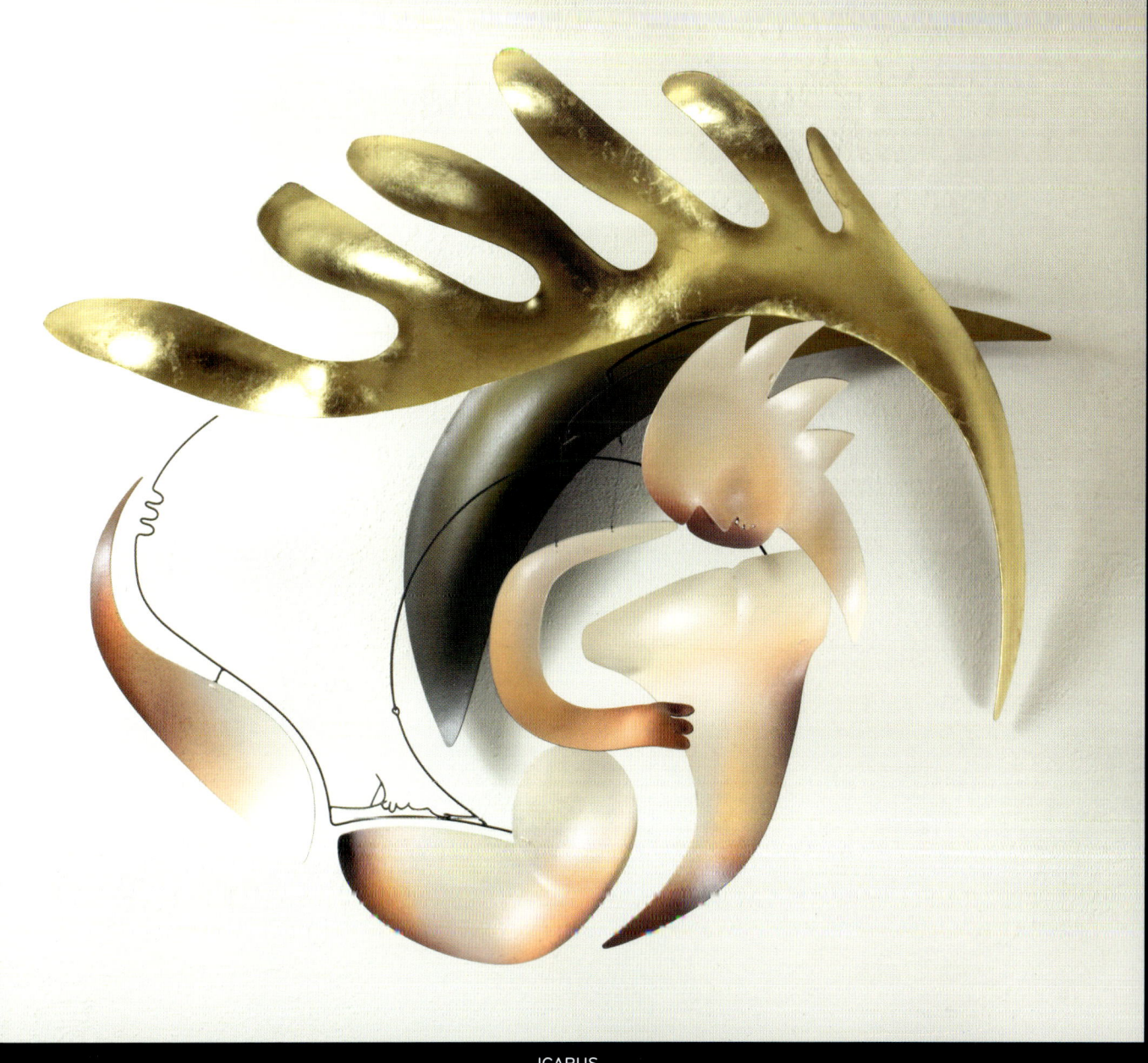

ICARUS
Wall-mounted mobile in brass and aluminum with steel wires, acrylic colors, and 23K gold leaf

REVERBERATING
GRAVITY
Hanging mobile in
brass and aluminum
with steel wires, oil
and acrylic colors,
and 23K gold leaf
68 x 55 x 58"
MD622

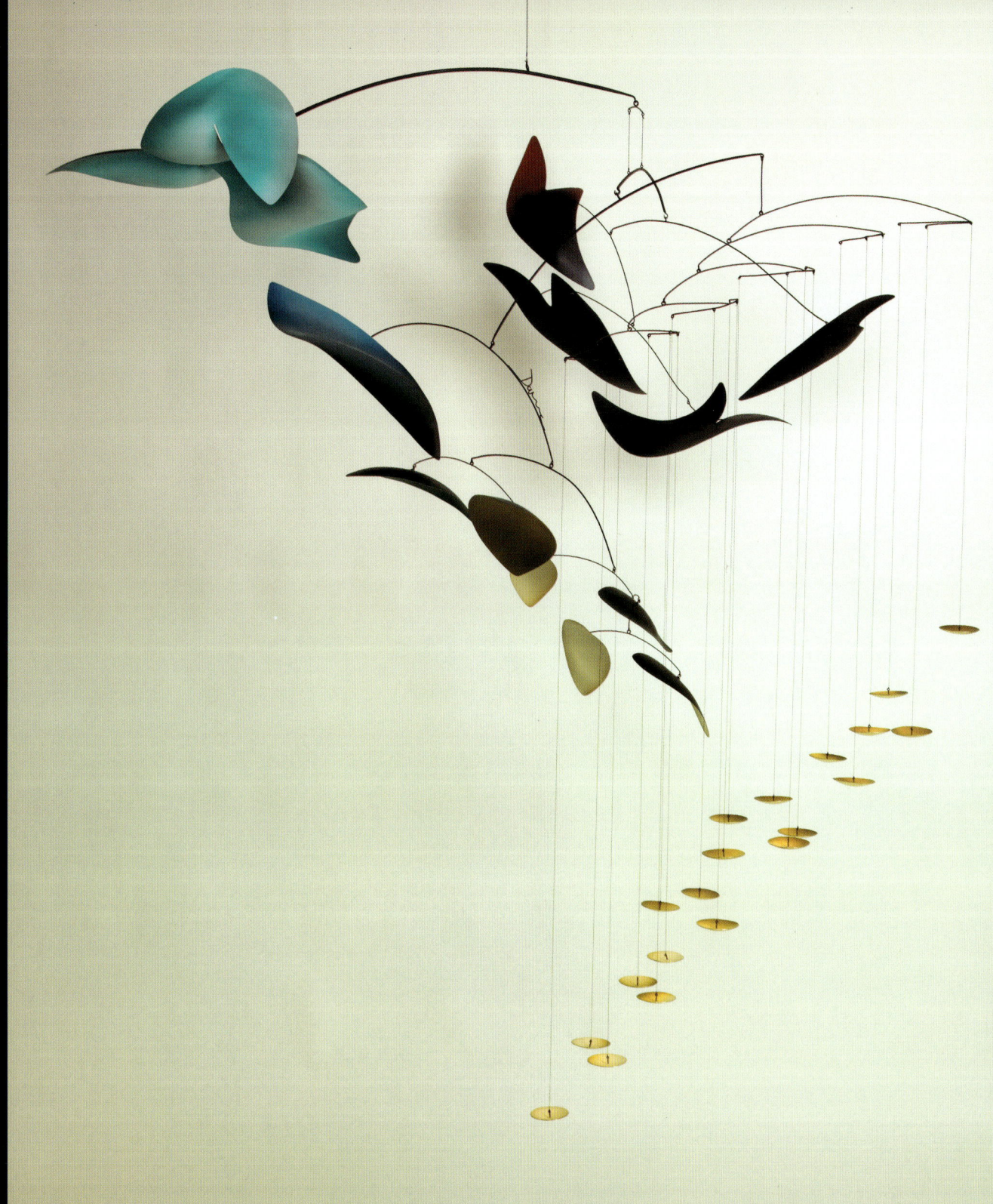

In many ways, Davis's mobiles pay homage to the interwar period of Modern Art. They celebrate the essential beauty of an art form where balance is achieved solely through the genius of the artist. Movement only comes from the breath of air or the gentle touch of a human being. The artist composes motion through the thoughtful interplay of individual elements, always cognizant of the synergy of the compiled elements with their surroundings. Each shape is like a stanza in a poem or a phrase in a song—economically crafted yet highly expressive, beautiful when unaccompanied but exponentially more powerful when taken in concert with its cohorts. *Reverberating Gravity* (p. 6) gracefully harmonizes weightier elements in its upper register with a series of delicate golden forms cascading downward, generating a gentle tension between hard edges and soft surfaces, substance and effervescence. Davis's artwork embodies many of the characteristics in Vasarely's manifesto: joy, beauty, peace, and harmony.

Lao Tzu philosophized that, "Knowing others is wisdom, knowing yourself is Enlightenment." The path to self-knowing is neither divined, straight, nor singular. Each individual must determine their own route, acknowledging the journey instead of focusing on the destination. For Mark Davis, art-making is an avenue of self-discovery and a vehicle for expressing his hopes and dreams. Joy is born from his art, and through it he delivers that joy to us. He once said, "My real training has been to follow and listen to my inner intuition, allowing my mind to open up to inner secrets." In his deepest understanding of himself, and in the outward expression of his artwork, Davis has chosen to privilege joy over everything else.

Davis's mobiles are an apt metaphor for the artist himself. Being an artist is the stable underpinning, the

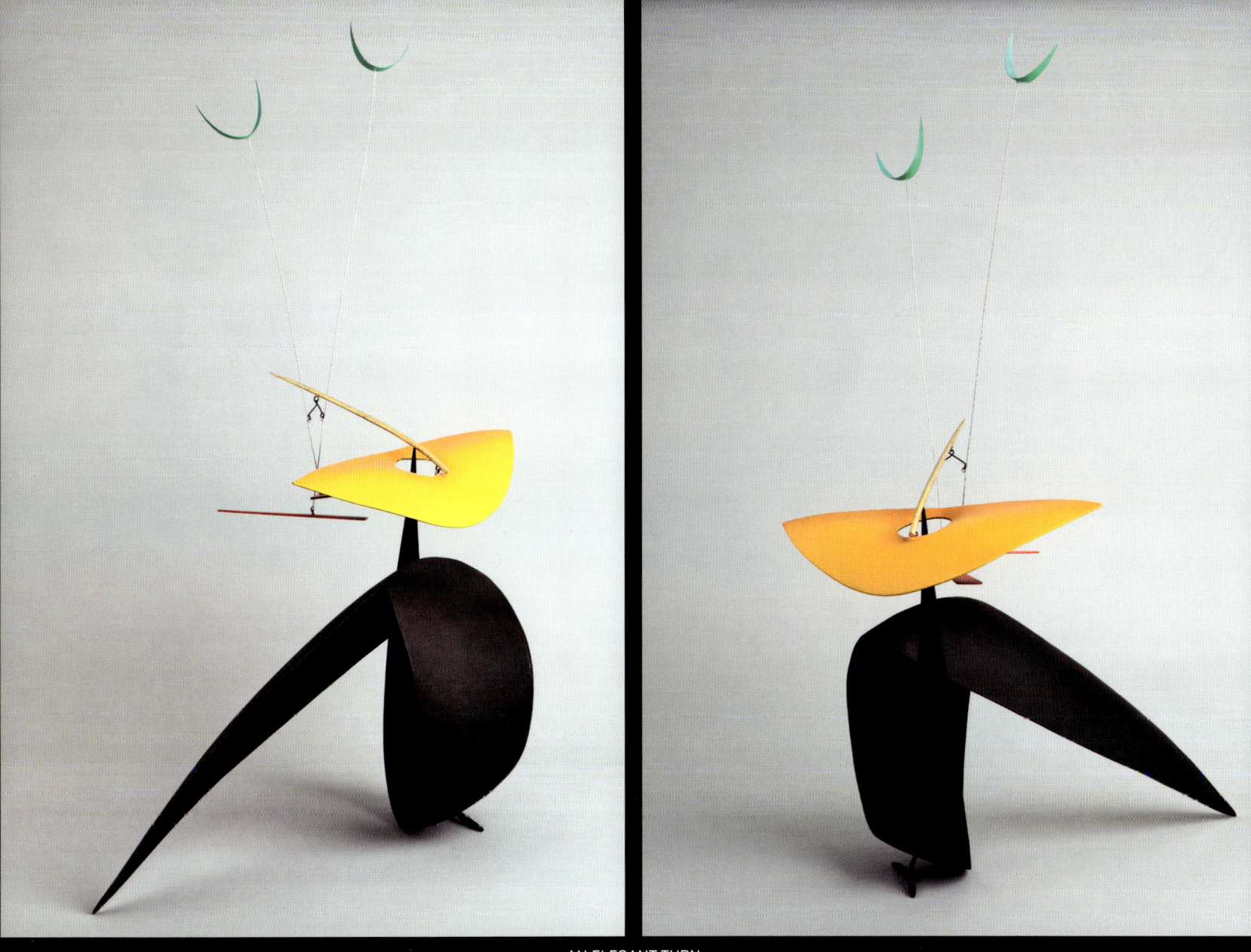

AN ELEGANT TURN
Standing mobile in steel and brass with stainless steel wires, and 23K gold leaf
29 x 16.5 x 12"
MD248

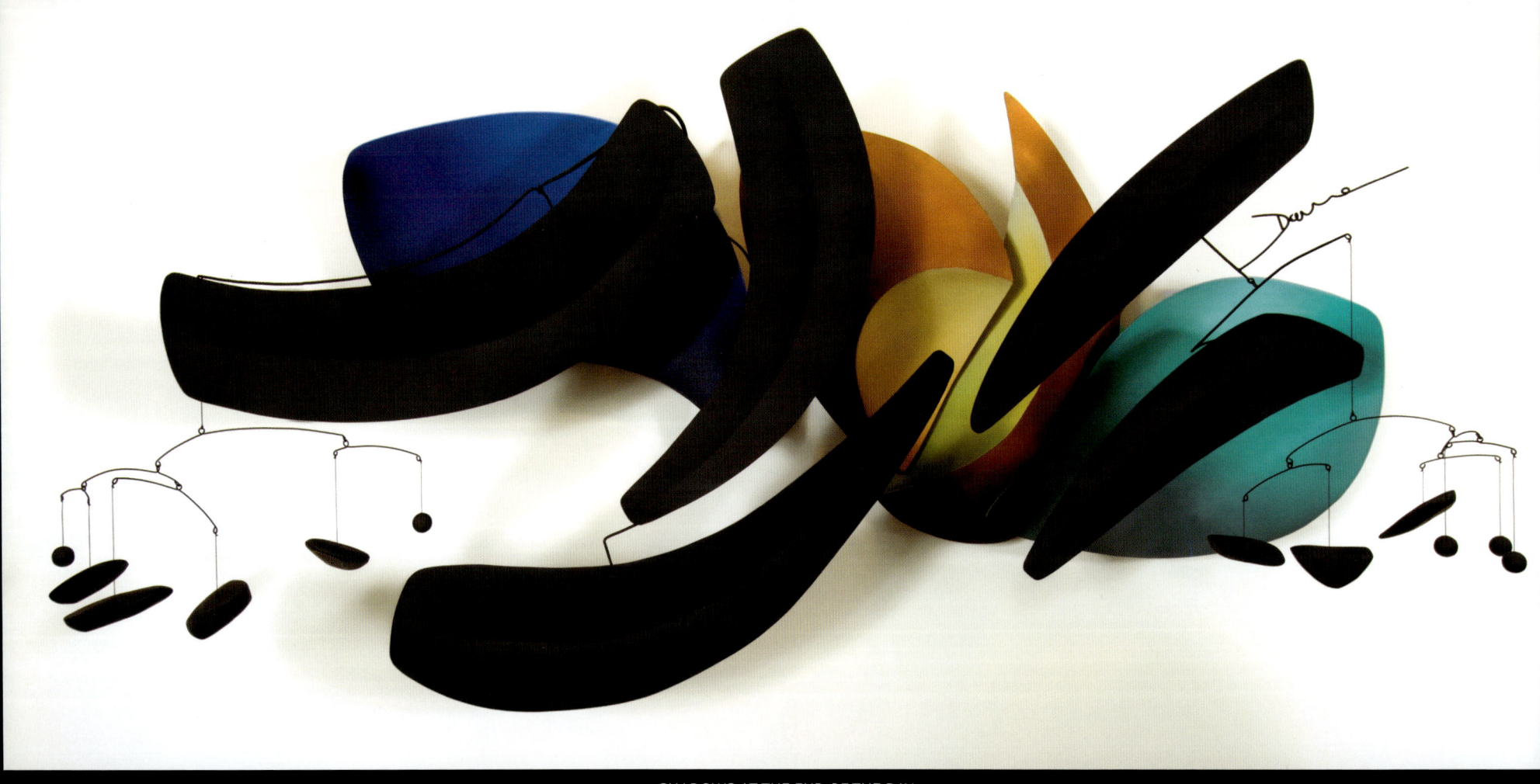

SHADOWS AT THE END OF THE DAY
Wall-mounted mobile in brass and aluminum with steel wires, and acrylic colors
23 x 46 x 12"
MD459

fulcrum, around which his world swirls. Energy shoots out from that concrete point, mimicking the soul. A playful tension emanates between balance and motion, strength and delicacy. He has written that, "Through abstract shapes I play with the concepts of space. My ideas come from organic life, the human form, and the external landscape, while deeply reflecting my internal landscape and dialogue. The work is playful, joyful, and always changing, and that is the way I see and experience life in all its complexities." Such bold and spirited artistic self-expression is the public face of a modest and private man who, like all of us, has experienced his share of setbacks and suffering. As thirteenth-century Persian poet and Sufi mystic Rumi wrote, "Why should I stay at the bottom of a well when a strong rope is in my hand?" This kind of purposefulness takes effort, though Davis is humble about his own accomplishments in this way.

Mark Davis was born in New Haven, Connecticut but grew up mostly near South Bend, Indiana. His father, Walter Davis, was an English professor who taught at Harvard, Yale, MIT, and Williams, and was head of the department at Notre Dame, then Brown in the 1980s. He received his doctorate from Yale in 1957, was a scholar of English Renaissance literature, and wrote on Elizabethan poetry and fiction. He was an active collector of Ancient Greek coins and one of sixteen elected members of The Society Historia Numorum in Boston. Davis's mother, Yolanda Leiss Davis, was a violin player, a concert musician, and a soloist. She gained a reputation for virtuosity in playing antique instruments like the Baroque and Renaissance viol da gamba and the rebec, another Renaissance stringed instrument popular from the thirteenth to sixteenth centuries. Yolanda was an expert in Medieval music, and while the family lived in Indiana, she played

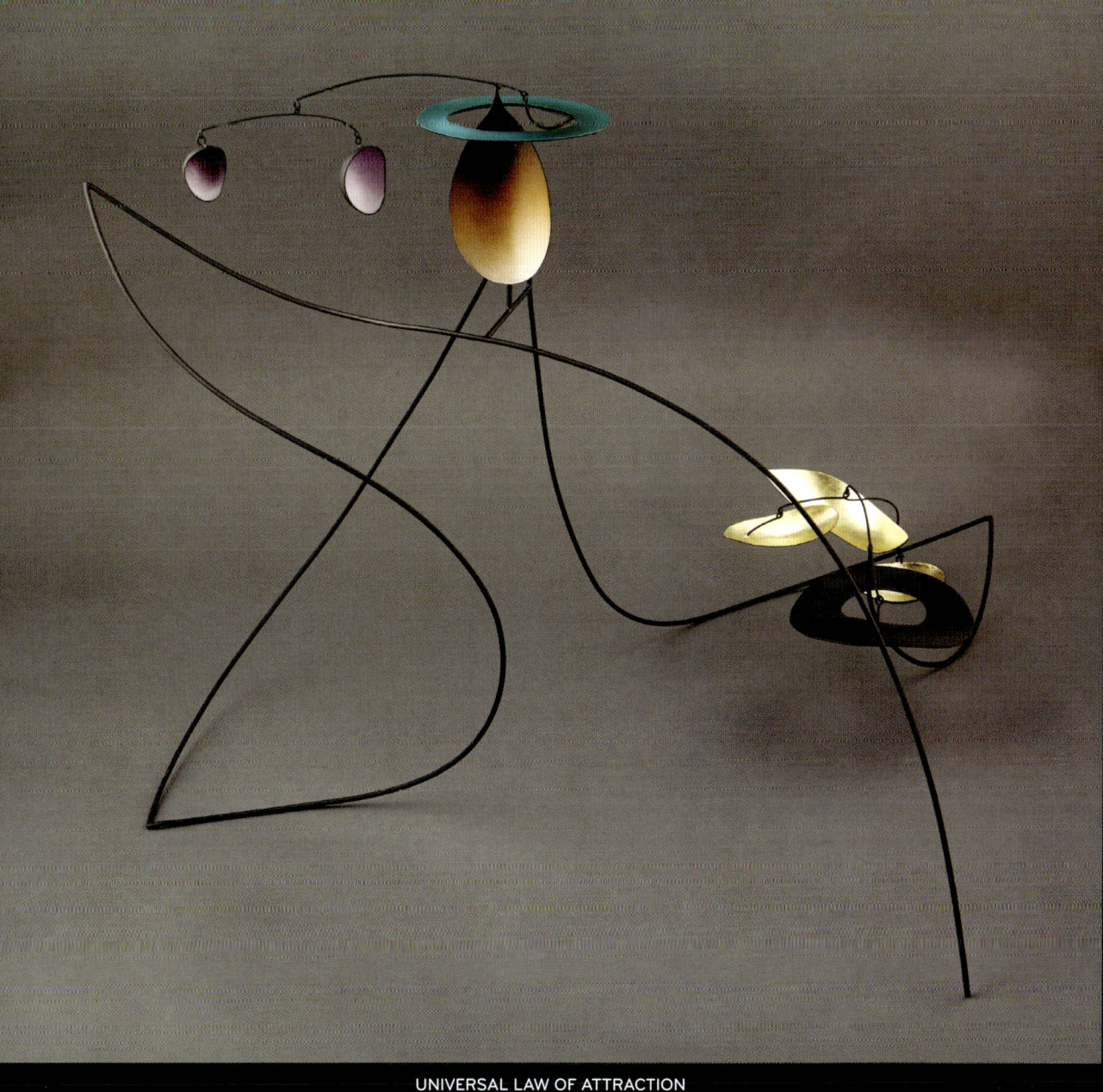

UNIVERSAL LAW OF ATTRACTION
Standing mobile in brass and aluminum with steel wires, oil and acrylic colors, and 23K gold leaf

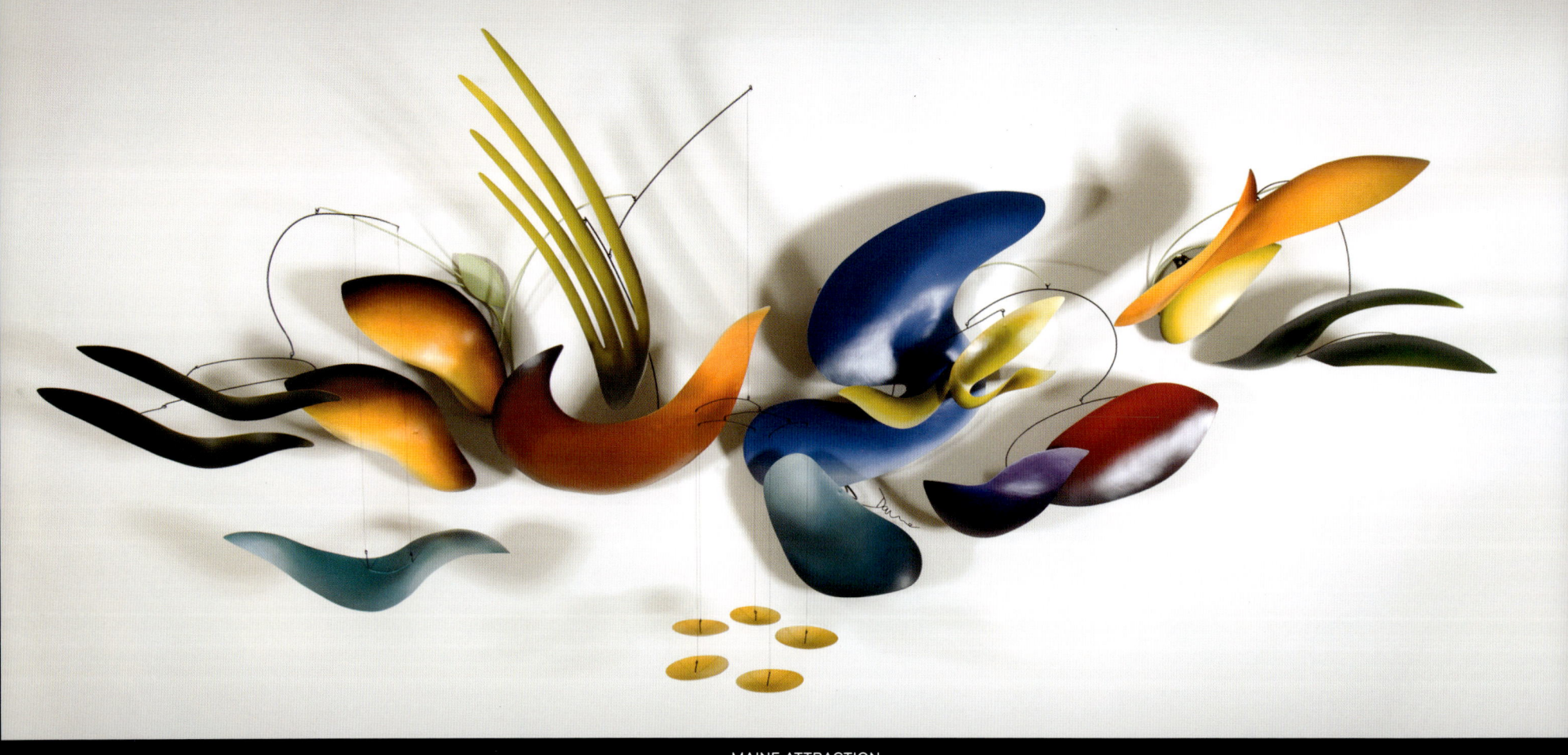

MAINE ATTRACTION

professionally in Chicago. Davis is the oldest of five children, including his sisters Alison, Catherine, and Elizabeth, and his brother Peter. Walter wanted the children to be intellectual, while Yolanda encouraged their creative pursuits. He was an academic. She was an elegant bohemian.

Yolanda suffered from extreme bipolar disorder, so life in the Davis household was touched by sadness and greatly affected by her frame of mind. Davis was generally a withdrawn but good, domestic, and thoughtful child. When he was eighteen, Davis left home to attend college and never returned. Shortly after, his mother passed away. Yolanda's death by suicide was a tragic end to her story and a mournful time for the family.

Throughout his youth, Davis was exposed to the arts, mostly the Medieval and Renaissance periods, which were of interest to his parents. From an early age, art-making came naturally and gave him purpose. He remembers enjoying the process of creation: puppets, wire constructions, woodcuts, and more. His dad had few tools, almost making a deliberate show of not being good with his hands. But Davis was resourceful. Using whatever materials he could find, such as eggshells and other delicate items around the house, he worked hours into the night with hardware-store wire and a pair of pliers. He was a gifted draughtsman and his realistic pencil drawings won local prizes throughout his youth. At ten-years-old, he found a book from which he learned to score and fold paper to make three-dimensional constructions. A few years later, at the local library in Indiana, Davis came across a book about Alexander Calder that spoke to him. He could hardly wait to get home and try assembling mobiles for himself. The young Davis had no trouble recreating the moving sculptures he saw in the book. On that day, he was given the gift of artistic language that he has worked with ever since.

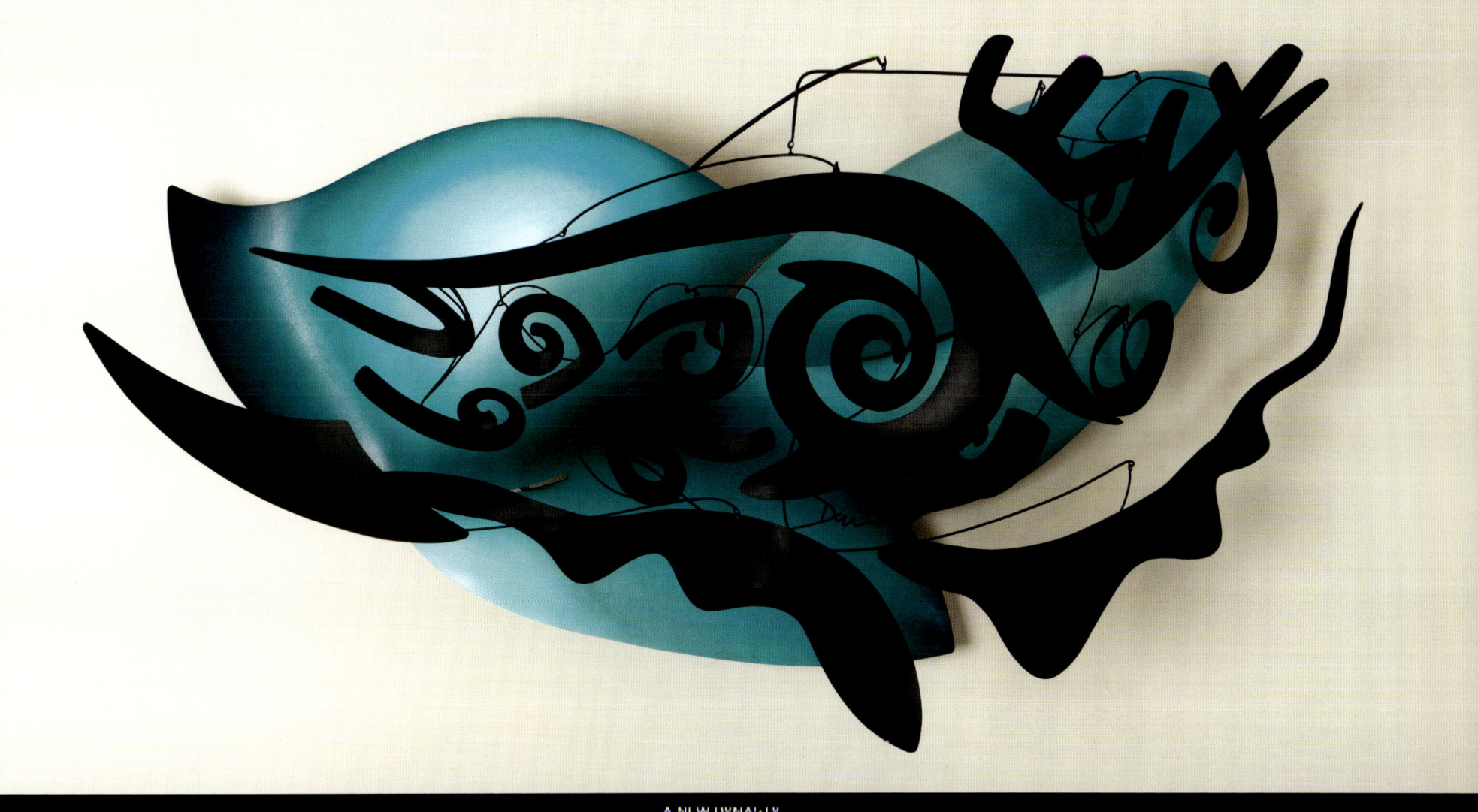

A NEW DYNASTY
Wall-mounted mobile in brass and aluminum with steel wires, and oil and acrylic colors
22.5 x 38.5 x 18"
MD629

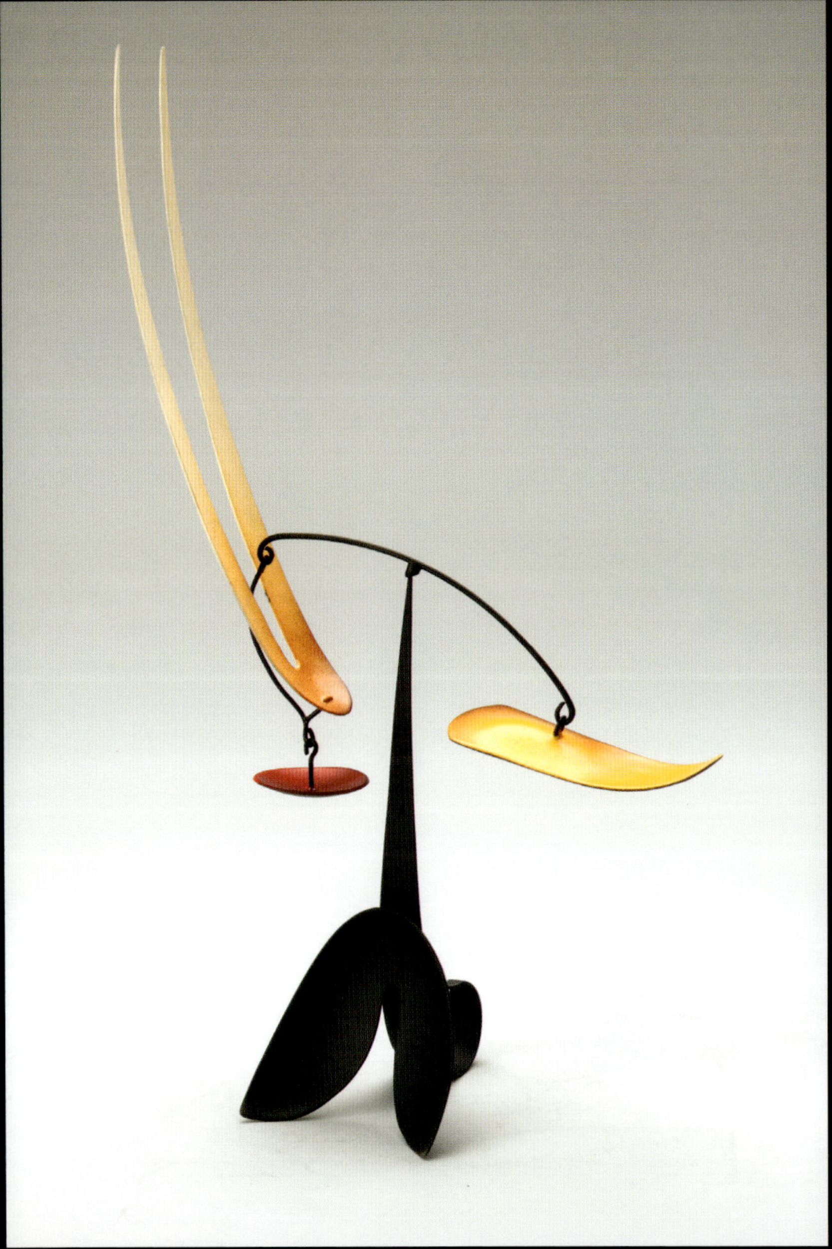

MISS ANGELIQUE
Standing mobile in brass and aluminum with steel wires, and oil and acrylic colors
11.5 x 7 x 2.5"

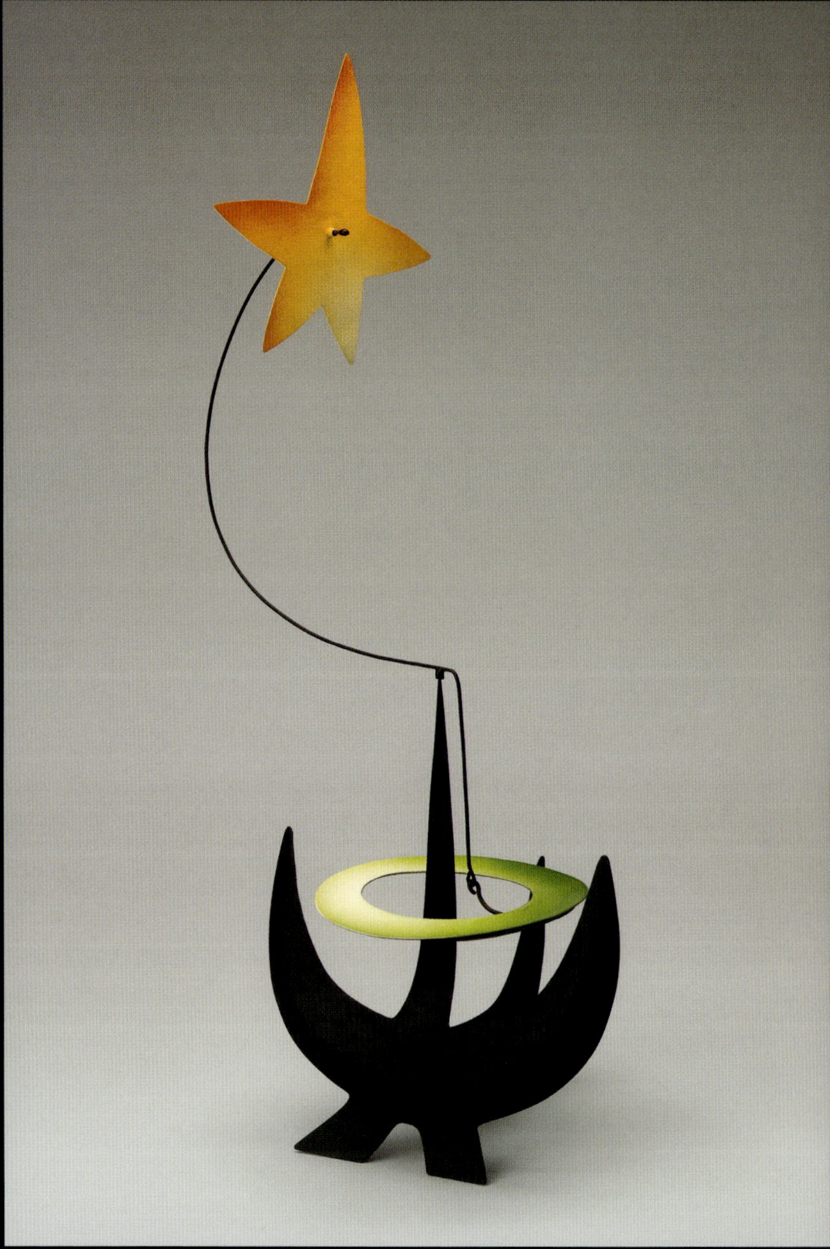

HOMAGE TO THE STAR
Standing mobile in brass and aluminum with steel wires, and oil and acrylic colors
18 x 9 x 6"

At fifteen-years-old, Davis began making jewelry in the style of Calder. Though better known for his iconic mobiles, Calder produced approximately 1,800 pieces of jewelry made of brass, silver, and gold. He embellished them with found objects such as sea glass, ceramic shards, and wood. Calder was not a trained jeweler, eshewing the traditional techniques of linking and soldering. He mostly gave the pieces to family and friends rather than selling them. His more primitive approach to jewelry as body ornamentation was influential for Davis, who experimented with a similarly innovative approach throughout high school. Davis's beautiful mother often proudly wore his work, and he had a small stint after high school selling jewelry at a local South Bend shop.

Pablo Picasso once said, "Every child is an artist. The problem is how to remain an artist once we grow up." For Davis, the notion of becoming a professional artist was never in his plan, if there even was a plan. It was important to his father that he attend college, though Davis had little interest. Mere consideration of college meant moving east. Davis wanted to escape an area he described as closed-minded, racially charged, and suffering from terrible unemployment. He insisted on moving to an area that embraced the progressive lifestyle he wished to live. His search for a creative school with a non-traditional curriculum brought him to Vermont's Goddard College in 1972. Despite the tolerant and artistic environment of the school, Davis still felt ill at ease. He was a hippie from the Midwest with long hair and mutton chops. By that time, his mother was residing in a state mental hospital, and he felt isolated. He dropped every class except weaving, and started squatting in a small, defunct jewelry studio on campus. He recalls one day when a young woman wandered in, sat down, and taught him how to solder.

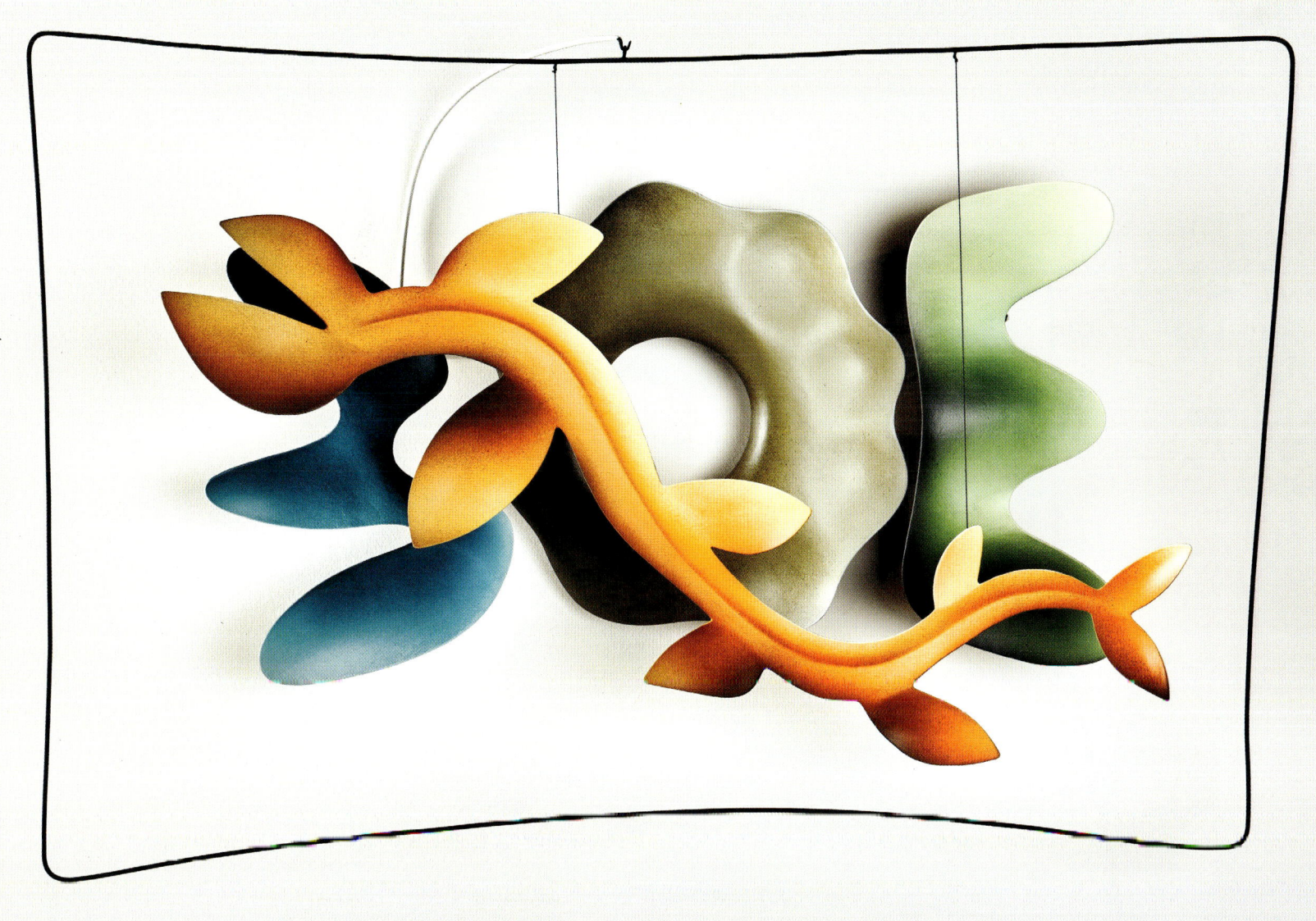

PIONEER
Wall-hanging mobile in brass and aluminum with steel wires, and oil and acrylic colors

EVENING MAJESTY
Hanging mobile in
brass and aluminum
with steel wires, oil
and acrylic colors,
and 23K gold leaf
72 x 75 x 60"
MD530

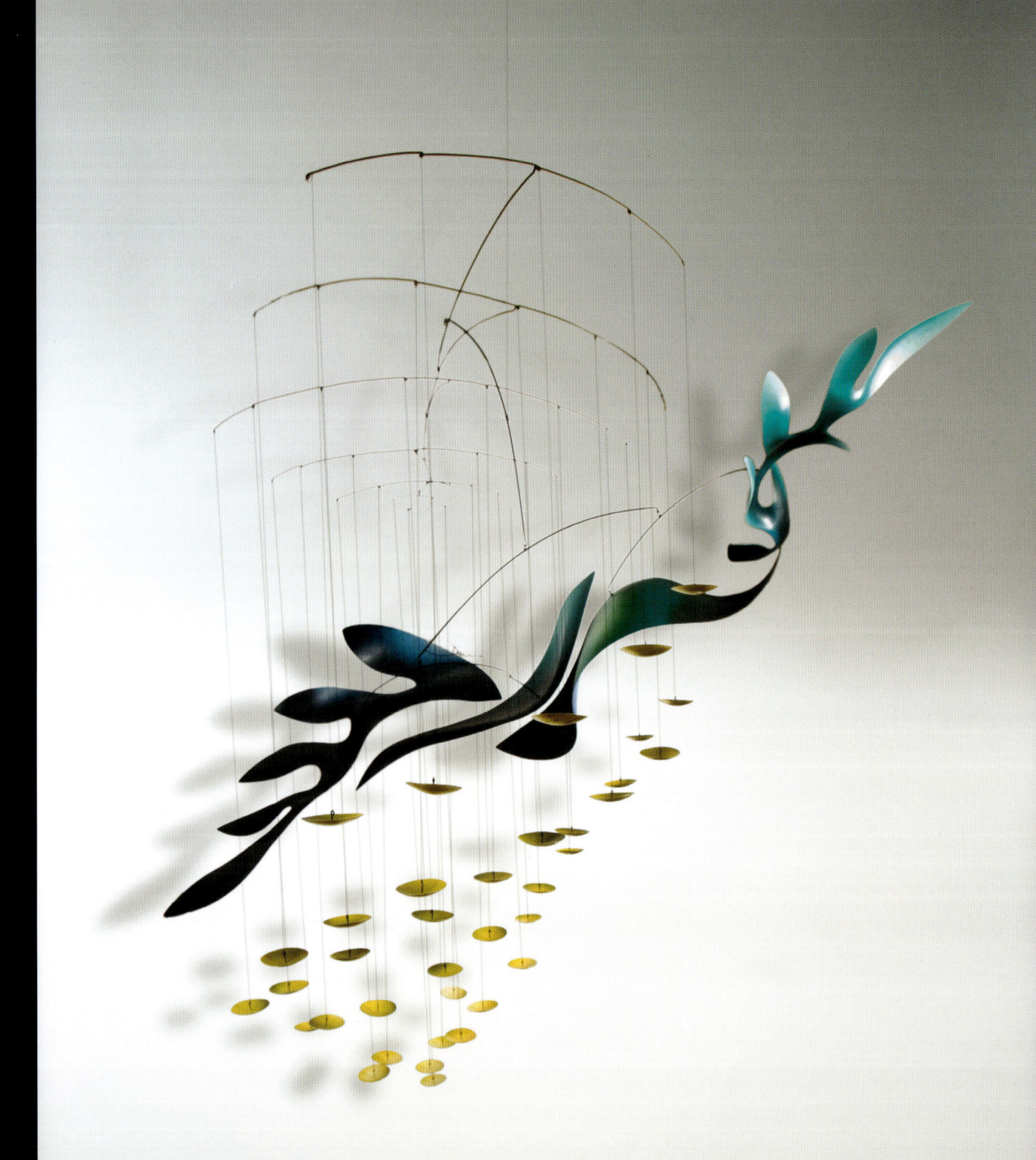

After only eight months at Goddard, Davis left school with a friend to start a restaurant in Worcester, Massachusetts, called The Struck of Loke. It was a beatnik spot that served vegetarian health food, something that was not quite traditional cuisine at the time. In his spare time, he continued to draw, mostly in pencil, only for his own enjoyment. He also continued to make wire constructions, emulating Calder and using innovative materials like Plexiglas and papier-mâché. As time went on, he began to bring more mindfulness to his jewelry, a hobby that he had continued in his spare time from work at the restaurant. When he met Peter, his partner for eleven years, they moved to the countryside of western Massachusetts, where Peter encouraged jewelry-making as a possible career.

Davis signed up for a three-week jewelry-making course at the Worcester Craft Center, where he learned to work with silver sheet and made an ambitious cuff, his first real piece of jewelry. To this day, this is the only formal training in metalwork the artist has received. From the start, Davis had an avant-garde aesthetic, creating body-art style jewelry like winged breastplates, architectural chokers, and oversized earrings that were strongly influenced by what he saw in New York City during the early 1980s. His dramatic pieces riffed on primitive African, pre-Columbian, Native American, and Greco-Roman motifs. He began to enjoy the process of working with metal and creating something fluid out of rigidity. He worked to coax the hard, inflexible material to respond to, and adorn, the soft contours of the female form. He befriended Robert Lee Morris, the acknowledged leader of the art jewelry movement, whose gladiator bubble collar had been featured on the cover of *Vogue* in 1976, and began showing his work in Morris's namesake SoHo gallery. Davis worked doggedly on his craft, and within three years felt confident enough to approach

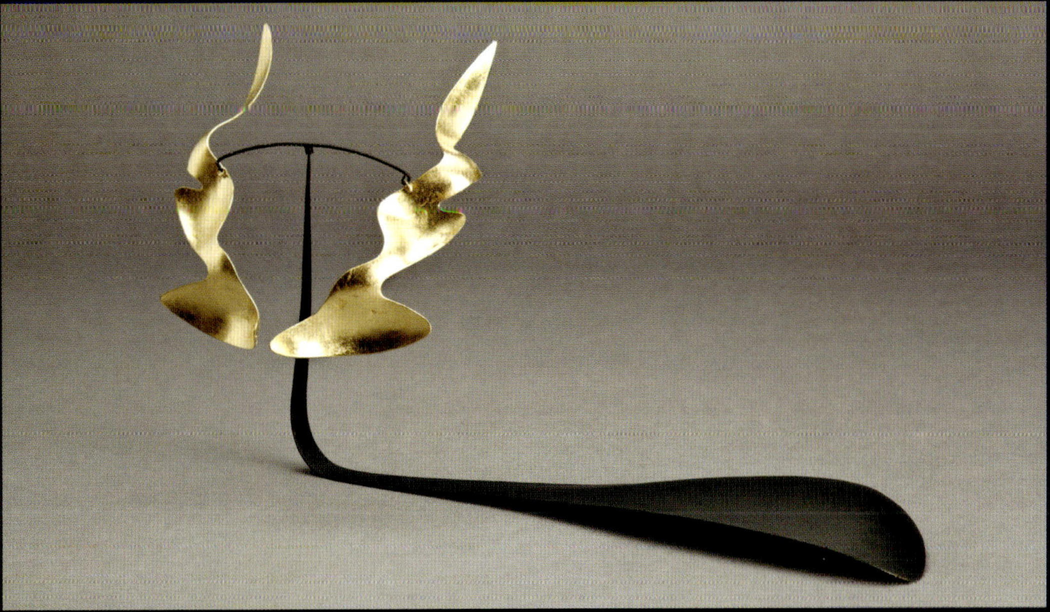

TURNING ANGELS
Standing mobile in brass with
oil colors, and 23K gold leaf
8 x 14 x 7"
MD660

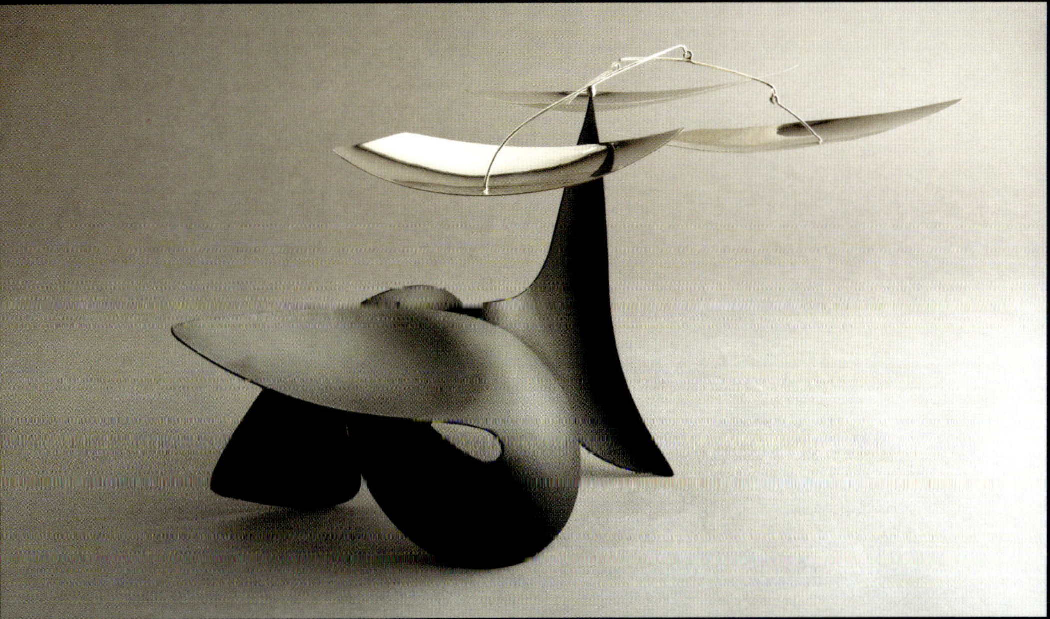

HEPHAESTUS
Standing mobile in oil painted
brass, and sterling silver
10 x 18 x 7"
MD670

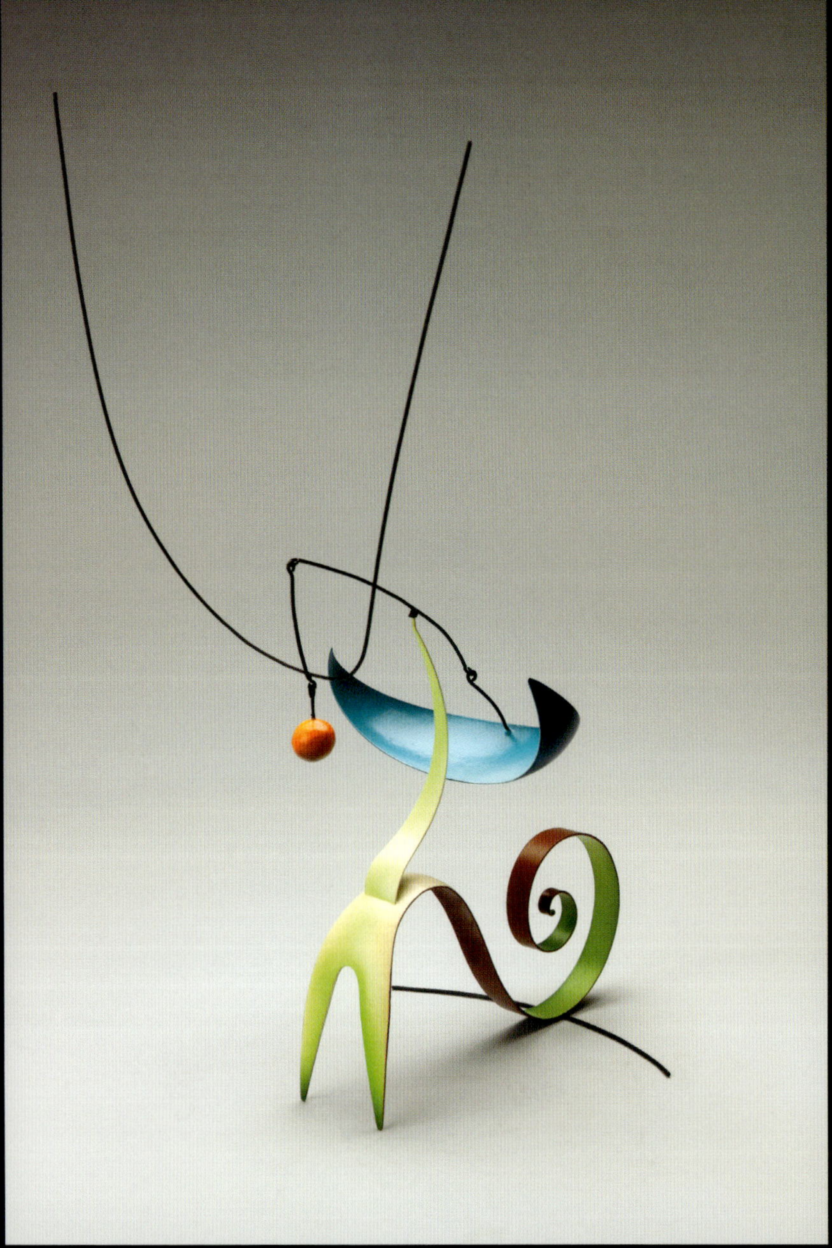

GATO
Standing mobile in brass and aluminum with steel wires, epoxy compound, and oil and acrylic colors
17.5 x 8 x 10"
MD582

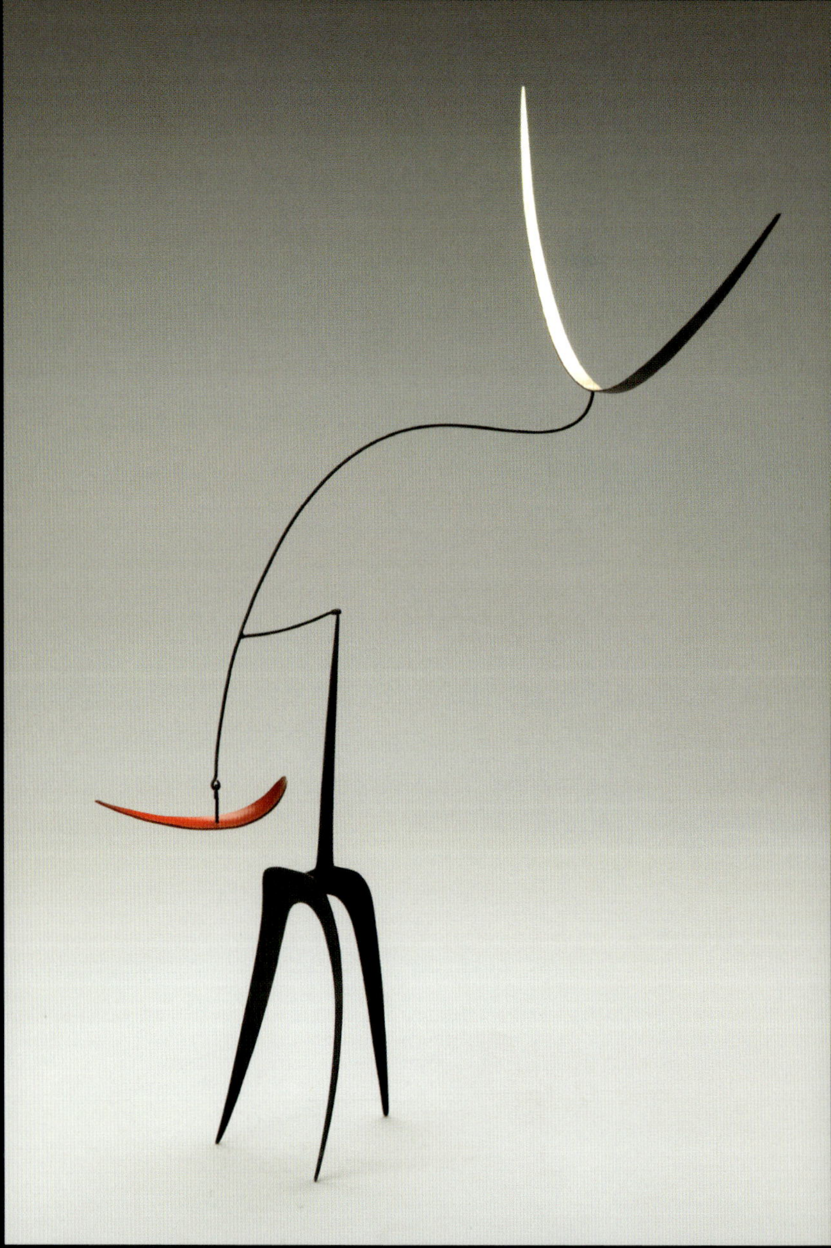

MORE CURIOUS
Standing mobile in brass and aluminum with steel wires, oil and acrylic colors, and 23K golf leaf
17 x 12 x 14"
MD632

Bloomingdale's in Chestnut Hill, Massachusetts, which gave him a solo show in conjunction with the opening of their apparel store. The once long-haired hippie felt like a fish out of water in the glitzy world of models and photo shoots. However, every piece in the show sold, which led him to regular business with Bloomingdale's and other New York department stores like Saks Fifth Avenue, Henri Bendel, and Macy's. He even had his own *Vogue* feature.

Along the way, Davis made the acquaintance of Gene Moore, the revolutionary window dresser. He designed approximately 5,000 windows for Tiffany & Co., and heralded the age of window artistry. Luminaries, including Robert Rauschenberg (1925-2008) and Jasper Johns (b. 1930), were invited to provide backdrop paintings and creative touches to displays. Davis and Gene were confidants, even traveling together to Italy in Gene's later years. Davis considered himself a jewelry designer and sought advice from Moore about how to amplify his success in the competitive New York market. Moore disparaged the cutthroat nature of the jewerly business in New York and instead encouraged Davis to leave the moniker of "designer" in favor of working as an independent artist.

This sage advice came in the late 1980's, when the taste for Davis's brand of sculptural jewelry was waning. His first mobiles explored design and function. Essentially standing, moving pieces of jewelery, they were constructed from sterling silver and had jewerly-like joints. He connected with a high-end design shop on Madison Avenue called the LS Collection. Every month, for two years, he would bring in a new collection that would promptly sell. As Davis's consciousness opened to the idea of being an artist, his creativity began to soar and his mobiles became more elaborate and colorful. Most importantly, he began to believe that his art could

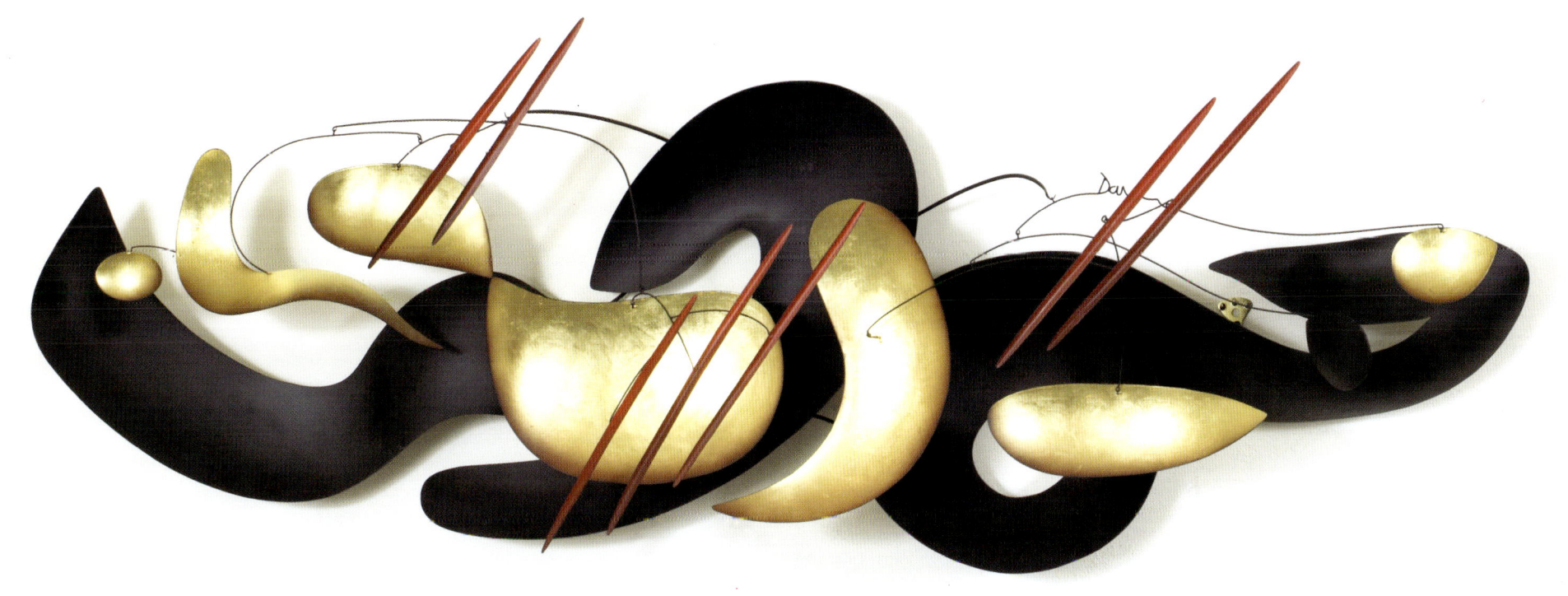

NIGHT JOURNEY
Wall-mounted mobile in brass and aluminum with steel wires, acrylic colors, and 23K gold leaf
58 x 20 x 15"
MD304

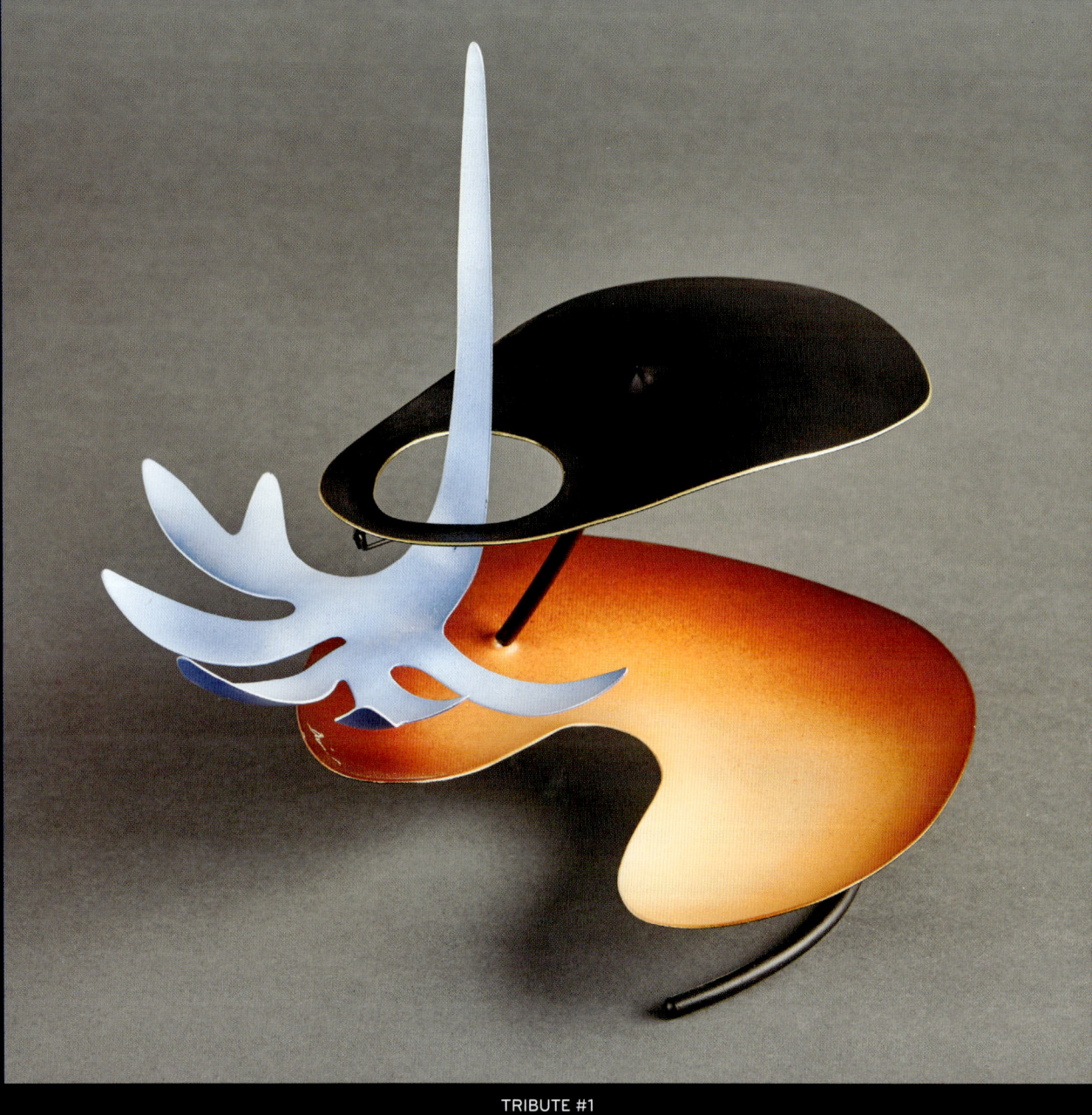

TRIBUTE #1
Standing mobile in brass and aluminum with steel wires, and oil and acrylic colors
11.5 x 14 x 7"
MD613

fuel introspection, stimulate an understanding of the world around him, and enrich the lives of those who viewed it.

It is virtually impossible to avoid comparisons to Calder when one works as a mobile artist, and Davis does not deny the influence. He recalls that he only began making hanging mobiles in 1998, after seeing the Calder show at the National Gallery of Art in Washington, D.C. Still, Davis has developed his own approach and spirit that differentiates him from this patrimony. Davis says that, "For most of my life I was totally excited by structural forms and three-dimensional objects. I always felt that Calder was using space as his 'background,' slicing through it with line and form. My mobiles were sculptural objects in a conventional sense. That has always felt like a big difference between his vision and mine." Structurally, the influence of sculptor Isamu Noguchi (1904-1988) is seen in works such as

Beside the Point (p. 33) and *Tribute #1* (p. 30), in which artfully curved elements emerge from solid, organic bases. Like Noguchi, Davis simultaneously embodies subtlety and boldness, modernity and tradition. There is also a philosophical affinity between Noguchi and Davis in their shared reverence for nature and her ample metaphorical capacities. Davis's mobiles abstractly allude to nature in its various incarnations—gentle breezes, tempestuous winds, lazy riverbeds, crashing waves, the sun's bright light, nocturnal shadows, stretching trees with sinuous limbs, vibrant gardens, and the breathtaking metamorphosis of insects.

Davis also brings a kinship with modernist painters to his mobiles, considering each work to be a painting in space. Color is paramount to form and motion, and the meaning of the work is as compelling as the finished piece. Though he never formally studied art history, he has always been a student of it through seeing,

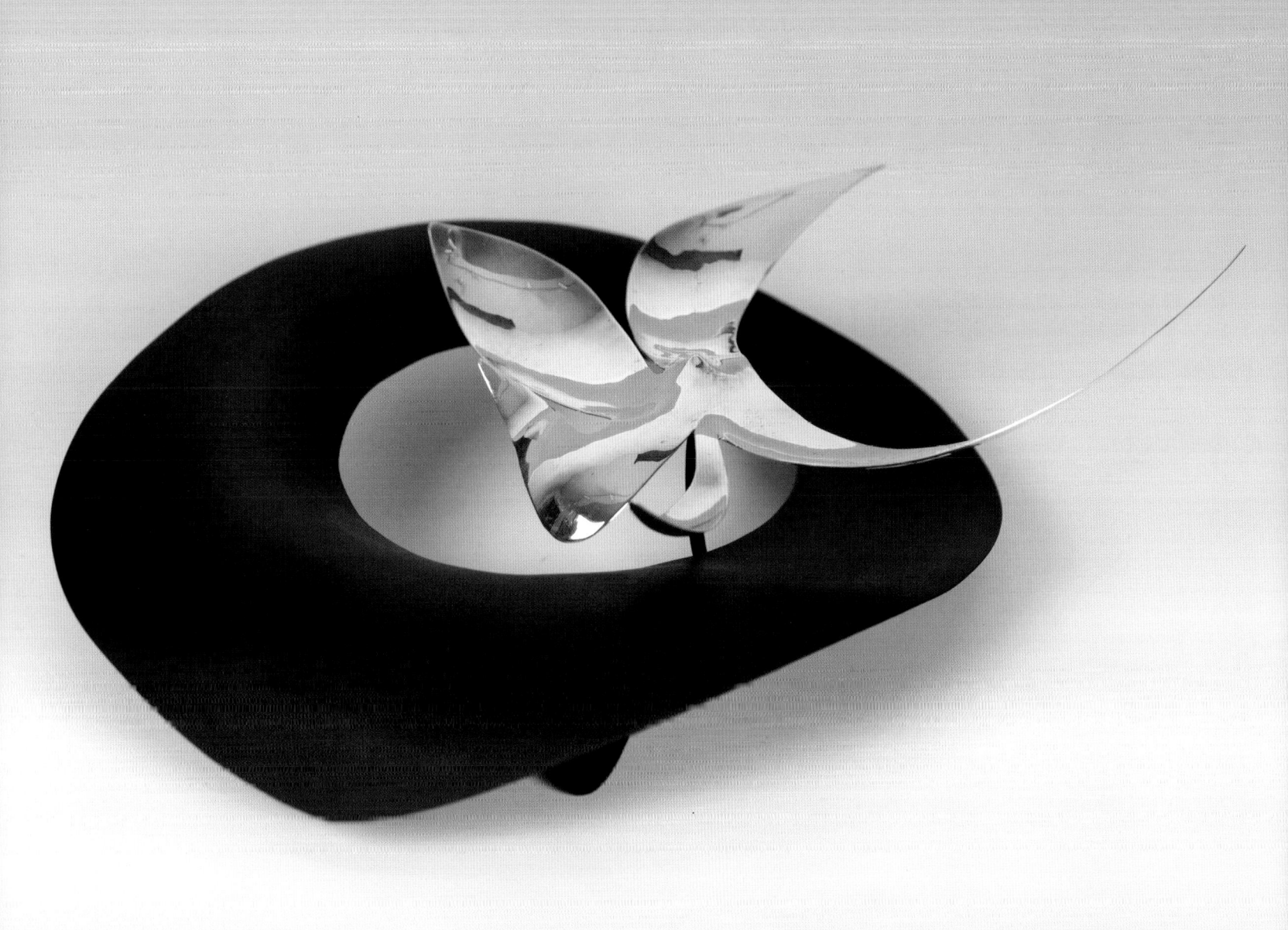

BESIDE THE POINT
Standing mobile in brass with oil color, and sterling silver
4 x 12 x 8.5"
MD555

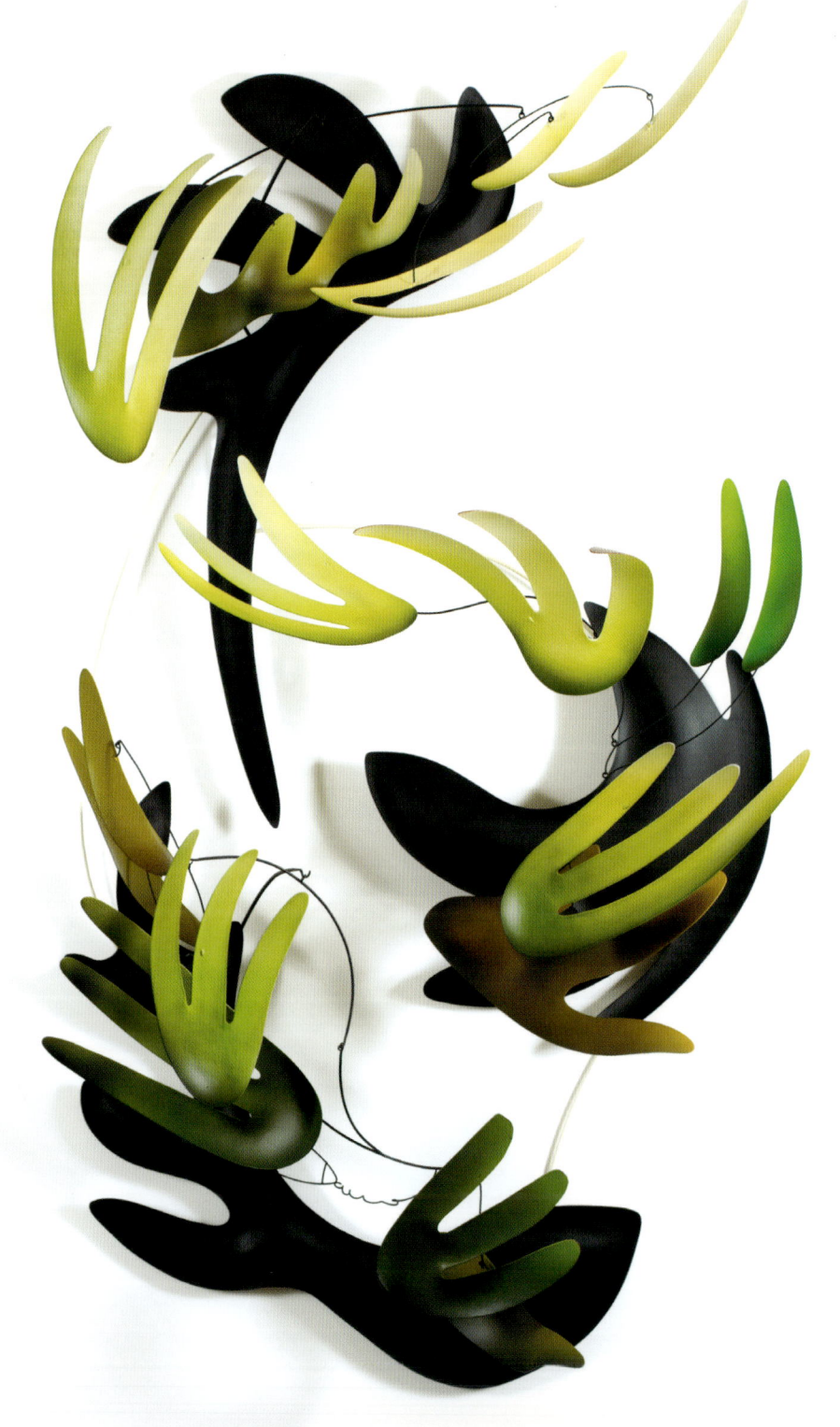

reading, and remaining open to learning. References to the landscape paintings of the American modernist Arthur Dove (1880-1946) are evident in a work like *Through the Trees* (p. 34), in which the lines, forms, colors, and gestures of nature are captured in an abstract composition of background, middle ground, and foreground. Nature's elements are recognizable yet abridged. The focus is meant to be less about their physical manifestation, and more about their connection to the spiritual world. *Jardin de Monsieur M* (p. 37) recalls the late cutouts of Henri Matisse (1869–1954) with colorful, limb-like foliage dancing exuberantly against the pyramidal backdrop. Davis is not necessarily creating a garden, but the feelings experienced when we encounter a brilliant, sun-lit garden.

The ability to be referential instead of literal creates a powerful touchpoint between artist and viewer, tapping into a deep place in the human psyche. It allows the artist to tell stories in alternative ways. Sometimes the narrative is linear, as found in *Reclining Nude by the Shore* (p. 38) or *The Serpent's Breath* (p. 41). Other times it is all-encompassing, as in *Whispering Wind* (p. 42) or *Invoking the Gods* (p. 45). Modernist artists, like Paul Klee (1879-1940) and Joan Miró, understood the persuasiveness and universality of elemental lines, colors, and forms. They tapped into a childlike naiveté that allowed viewers to disconnect from the exigencies of daily life, and experience the emotions of simply being alive. *The Perfect Moment* (p. 46), and *Tribute #3* (p. 49) are a few of the many mobiles in which Davis pays homage, both aesthetically and philosophically, to these forbears. As he has said, "In the journey my work has taken in the last few years, there is a growing understanding that these artists are a link to my inner world. Comforting voices that keep me company during those hours at my workbench. Struggling with the

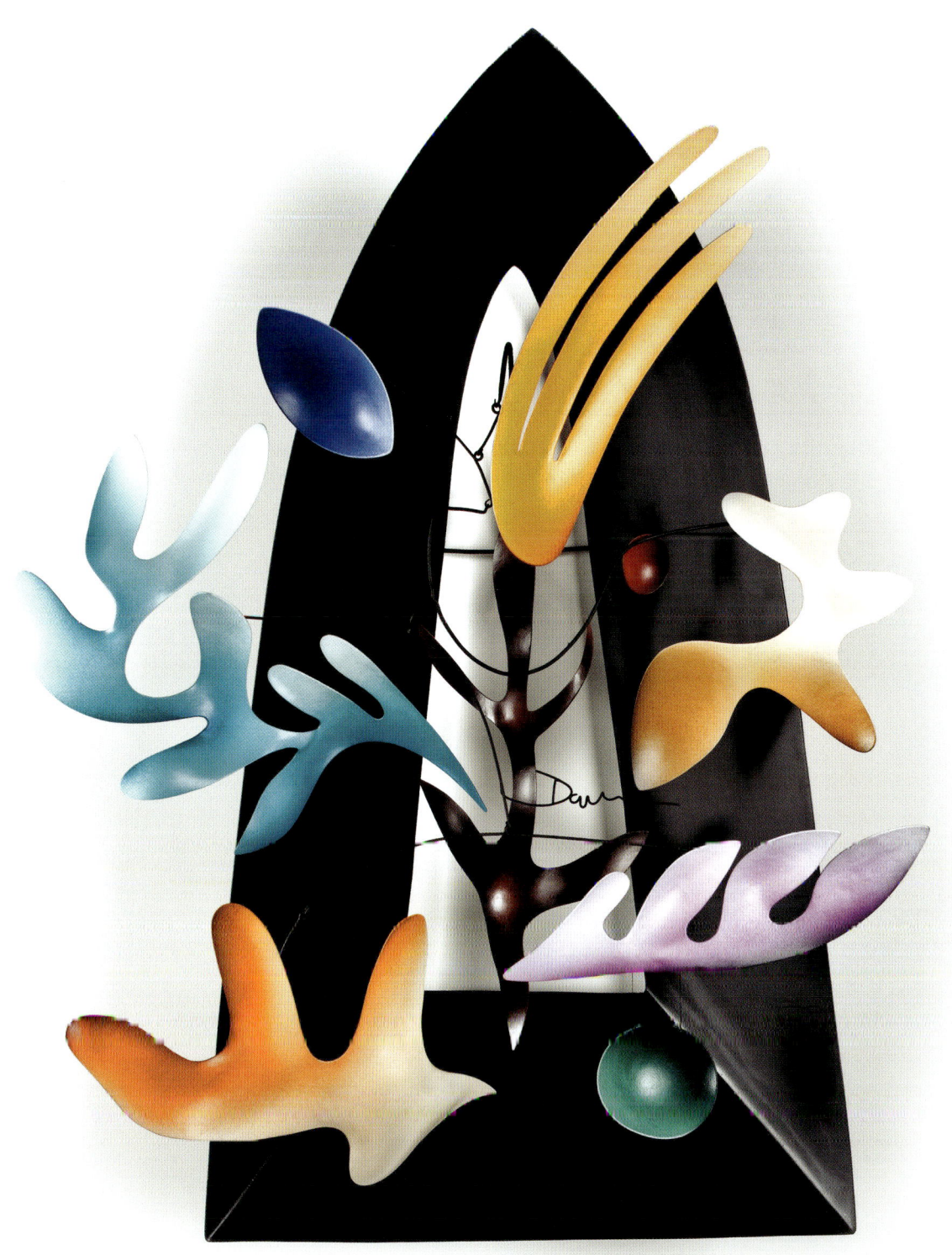

JARDIN DE MONSIEUR M
Wall-mounted mobile in
brass and aluminum with
steel wires, nylon cord, and
acrylic colors
33 x 26 x 12"
MD709

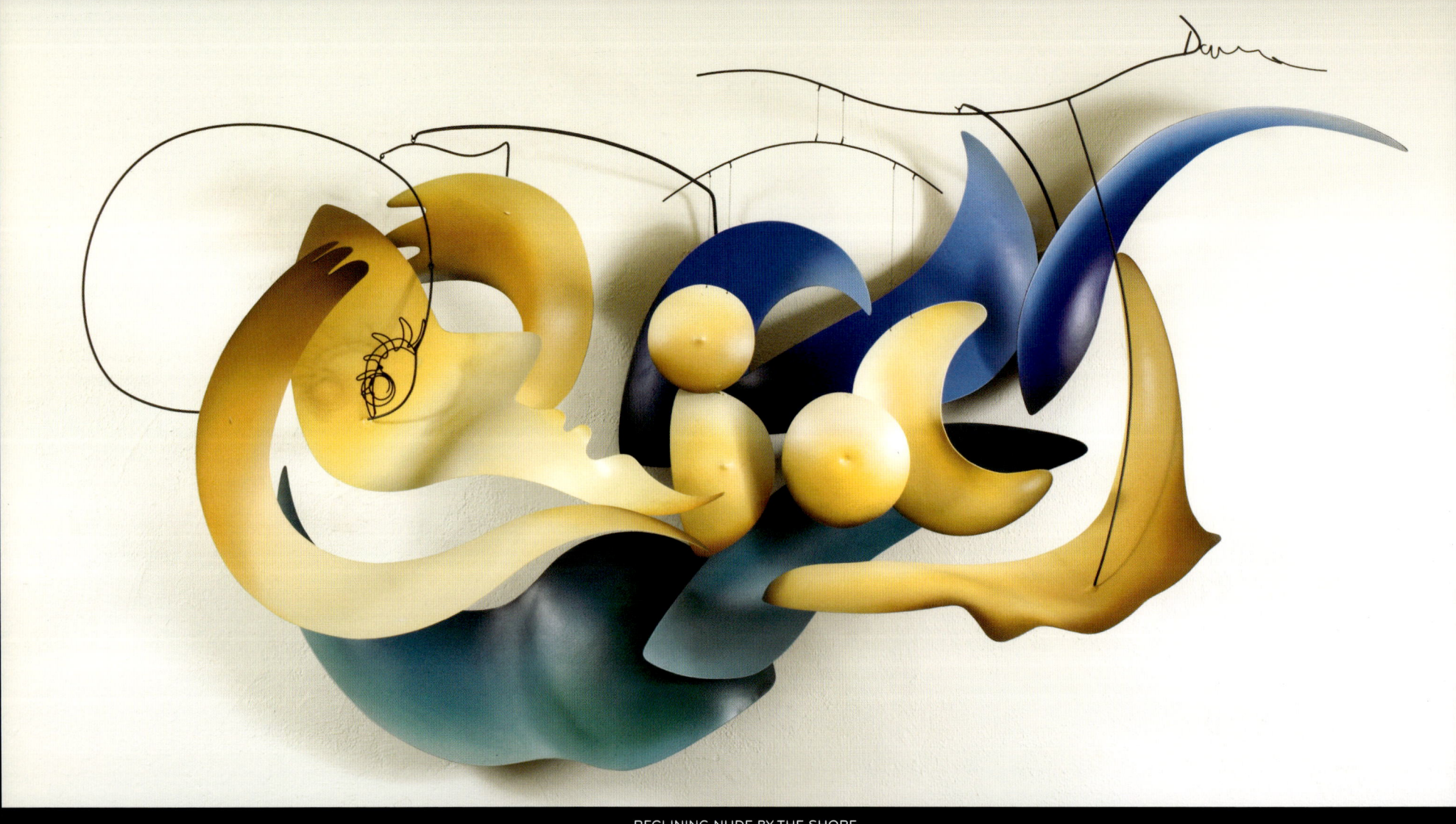

RECLINING NUDE BY THE SHORE
Wall-mounted mobile in brass and aluminum with steel wires, and acrylic colors
26 x 48 x 20"
MD391

same issues...feeling overcome by spiritual joy at the discovery of a new way of containing and organizing the swirling energies, the beauties, and terrors inherent in the condition of being human."

The recent *Tribute* series acknowledges the artist's connection to the colorists of previous eras, which is at once innate and also outwardly expressed in the work. As Davis explains,

"As I worked, I began to use more color. Finally, I discovered working with an airbrush, where I could mix my own colors, and suddenly the subtle and exciting color combinations added another layer to the objects I was making. I began to really explore color in my work. I realized that the study of color as a concept was something I had not explored yet, and I felt completely out to sea. So

I picked up a book of Vincent van Gogh paintings and really, really looked at his color combinations. I was struck with how he used opposing colors together to give the image depth and how I could do this with my mobiles. I also realized that in painting, the colors lie next to each other to give them new power. My mobiles are a "grouping" of disparate elements, so each has its own color identity. As the piece moves, the color combination changes. This brought about a real challenge, one I have been working on for the last fifteen years. I have always used the influences of others in subtle ways to incorporate a new idea of color or form into my work, but with the Tribute series, I wanted to make a statement that was more direct in honoring these influences."

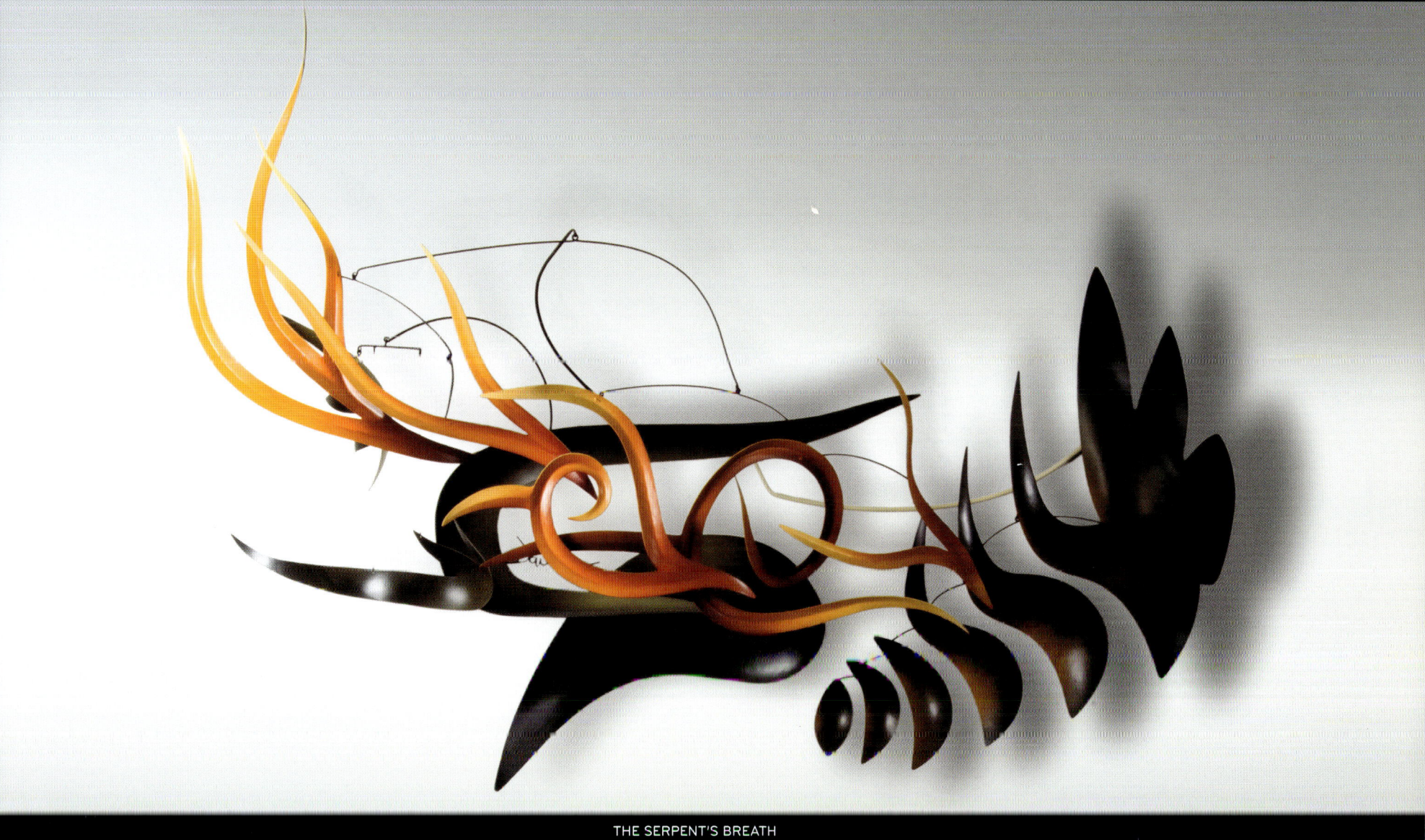

THE SERPENT'S BREATH
Wall-mounted mobile in brass and aluminum with steel wires, and oil and acrylic colors
32 x 45 x 12"

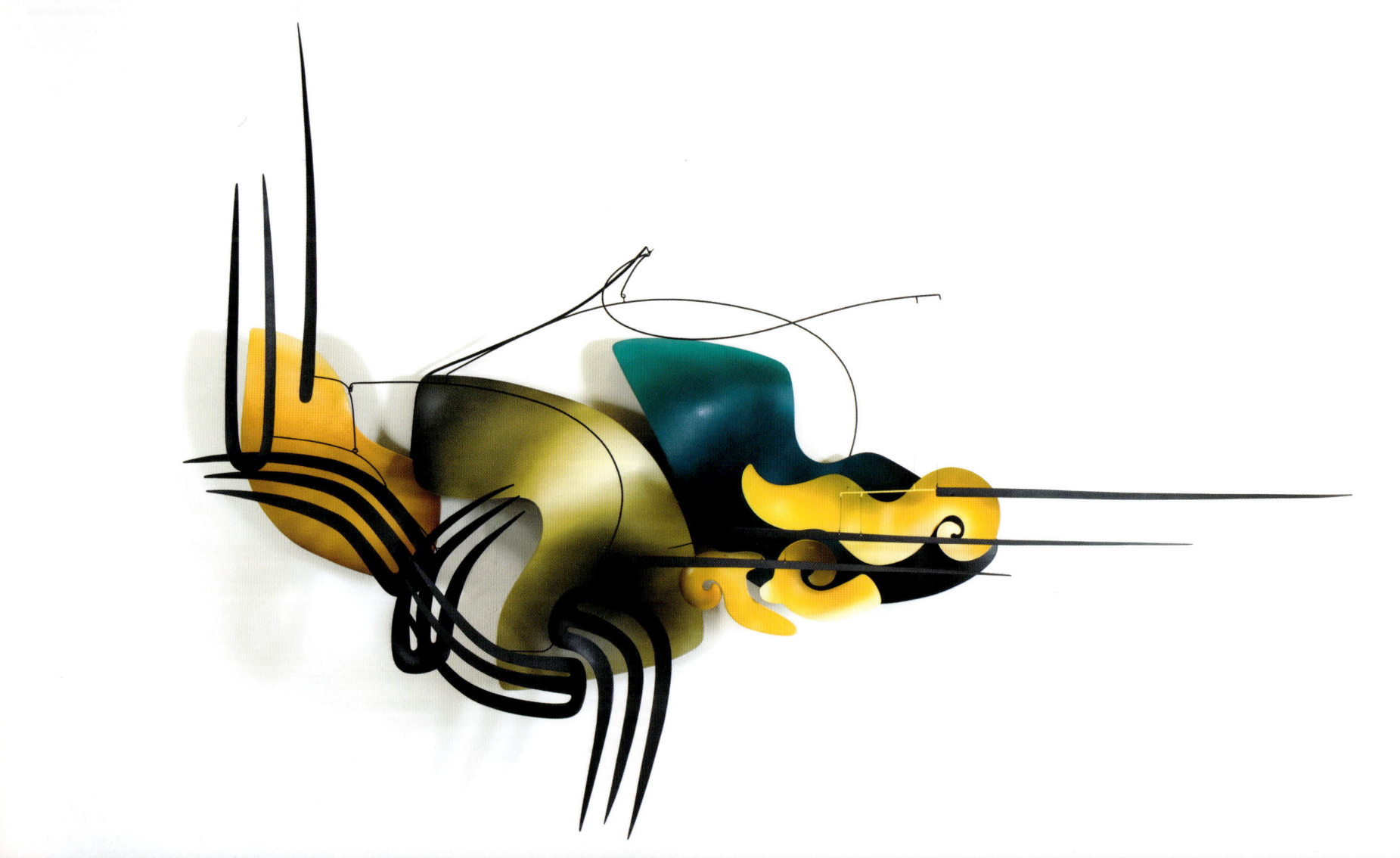

WHISPERING WIND
Wall-mounted mobile in brass and aluminum with steel wires, and acrylic colors
34 x 50 x 15"
MD475

Gabriel García Márquez wrote, in *Love in the Time of Cholera*, "He allowed himself to be swayed by the conviction that human beings are not born once and for all on the day their mothers give birth to them, but that life obliges them over and over again to give birth to themselves." Becoming an artist gave Mark Davis that chance at rebirth. While living in western Massachusetts in the late 1980s, Davis became friends with Jim Schantz, a Berkshire-based pastel artist. Schantz introduced Davis to a gallery owner in Boston named Bernard Pucker. Pucker Gallery included four pieces in a group show, and thus began their decades-long relationship. Davis moved to Boston in 1992, and although he was on the hunt for a live-work artist's loft space, he purchased an old Victorian home in 1999, gutting out most of the top two floors for his workshop and studio. His home reflects the same philosophies that fuel his work, though aesthetically it could not be more disparate. It combines his upbringing around the Renaissance and the Medieval with his love of salvaging and what he calls "curating orphan objects." Brimming with an extraordinary assembly of antiques, furnishings, religious icons, and Oriental rugs creatively grouped and often repurposed, the home is more cabinet of curiosities than abstract modern. But like Davis's mobiles, diverse objects work in charming harmony and evoke a sense of comfort and belonging.

The threshold into the studio and workshop crosses from Davis's inner sphere to his outer persona. It is also filled to the brim with large sheets of metal in varying thicknesses, discarded half-shaped forms, composite mobiles in mid-creation, delicate jewelers' tools and soldering equipment, hammers, cutters, and anvils, railroad ties and English wheels. On the third floor is the heavy machinery and the spray painting booth. Though these objects are of a very different purpose than the

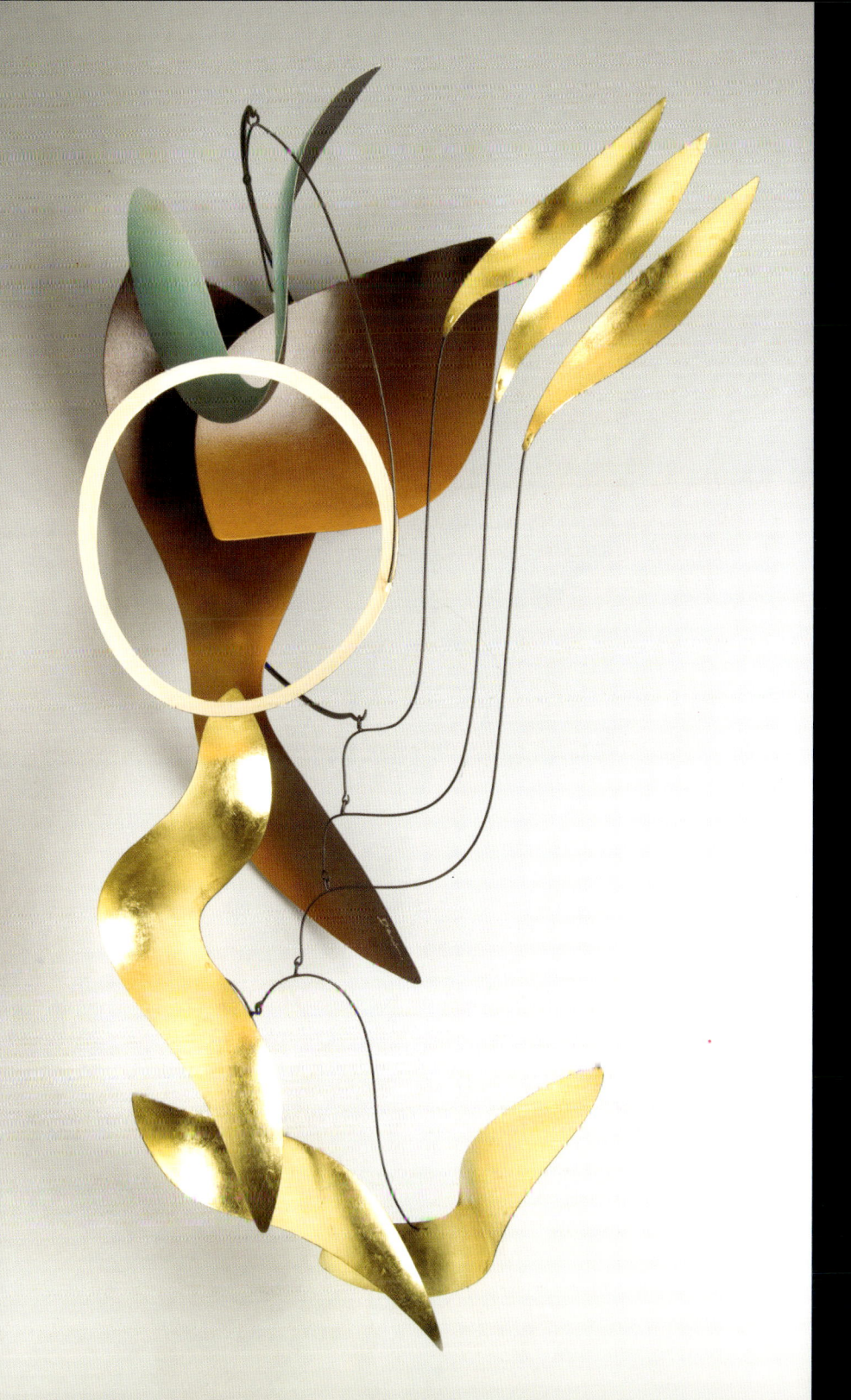

INVOKING THE GODS
Wall-mounted mobile in brass and
aluminum with steel wires, oil and
acrylic colors, and 23K gold leaf
29 x 14 x 7"
MD517

THE PERFECT
MOMENT
Standing mobile in
brass and aluminum
with steel wires, and oil
and acrylic colors
24 x 23 x 26"
MD666

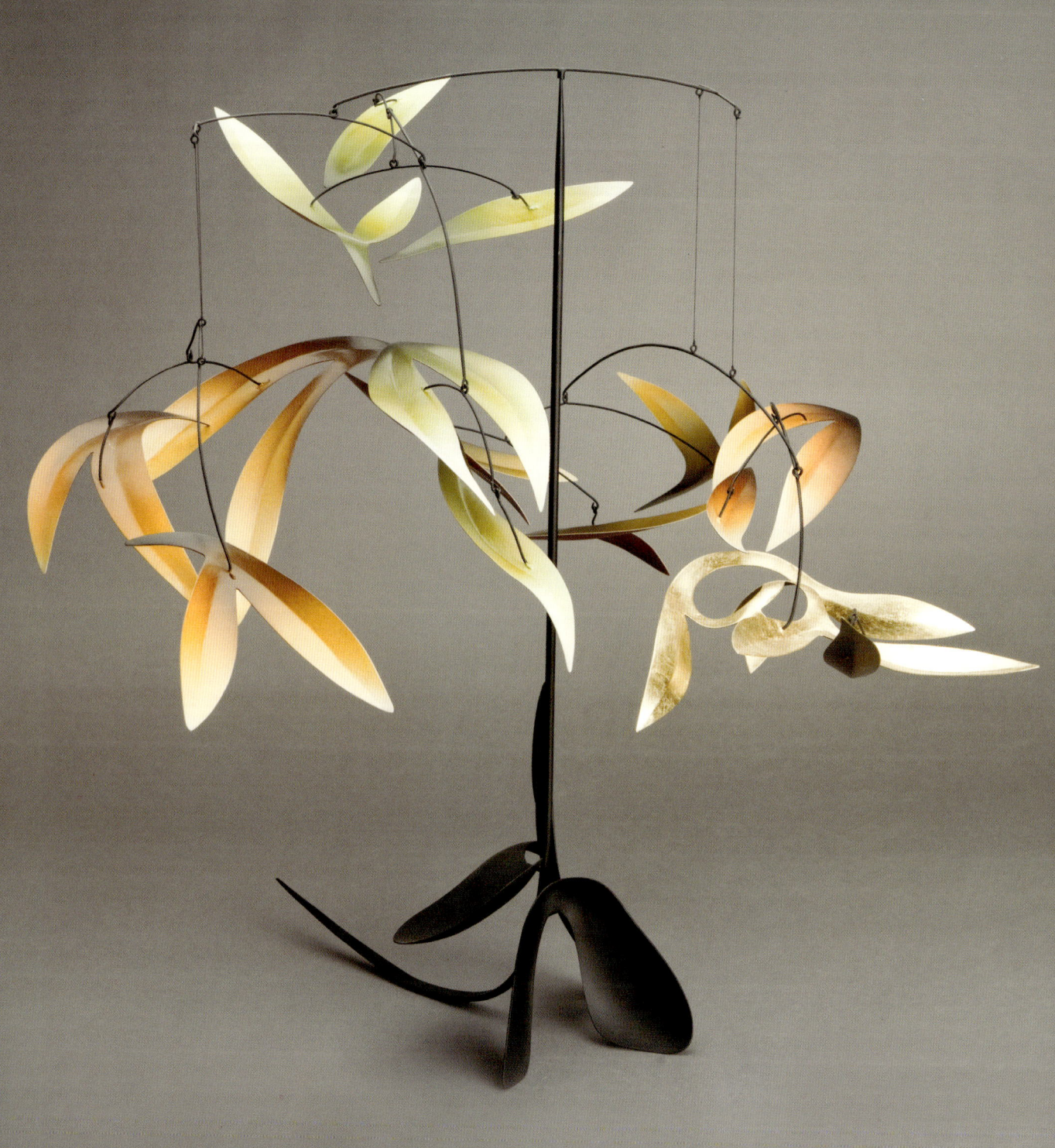

décor of the rest of his home, they are similarly a source of well-being for the artist. They are also a source of purpose for a man who never considers it work to go to the studio. He puts on music (albums range from the B-52s, to Tom Waits, and Aretha Franklin, and occupy one corner of the room), set to accomplish something every day, and lets the creative alchemy flow.

Davis has always enjoyed the discipline of working with a single material—metal—and is particularly drawn to its elemental and lasting qualities. He uses sheet metals of different weights and compositions like steel (the heaviest), brass (the most difficult to manipulate), aluminum (the lightest), and gold and silver (the easiest to shape, hence its popularity in jewelry). Flat sheet metal is formed by traditional silversmithing methods such as planishing, whereby the piece of metal is hammered out on an old railroad tie with different depressions creating different contours. Rolling the metal back and forth through the English wheel (a tool originally made for the auto industry) shapes and smooths the metal. His is not a spontaneous art, which makes it all the more impressive that the final product feels so effortless and expressive.

Ideas and inspiration come from everywhere and anything. Therefore, Davis keeps a sketchpad close by to record fleeting shapes and ideas. When he begins a new work, he might sketch something or use an old castaway as a new beginning, thinking about a few strong sets of shapes then adding lyrical counterparts. This stage is often done in cardboard to allow for maximum fussing. However, more often than not, the final product deviates greatly from the basic concept or sketch from which it was born. According to Davis, "The balancing is done by intuition at first, and then as the piece progresses, I am able to fine-tune the balance. Initially, my vision is to see the various elements floating

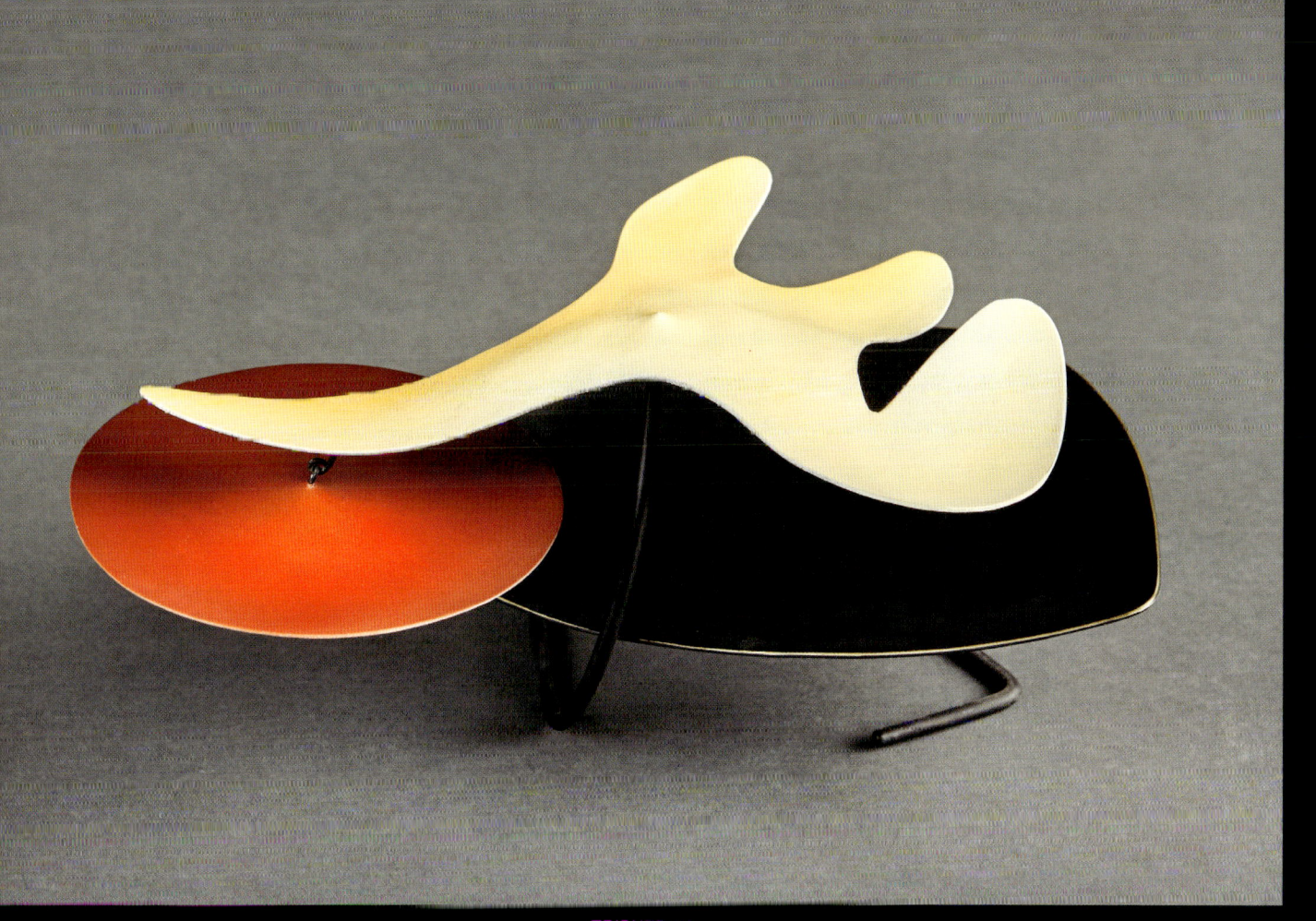

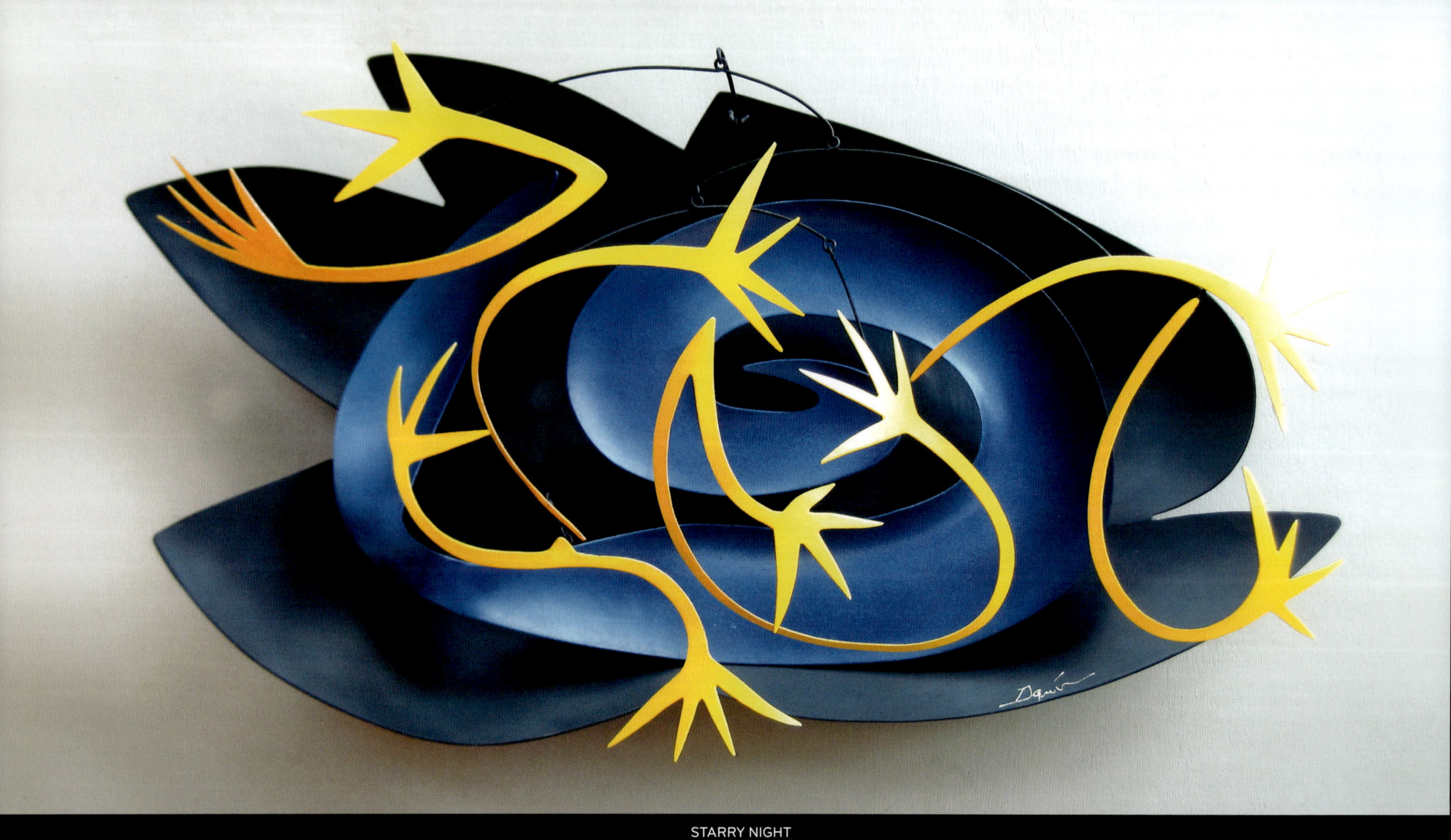

STARRY NIGHT
Wall-mounted mobile in brass and aluminum with steel wires, and oil and acrylic colors
10 x 21 x 8"
MD713

in space, relating to, but not anchored to the earth. By completion, each piece becomes its own very personal universe." At first, all of the pieces are finished with temporary joining arms so Davis can adjust them to fine-tune the aesthetics and mechanical balance. He finds the center of gravity, then a pinpoint or dimple is needed and the weights of the pieces keep everything perfectly balanced. This creative process is emblematic of the virtuosity of Mark Davis and metaphorical to his life—taking something heavy and countering it with lightness, appreciating how separate elements must work in tandem to create balance, and bringing something colorful and joyful into the world. Art is the "pinpoint" or the "dimple" around which Davis's life is kept in balance.

The fulfilment Davis feels through being an artist is something he purposefully and effortlessly shares with each viewer who encounters his work. The mutual relationship between artist and viewer has become increasingly valuable to Davis, who has been involved in many collaboration-based and larger-scale private and public projects for the past eight years. Working collaboratively with people brings a new level of creative output, while also giving Davis more direct feedback on the positive impact his work has on others. *Healing Waters* (p. 98) is one example of a large-scale commissioned piece. It was installed in 2012 in the outer entrance to the Ann and Robert H. Lurie Children's Hospital in Chicago. It is a suspended sculpture of painted blue and green steel and carbon fiber molded plates, measuring 70 feet long, 30 feet wide, and 10 feet tall. Its undulating panels evoke calming ocean waves, transporting all those who enter the hospital to a more peaceful place. The humble Davis sometimes calls upon the parables of Greek and Roman mythology like Icarus and Apollo and Daphne in his work,

A GLOW ALONG THE
SHORELINE
Standing mobile in
painted brass, and
sterling silver
22 x 28 x 20"
MD603

53

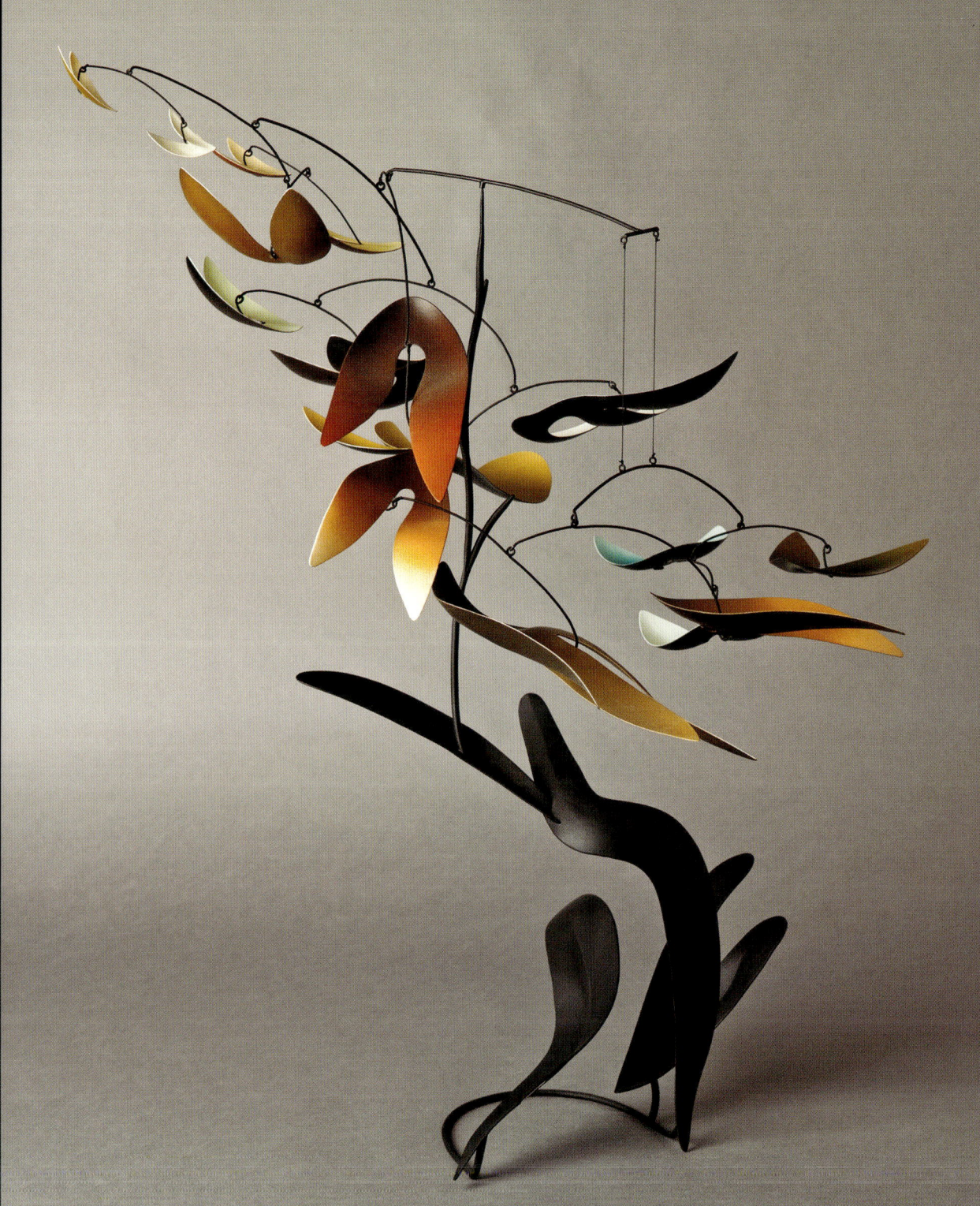

EARLY MORNING
RAPTURE
Standing mobile in
brass and aluminum
with steel wires, and oil
and acrylic colors
30 x 20 x 20"
MD693

perhaps cautioning himself against the pitfalls of vanity or self-aggrandizement. But, working in large-scale public venues has redoubled Davis's commitment to bring joy where there is heaviness, and disseminate his inspirational art to an even wider audience. He wanted it to appear in places characterized by grief and hardship, or defined more by banality than revelry.

Henri Matisse once wrote, "What I dream of is an art of balance, of purity and serenity devoid of troubling or depressing subject matter—a soothing, calming influence on the mind, rather like a good armchair which provides relaxation from physical fatigue." Mark Davis literally achieves this balance in his varicolored mobiles, paying homage to subjects from nature to the human gesture, deftly playing substance against grace, carefully considering the reciprocity of stillness and movement, positive and negative, light and shadow. Davis also achieves this balance with his humanity—funny and sincere but tough, he is a man of simultaneous strength and fragility, afflicted by his demons but mindfully choosing to see joy all around him. Through his mobiles, Davis communicates the many complexities of the human spirit in a way that words never could, helping the viewer to achieve their own inner balance, then tipping our scales towards a more contented place.

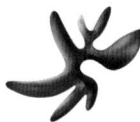

Jeanne V. Koles is an independent consultant who does project management, design, and writing for museums and the cultural sector.

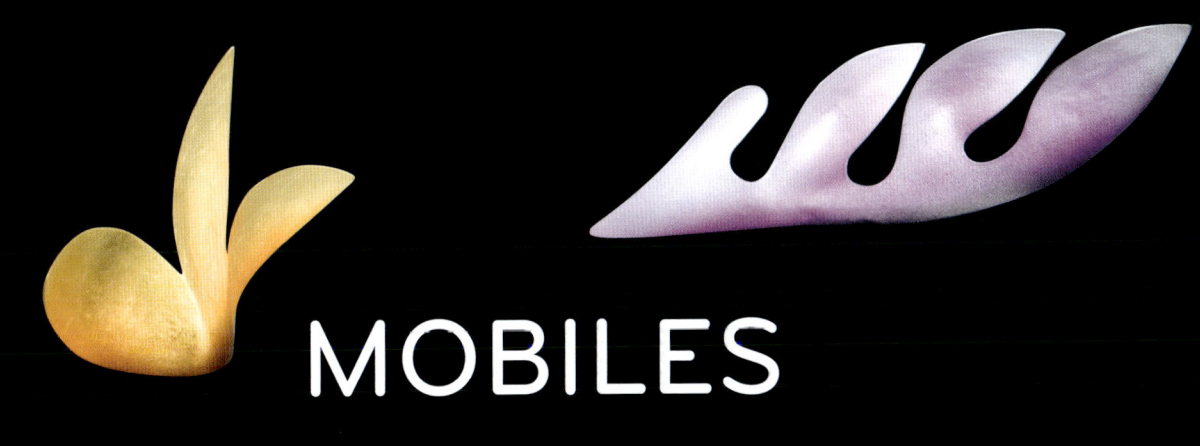

MOBILES

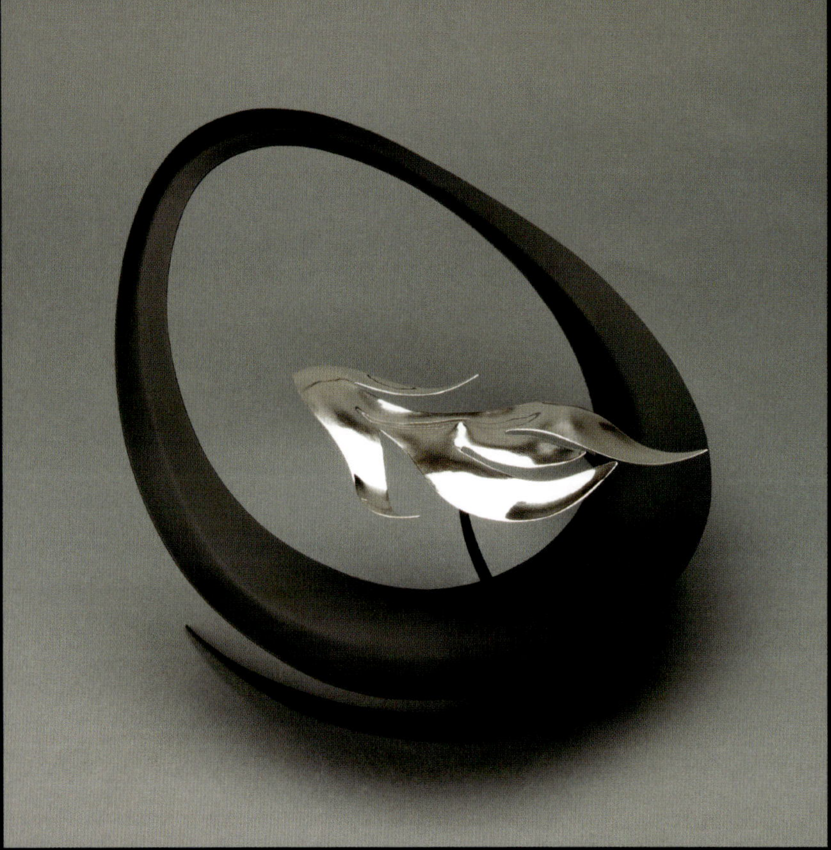

COOL HEAT
Standing mobile in oil painted brass, and sterling silver
7 x 12 x 10"
MD563

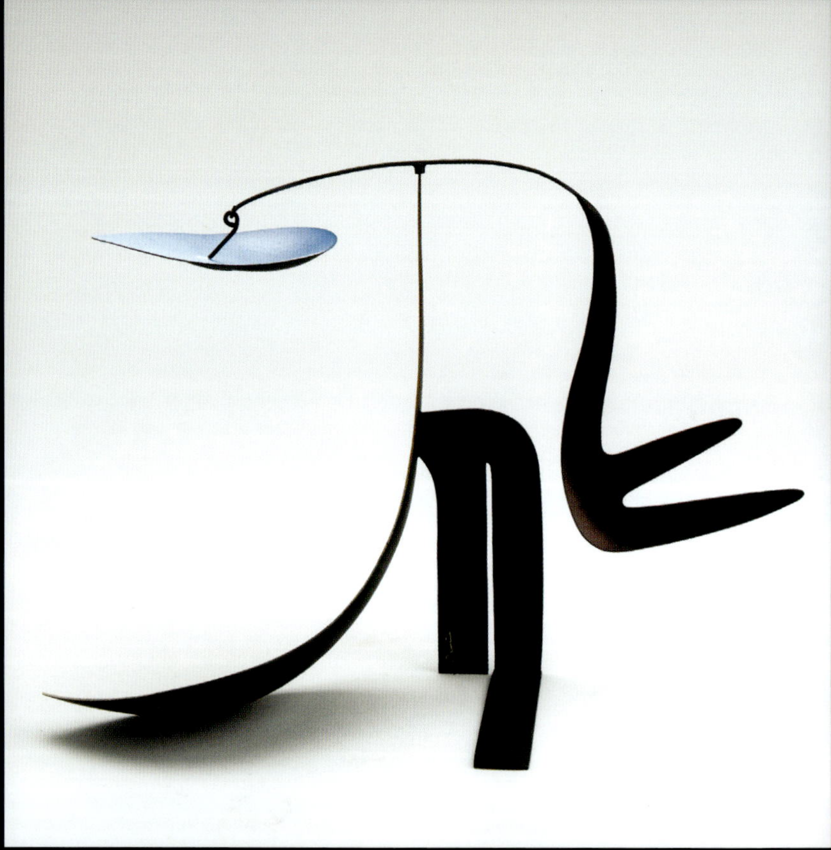

GONDOLIER
Standing mobile in brass and aluminum with steel wires, and oil and acrylic colors
8 x 11 x 4"
MD592

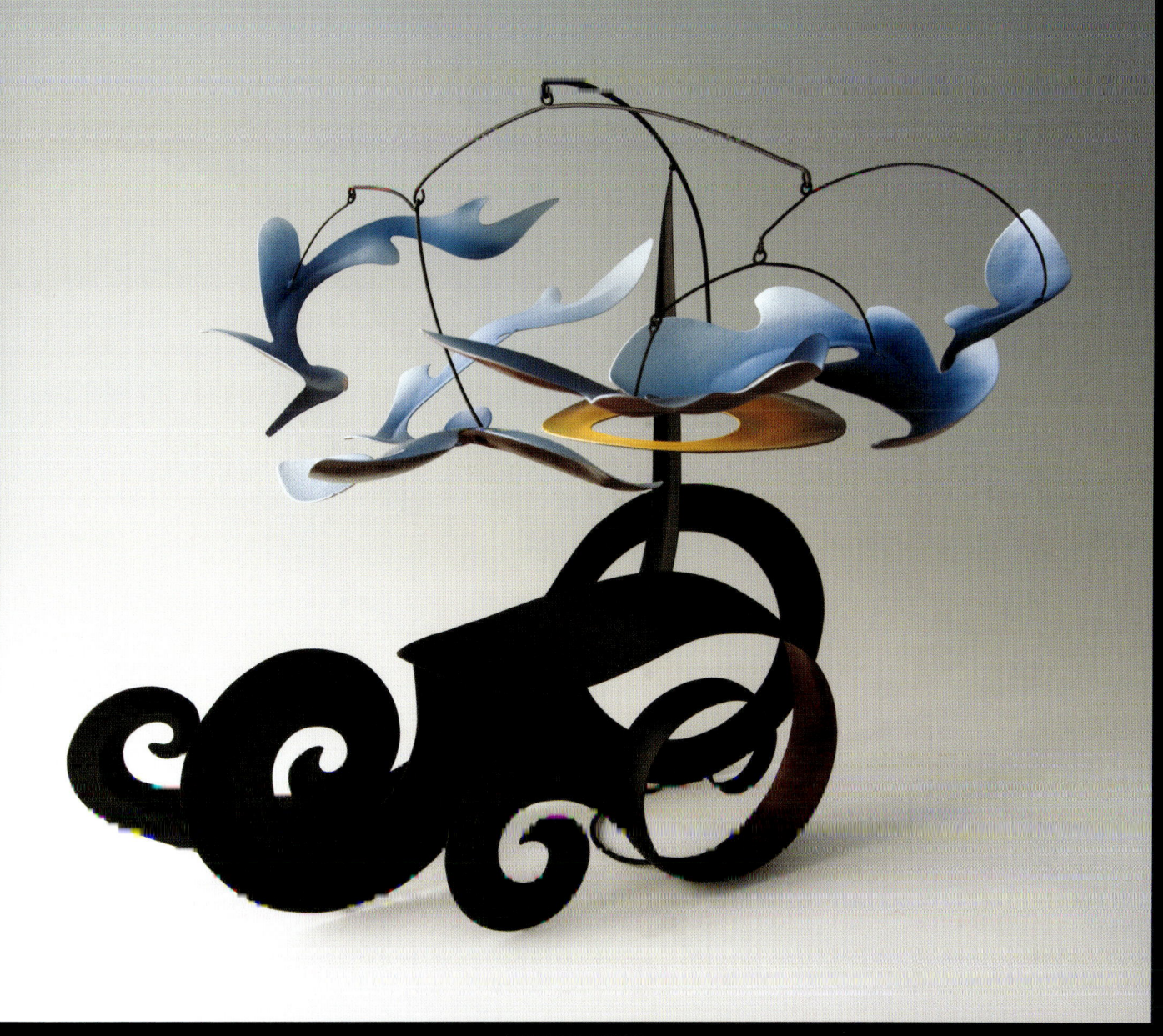

EZEKIEL'S VISION
Standing mobile in brass and aluminum with steel wires, and oil and acrylic colors

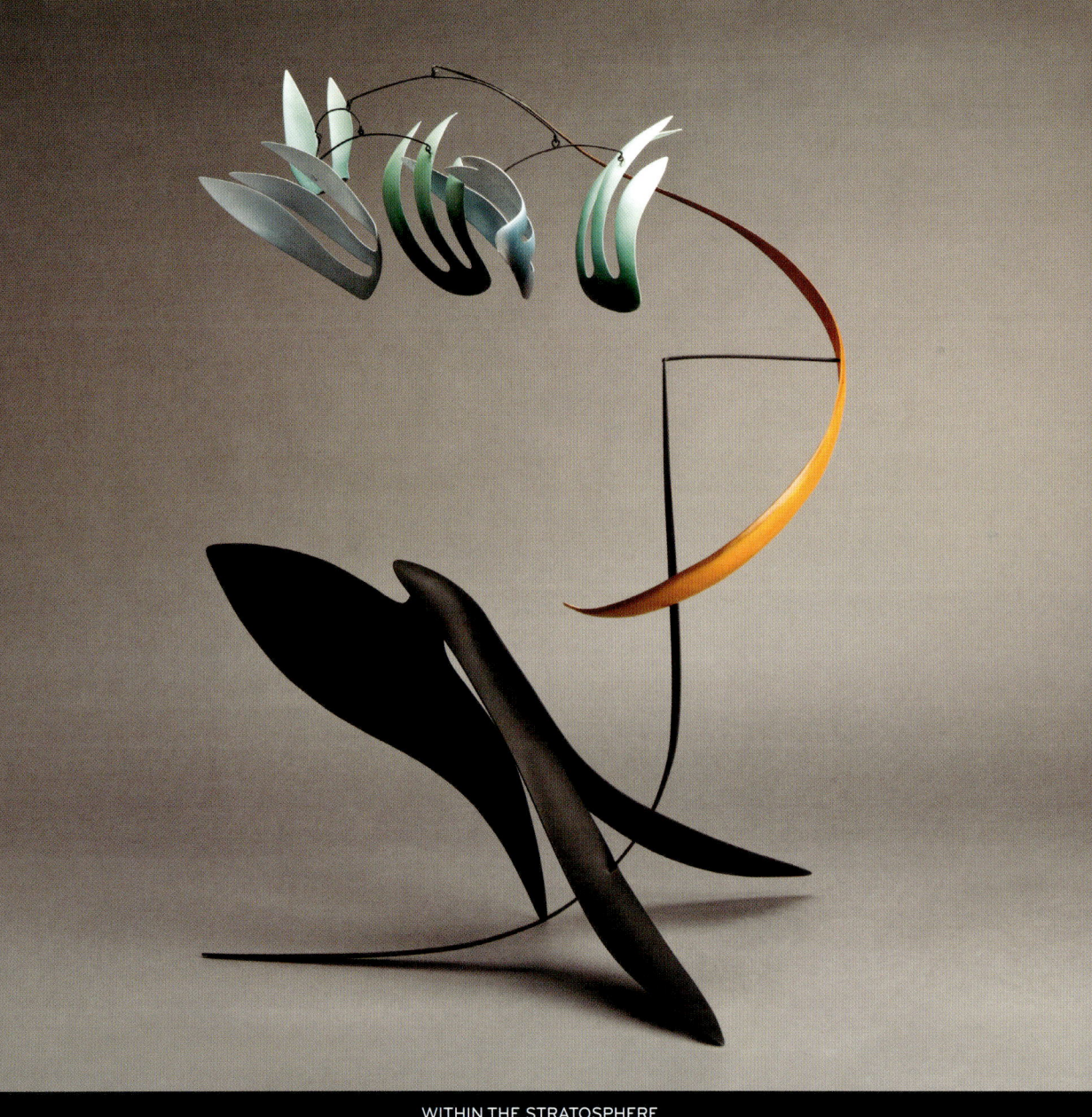

WITHIN THE STRATOSPHERE
Standing mobile in brass, silicon bronze, and aluminum, with steel wires, and oil and acrylic colors

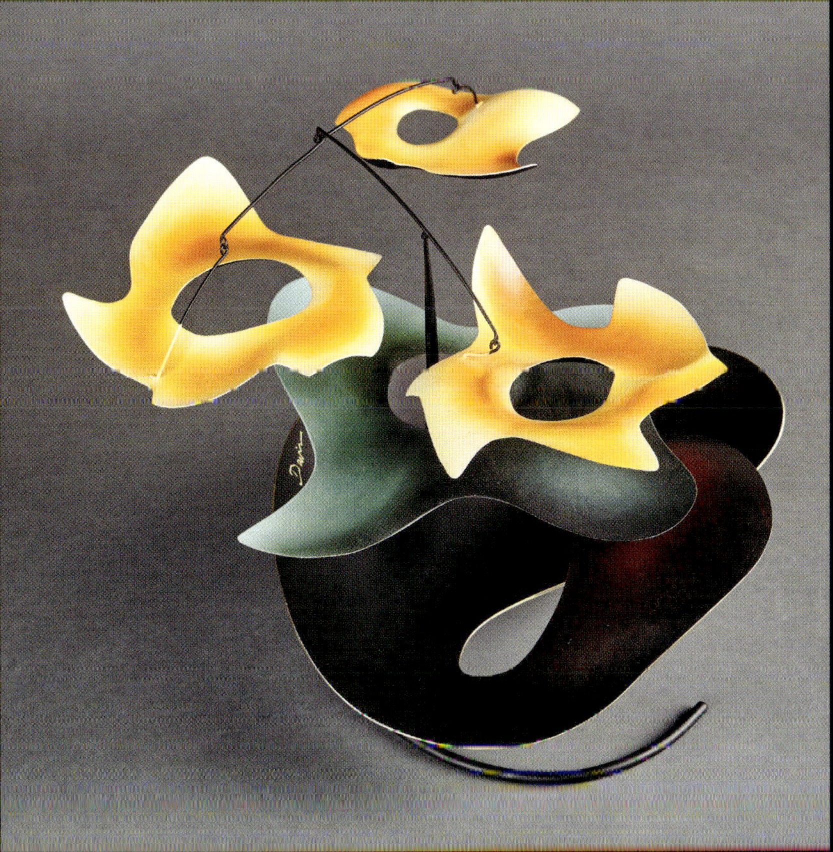

TRIBUTE #7
Standing mobile in brass and aluminum with steel wires, and oil and acrylic colors
11 x 15 x 14"
MD621

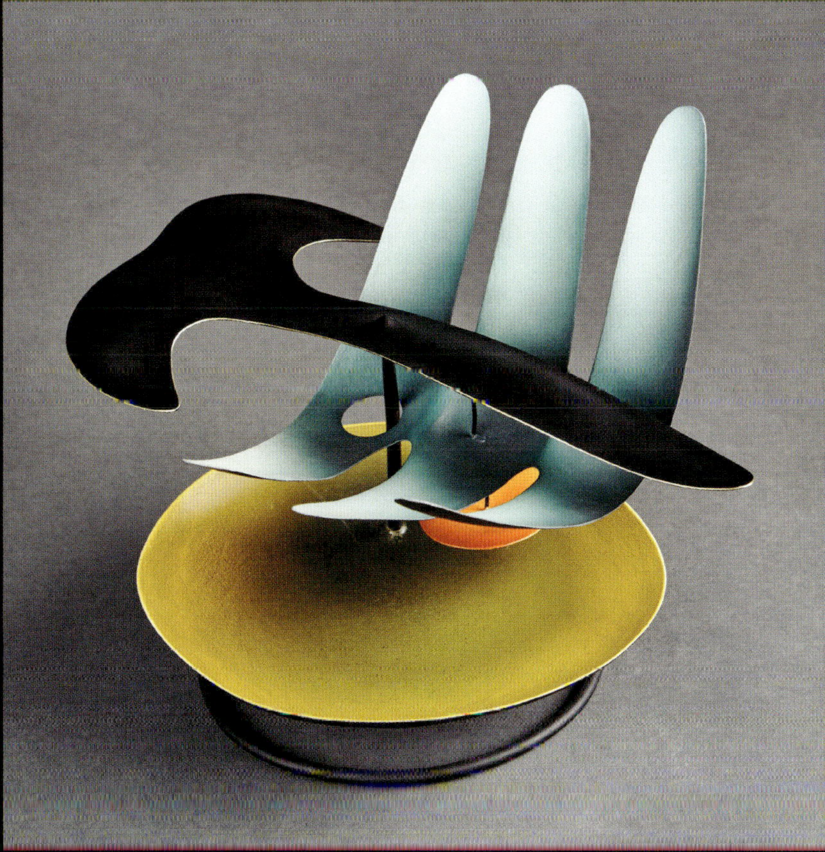

TRIBUTE #6
Standing mobile in brass and aluminum with steel wires, and oil and acrylic colors
10 x 13 x 9"
MD620

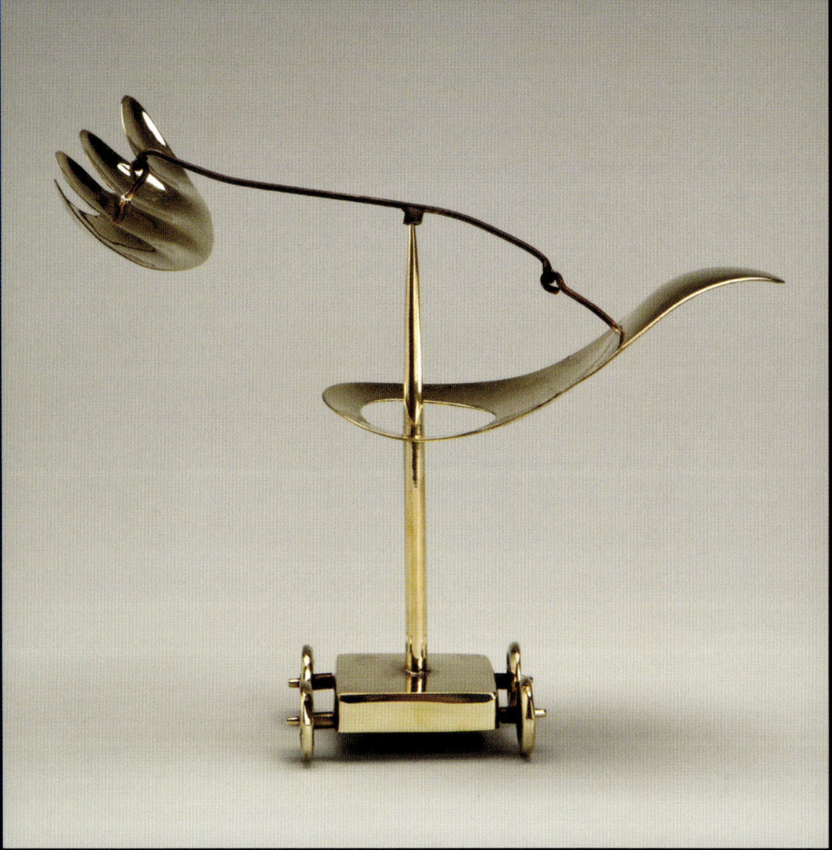

RISE AND FALL
Standing mobile in polished brass
7 x 9 x 5.5"

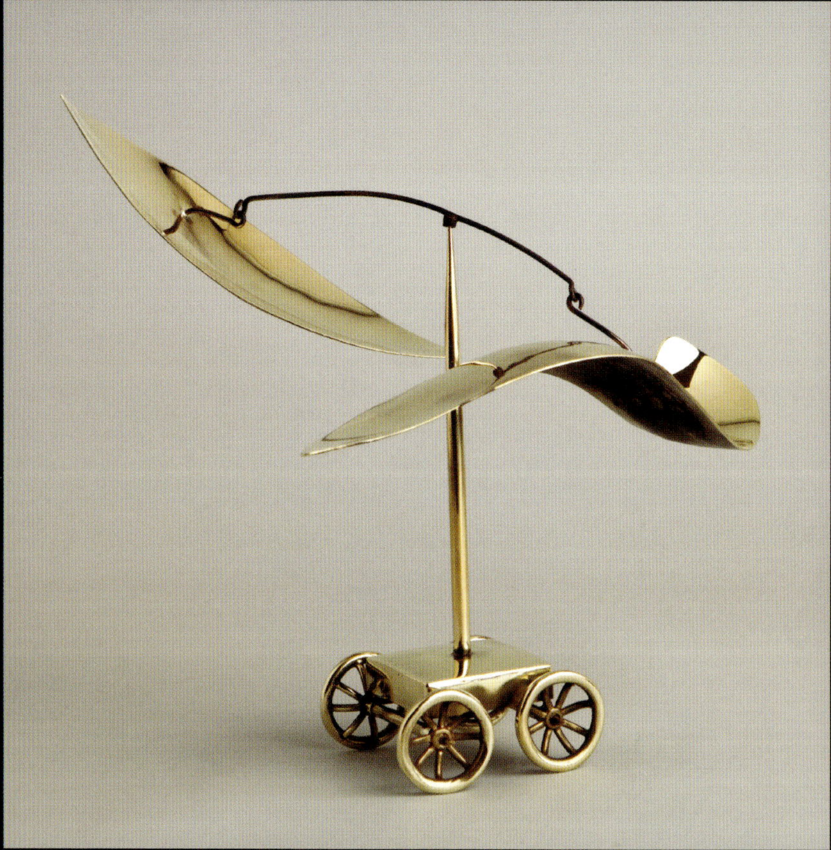

DREAM ON
Standing mobile in polished brass
9 x 11 x 8"

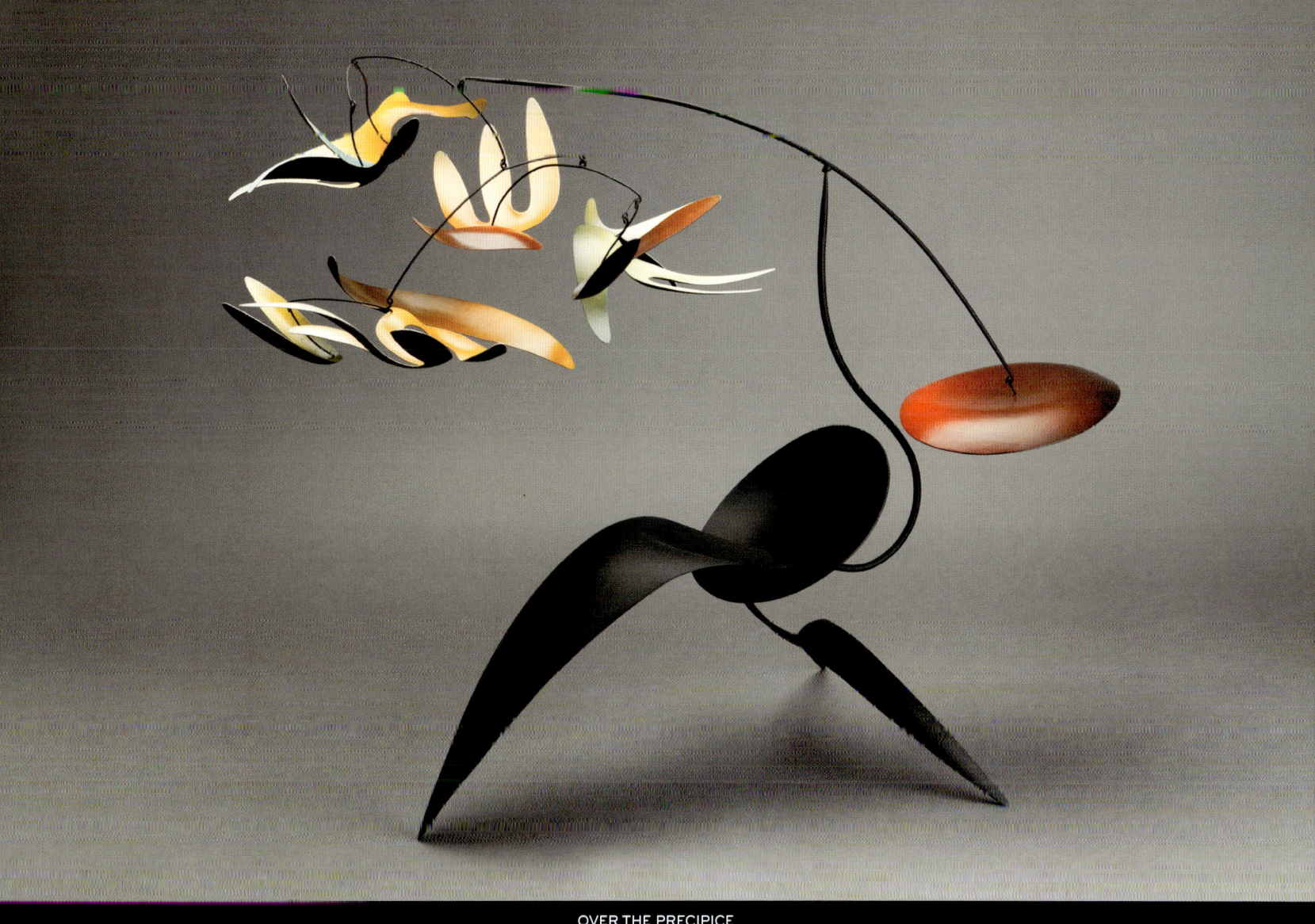

OVER THE PRECIPICE
Standing mobile in brass and aluminum with steel wires, and oil and acrylic colors
30 x 22 x 23"
MD678

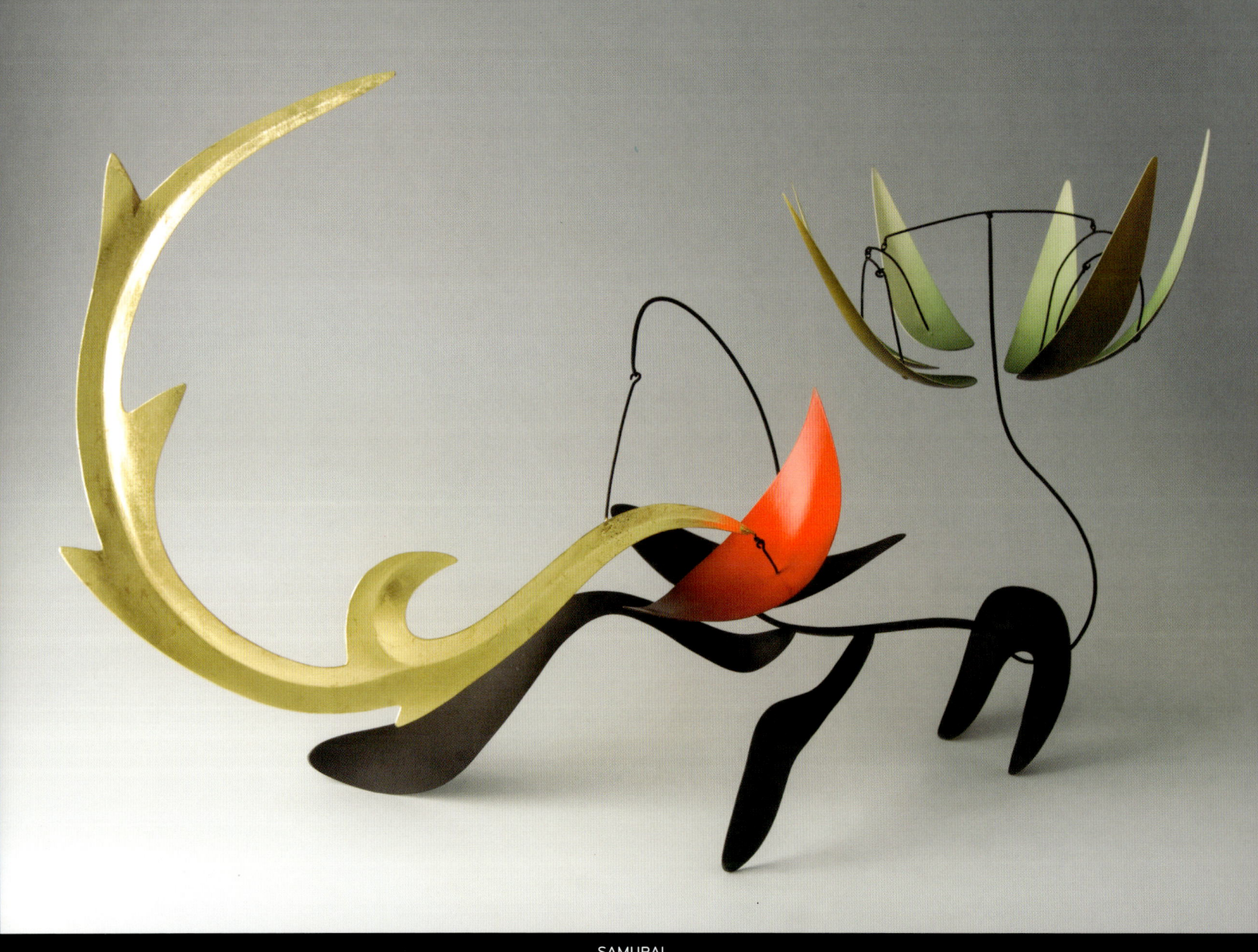

SAMURAI
Standing mobile in brass and aluminum with steel wires, oil and acrylic colors, and 23K gold leaf

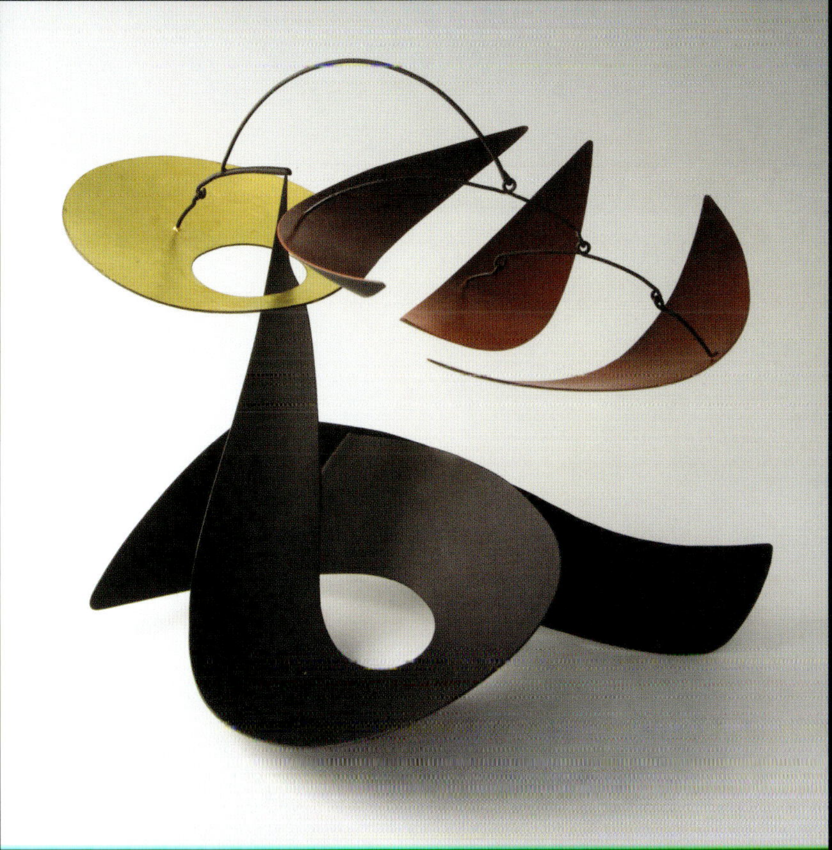

KANJI III
Standing mobile in brass and aluminum with steel wires, oil and acrylic colors, and 23K gold leaf
10 x 14 x 12"
MD529

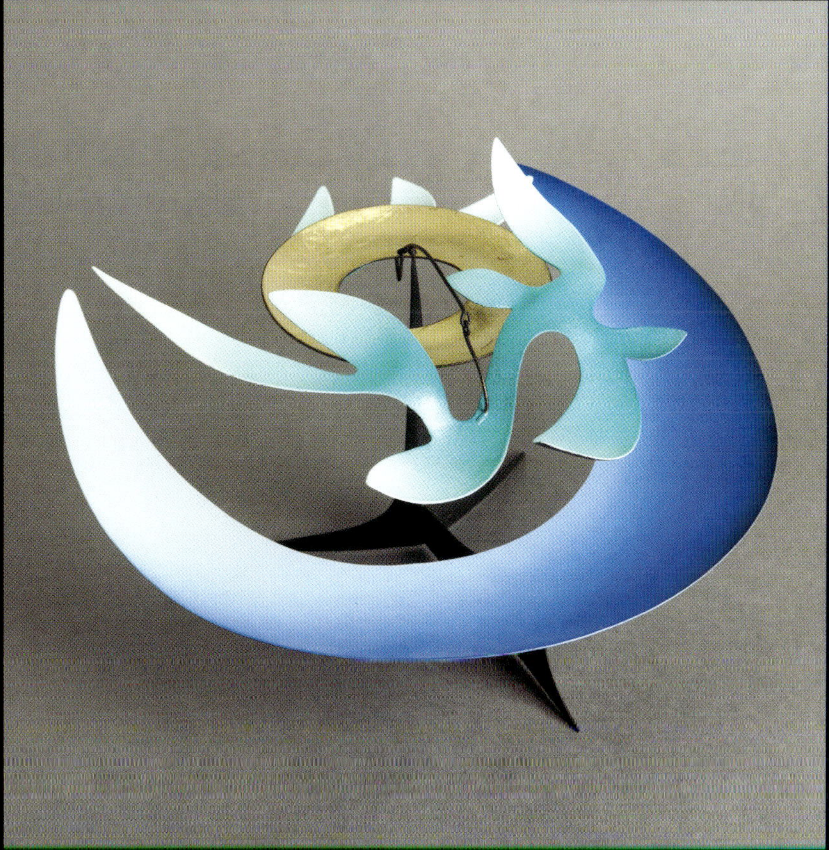

BLUE DANUBE
Standing mobile in brass and aluminum with steel wires, oil and acrylic colors, and 23K gold leaf
8 x 12 x 12"
MD692

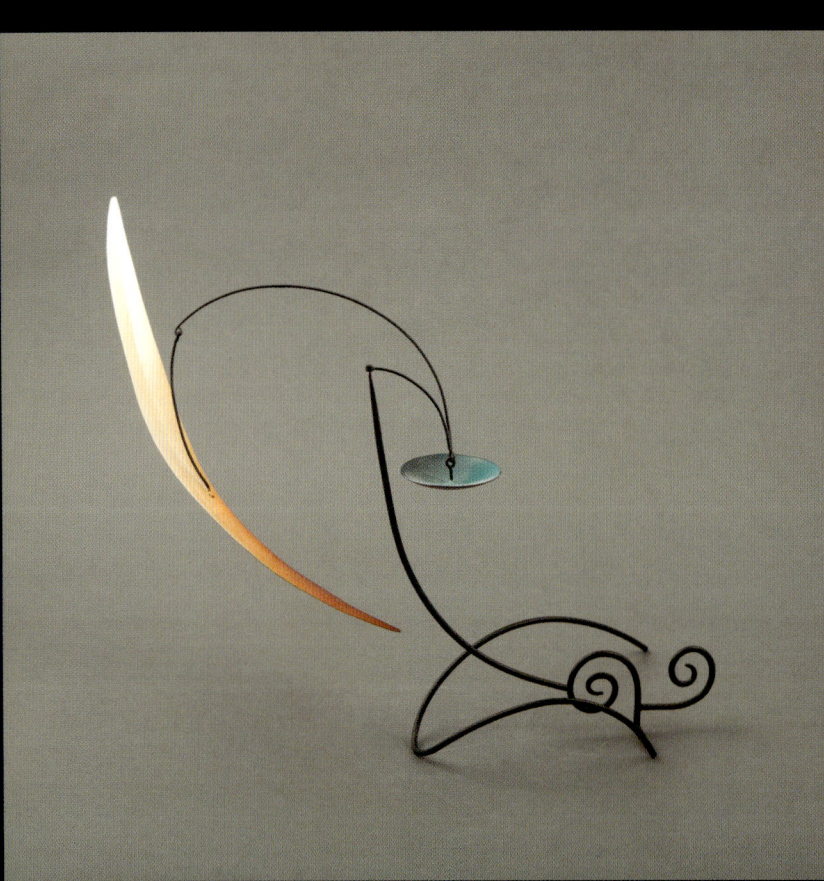

HAPPY TRAILS
Standing mobile in brass and aluminum with steel wires, and oil and acrylic colors
12 x 12 x 8"
MD731

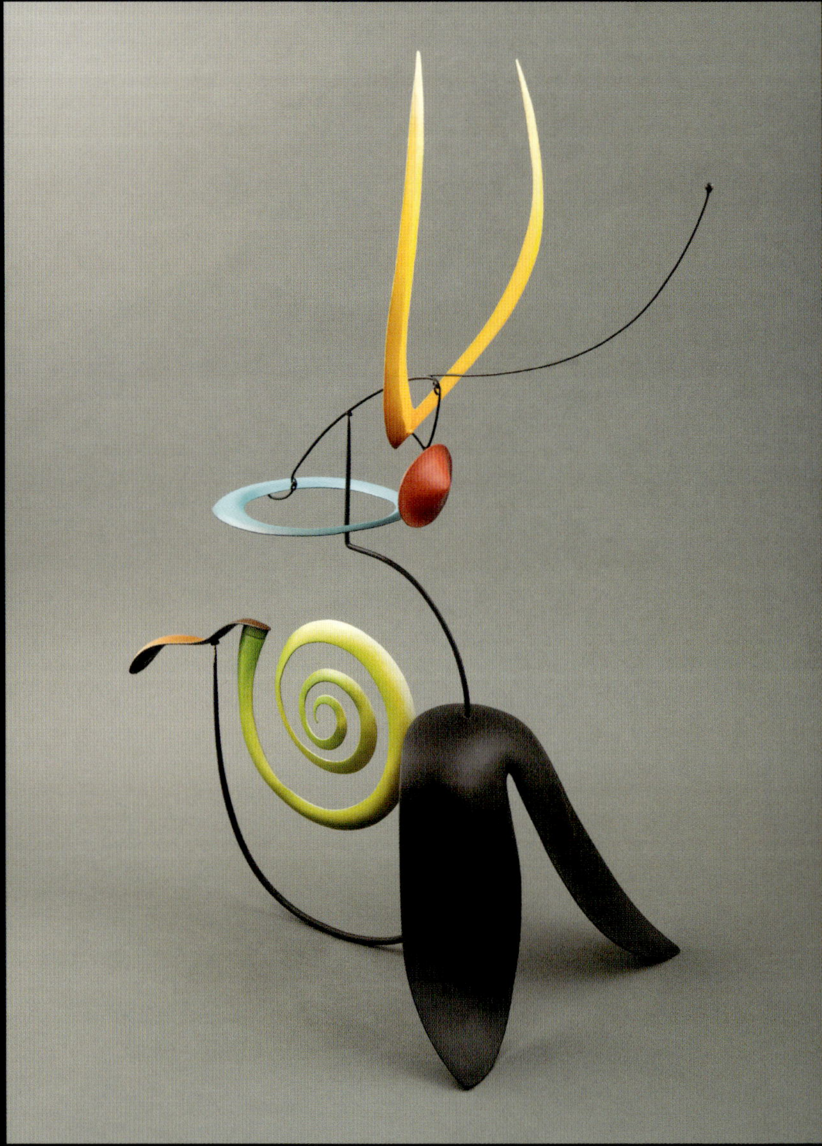

THE NIGHT BRIGADE
Standing mobile in brass and aluminum with steel wires,
oil and acrylic colors, and 23K gold leaf
24 x 21 x 10"
MD729

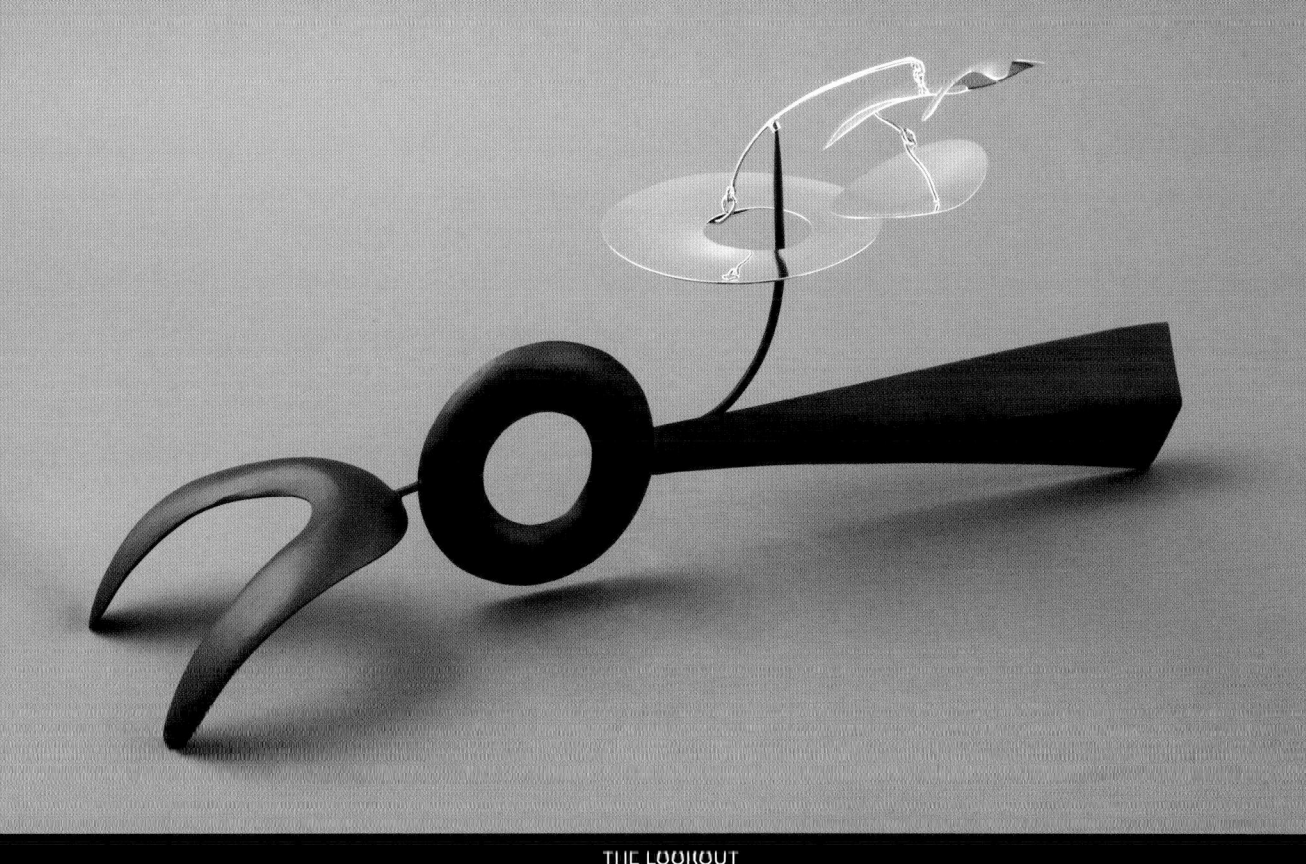

THE LOOKOUT
Standing mobile in painted brass, and sterling silver
9 x 18 x 9.5"
MD730

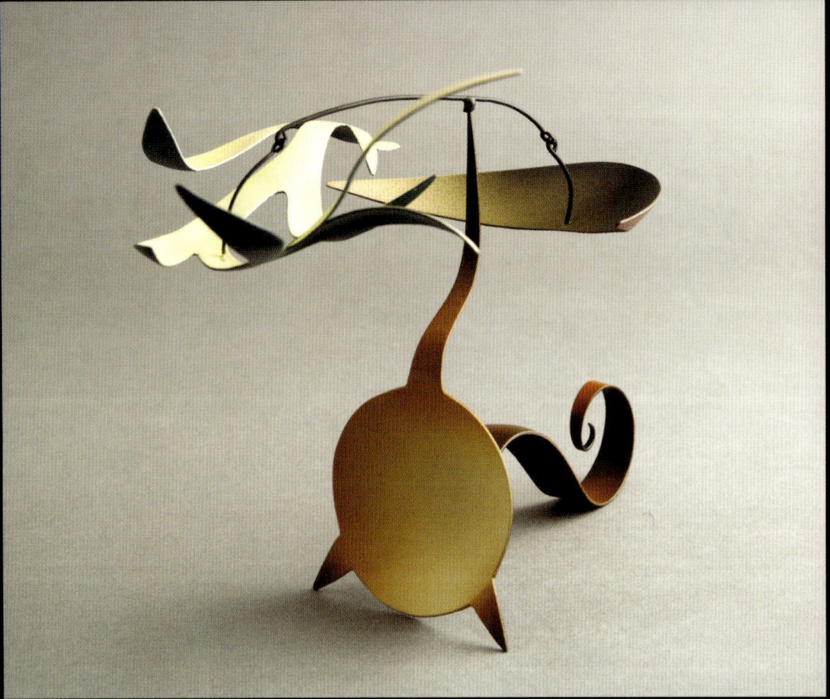

SEA AND FOREST
Standing mobile in brass and aluminum with steel wires, and oil and acrylic colors
8 x 8 x 8"
MD671

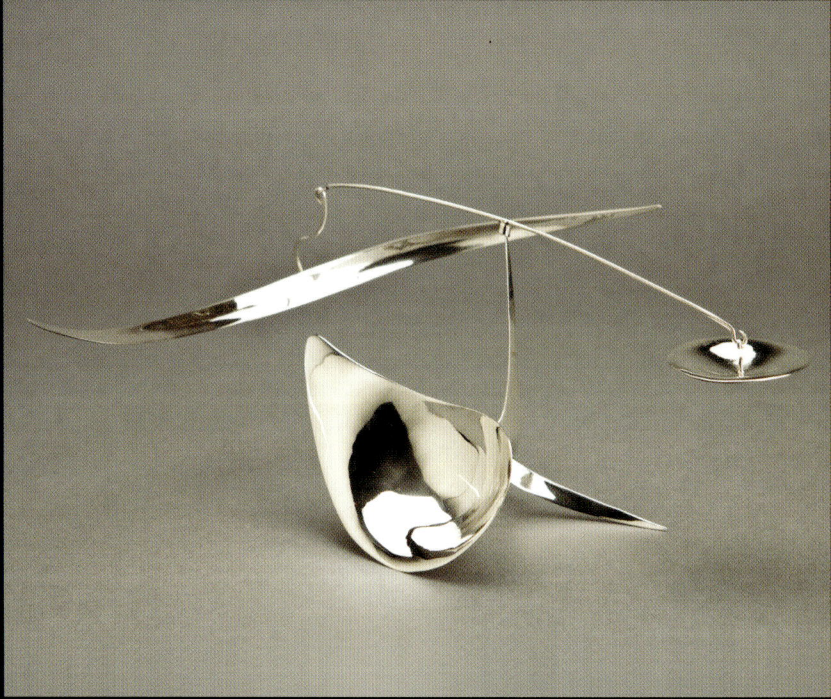

LOOKING INWARD FROM ABOVE
Standing mobile in polished sterling silver
4.5 x 9 x 9"
MD636

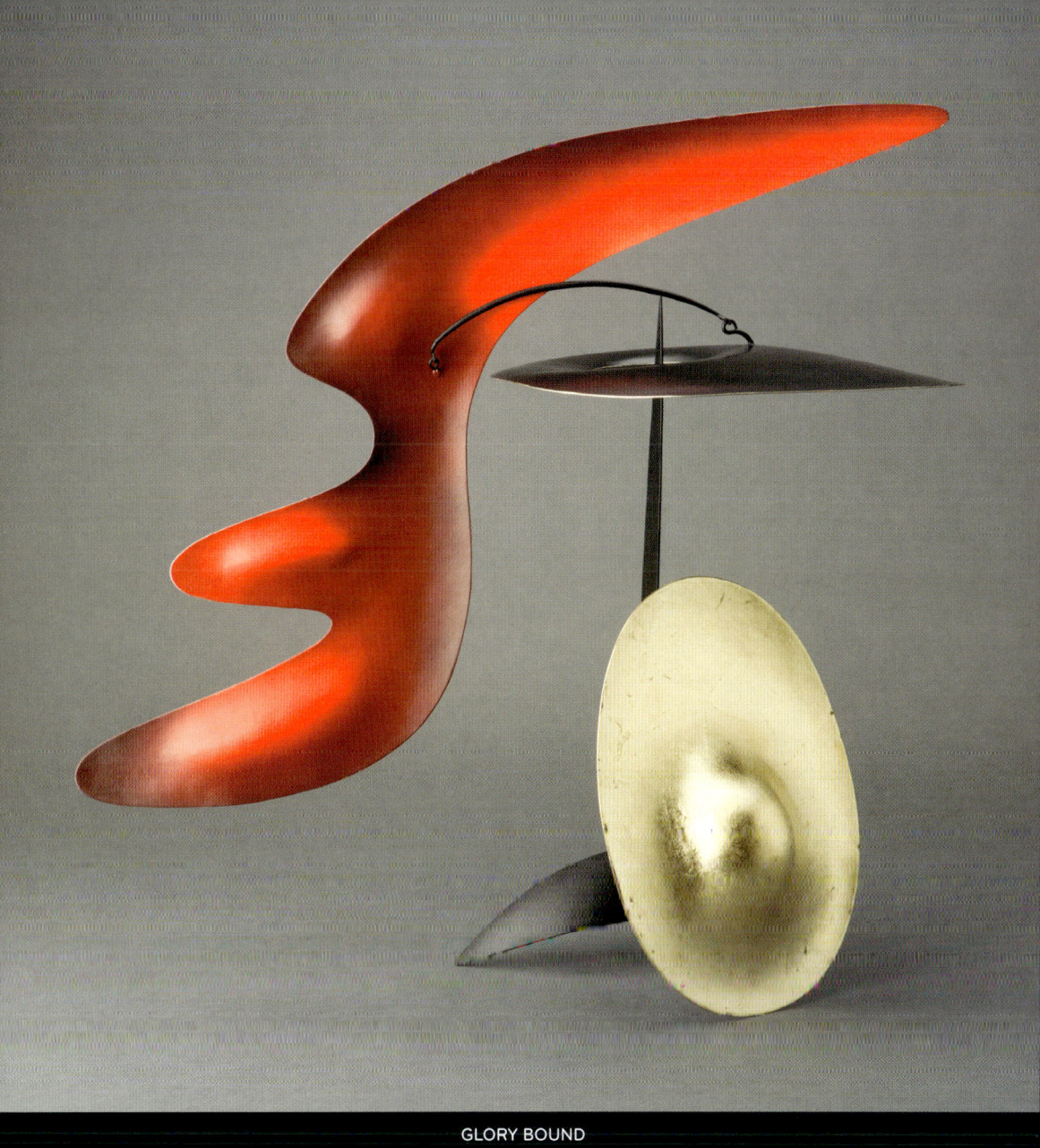

GLORY BOUND
Standing mobile in brass and aluminum with steel wires, oil and acrylic colors, and 23K gold leaf
19 x 21 x 11"
MD712

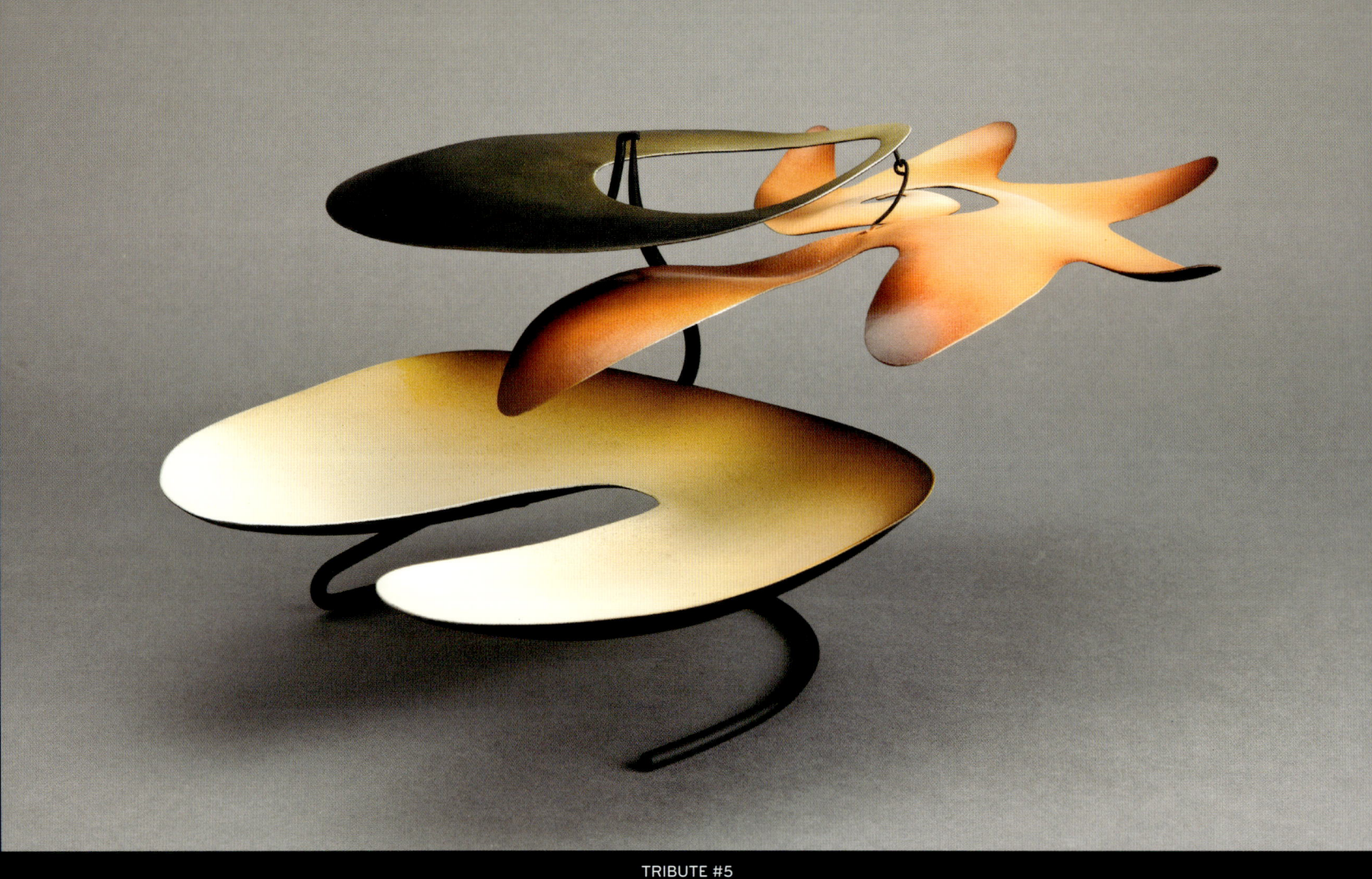

TRIBUTE #5
Standing mobile in brass and aluminum with steel wires, and oil and acrylic colors
8 x 17 x 12.5"
MD619

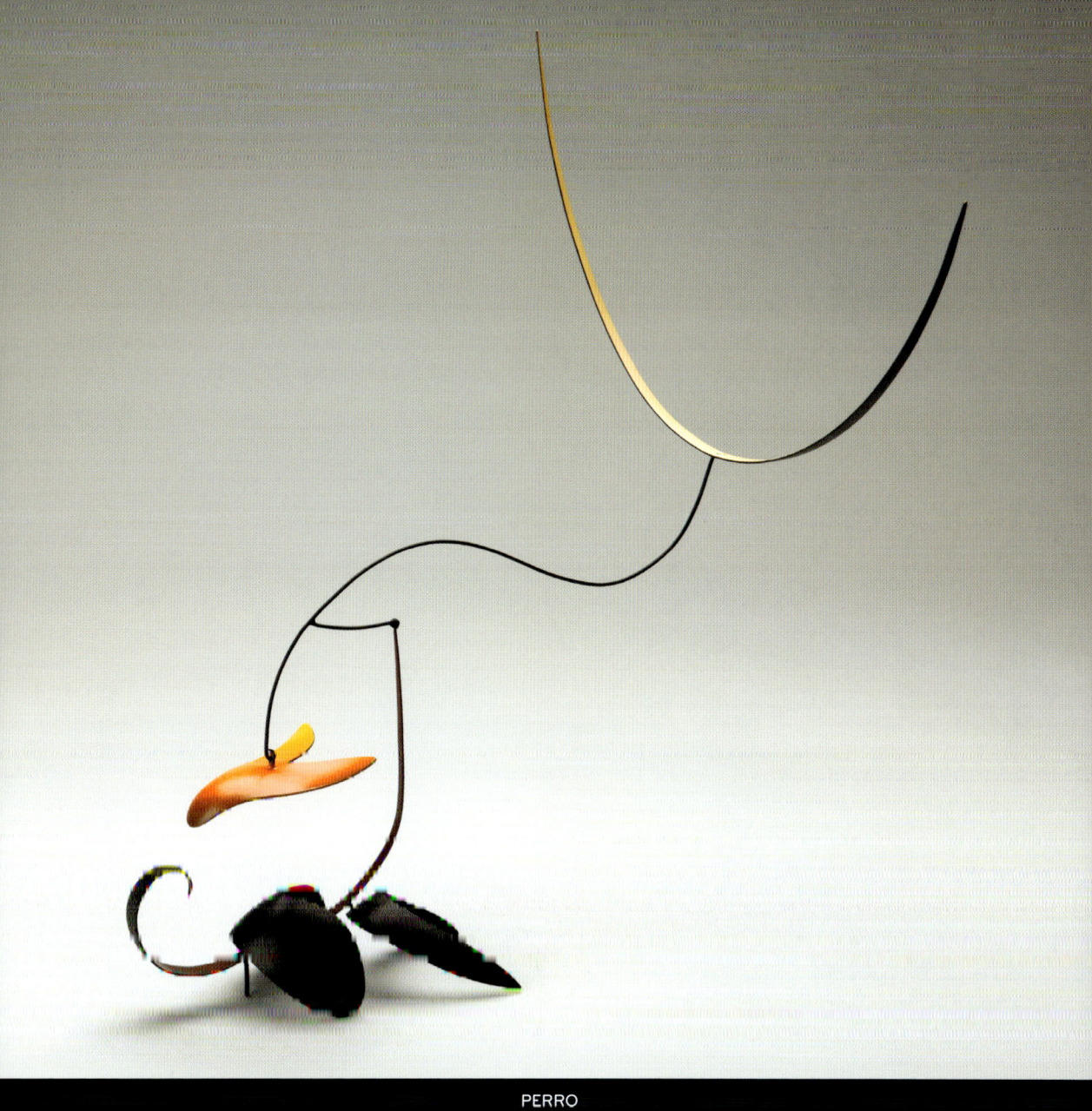

PERRO
Standing mobile in brass and aluminum with steel wires, and oil and acrylic colors

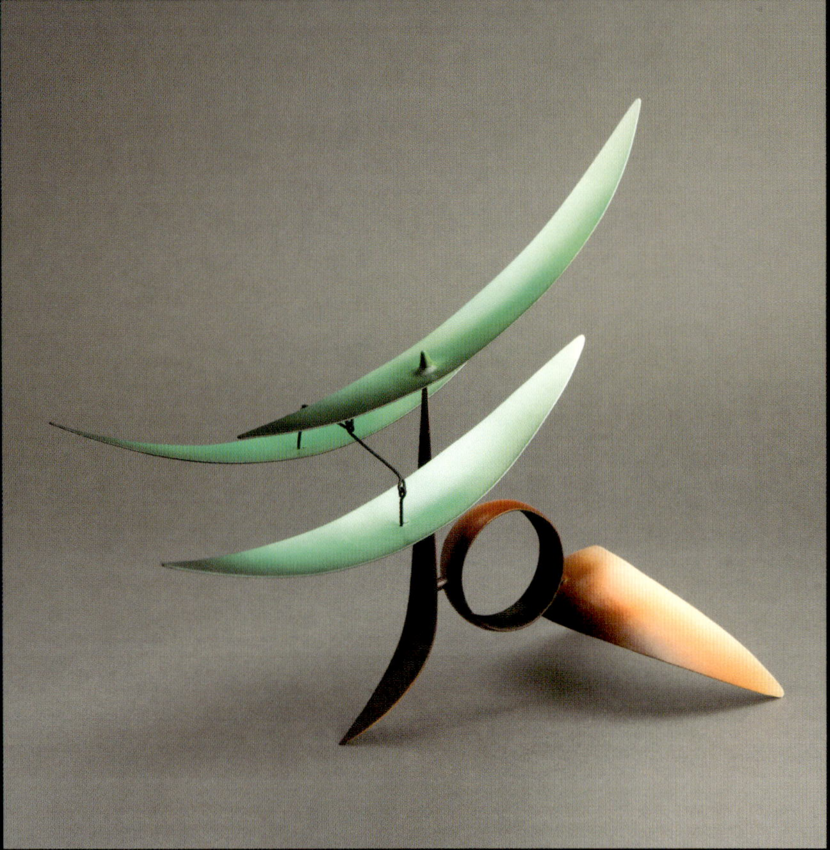

THE FORTRESS
Standing mobile in brass and aluminum with steel wires, and oil and acrylic colors
13 x 16 x 7"

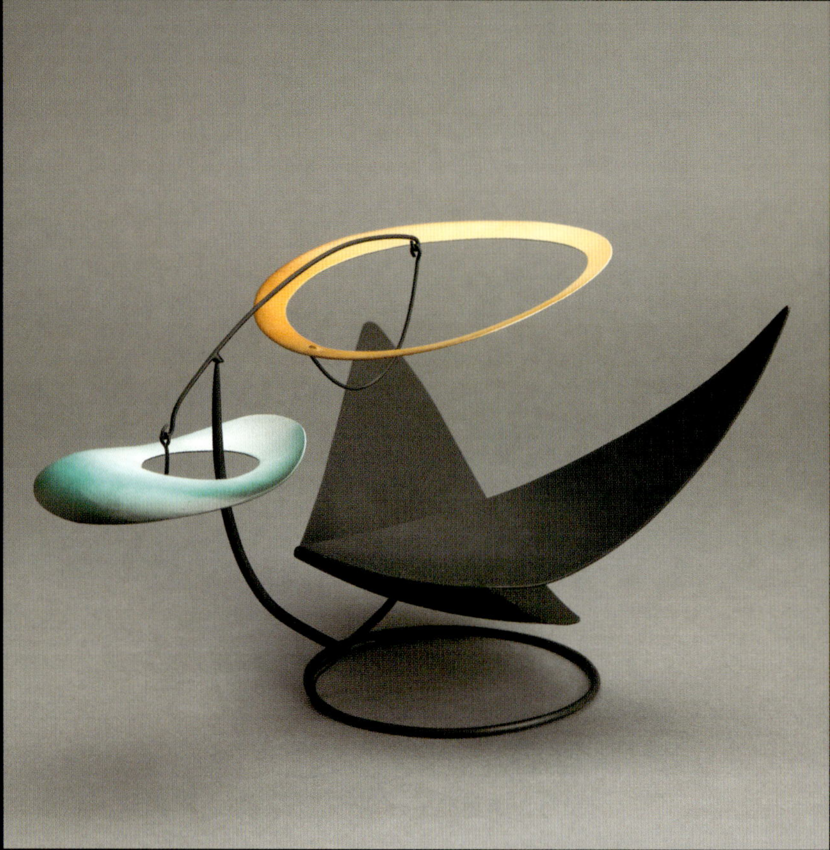

SOARING
Standing mobile in brass and aluminum with steel wires, and oil and acrylic colors
7.5 x 16 x 9"

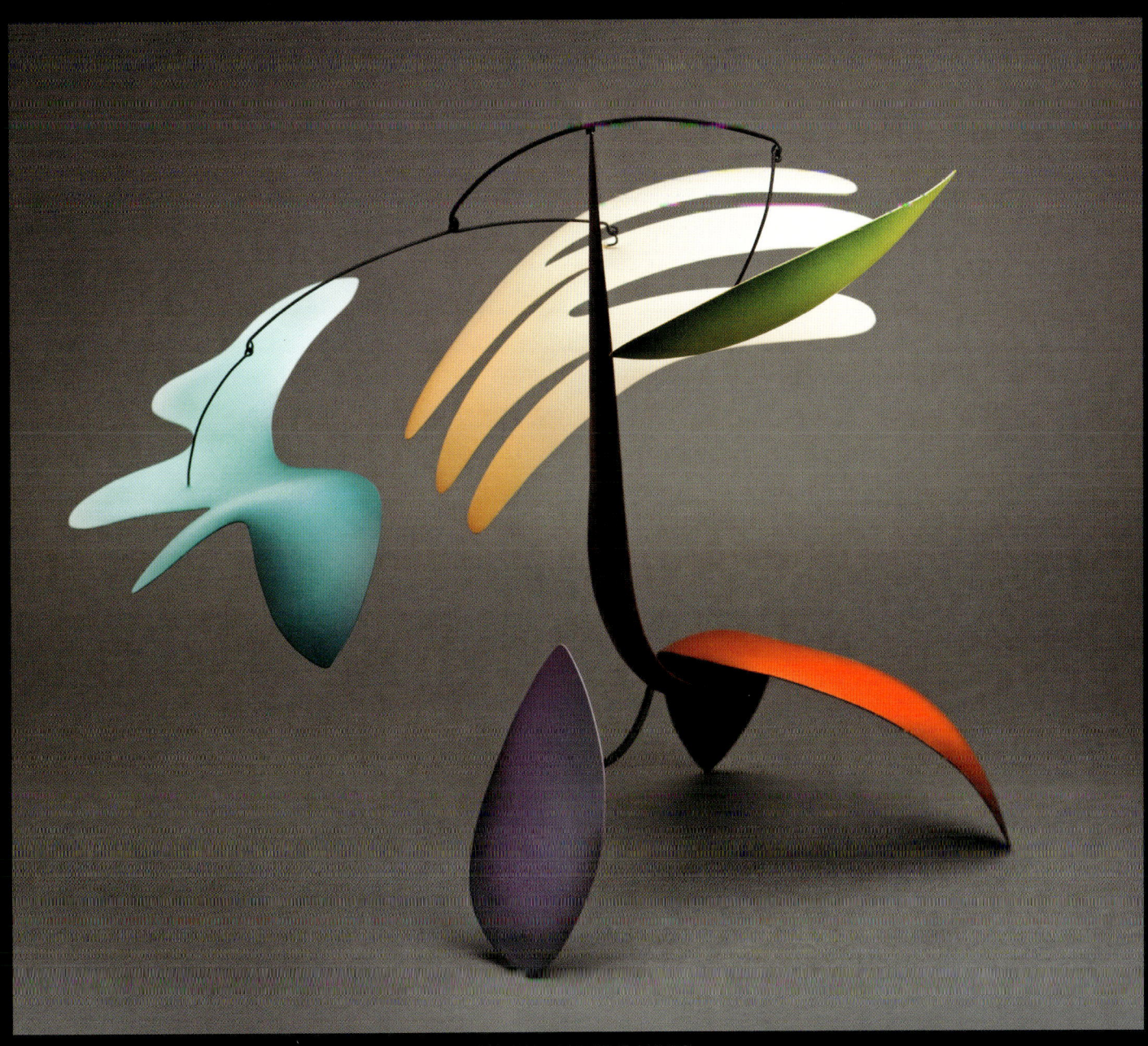

THE RHYTHM OF THE SAINTS
Standing mobile in brass and aluminum with steel wires, and oil and acrylic colors
18 x 18 x 20"
MD700

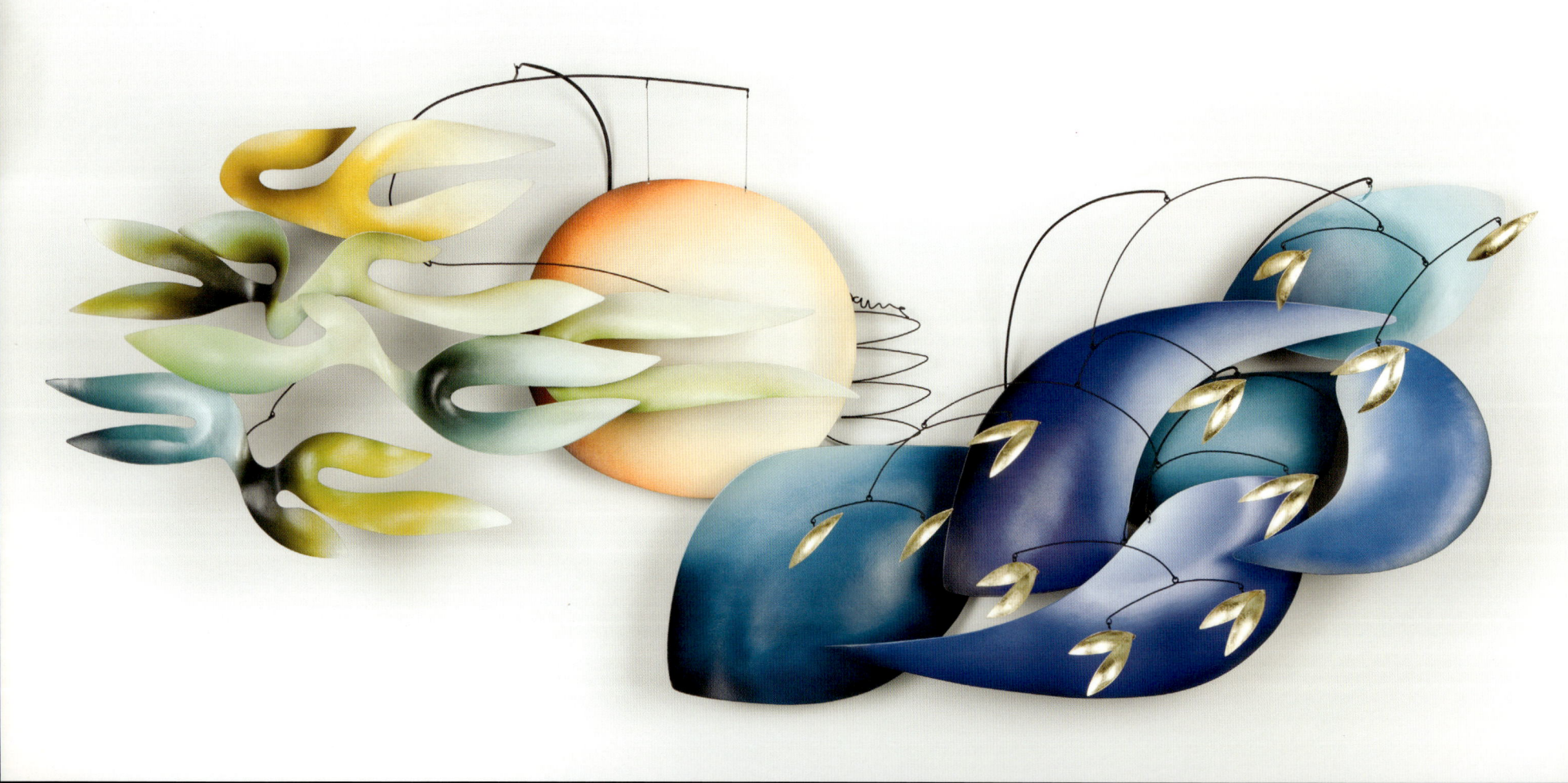

DAY'S JOURNEY INTO NIGHT
Standing mobile in brass and aluminum with steel wires, oil and acrylic colors, and 23K gold leaf
27 x 52 x 12"
MD728

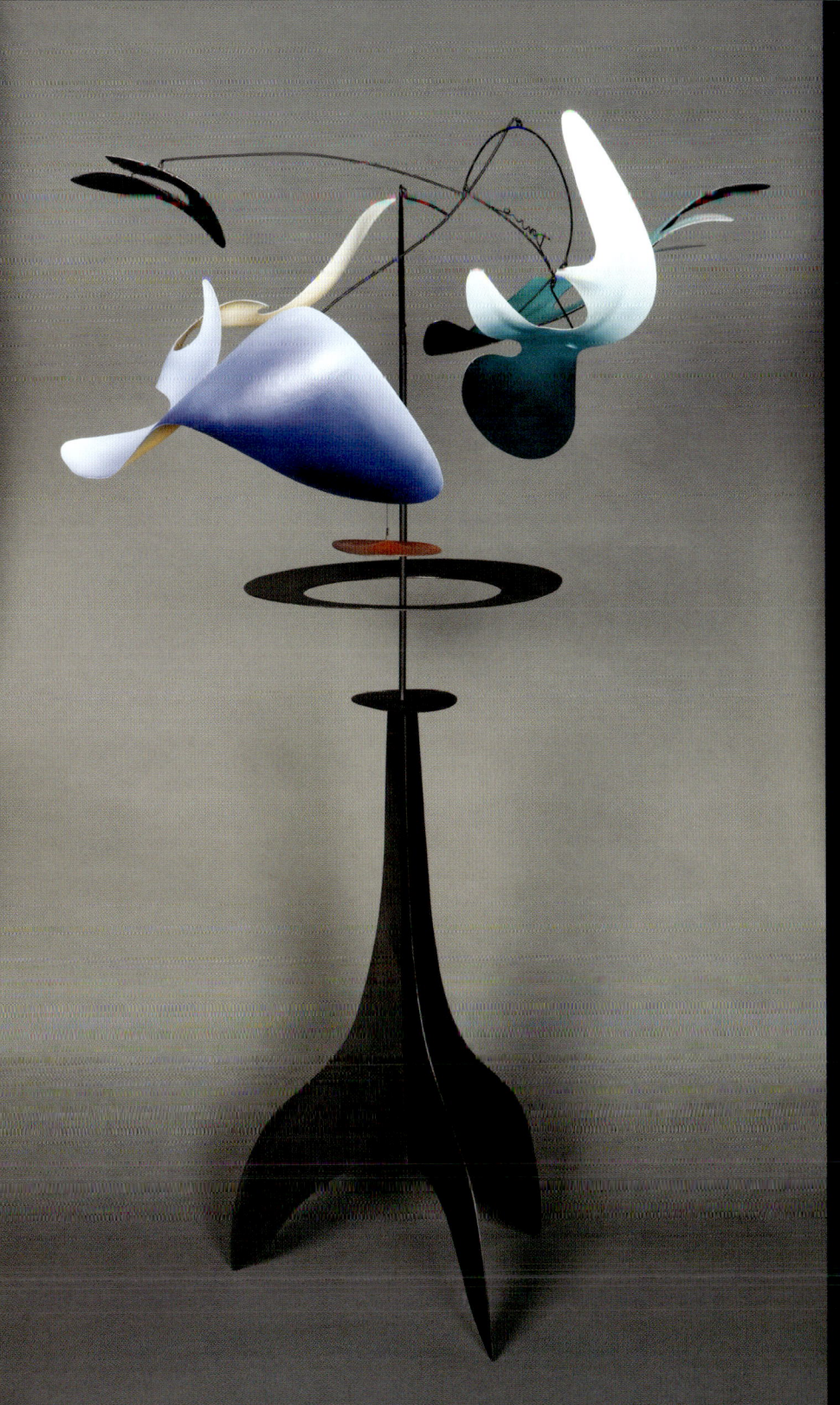

A CALLING FROM ABOVE
Standing mobile in brass and aluminum
with steel wires, and oil and acrylic colors
61 x 30 x 36"
MD733

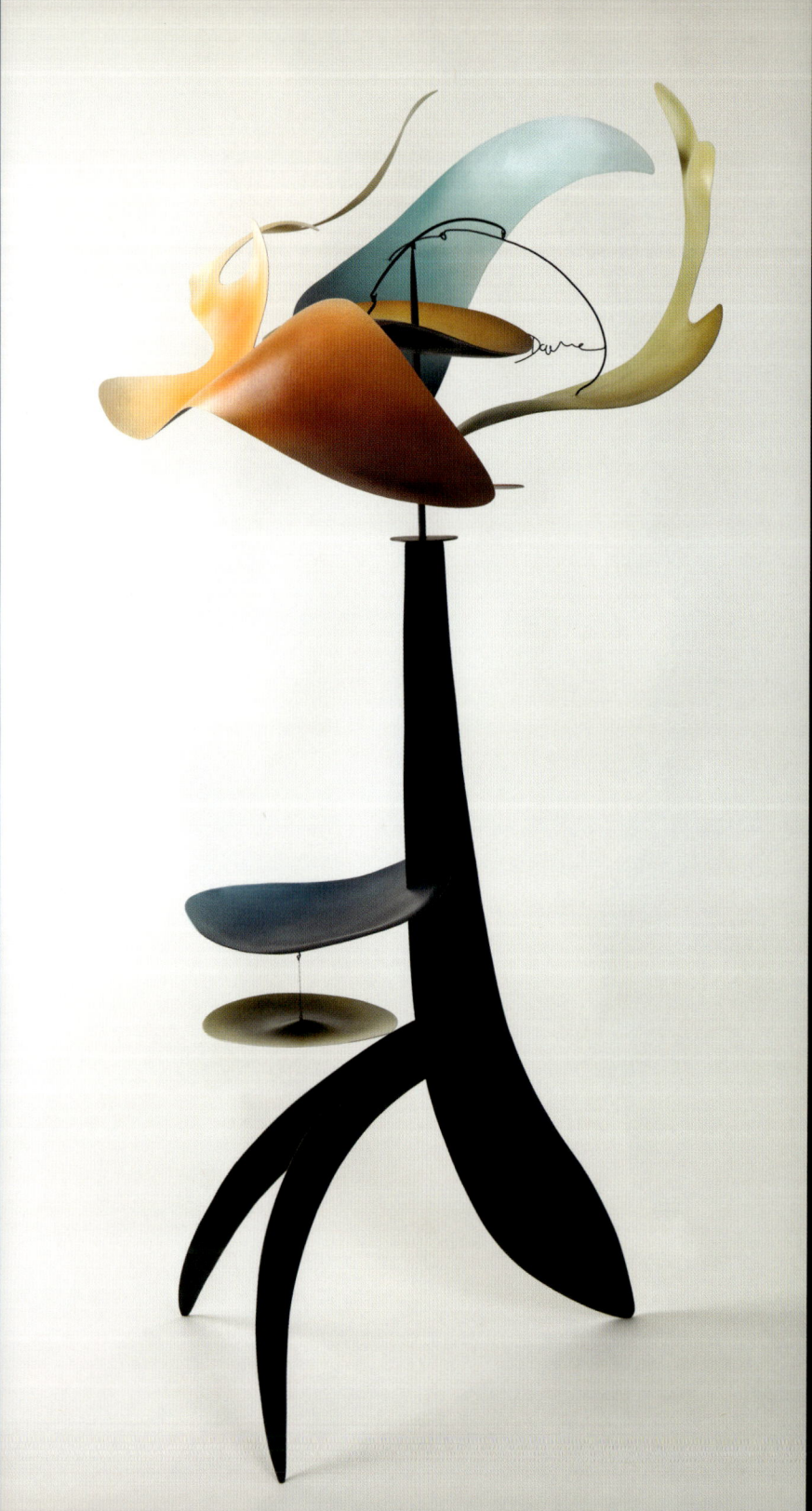

VIGOROUS GROWTH
Standing mobile in brass,
steel, and aluminum, with
oil and acrylic colors
60 x 32 x 24"
MD655

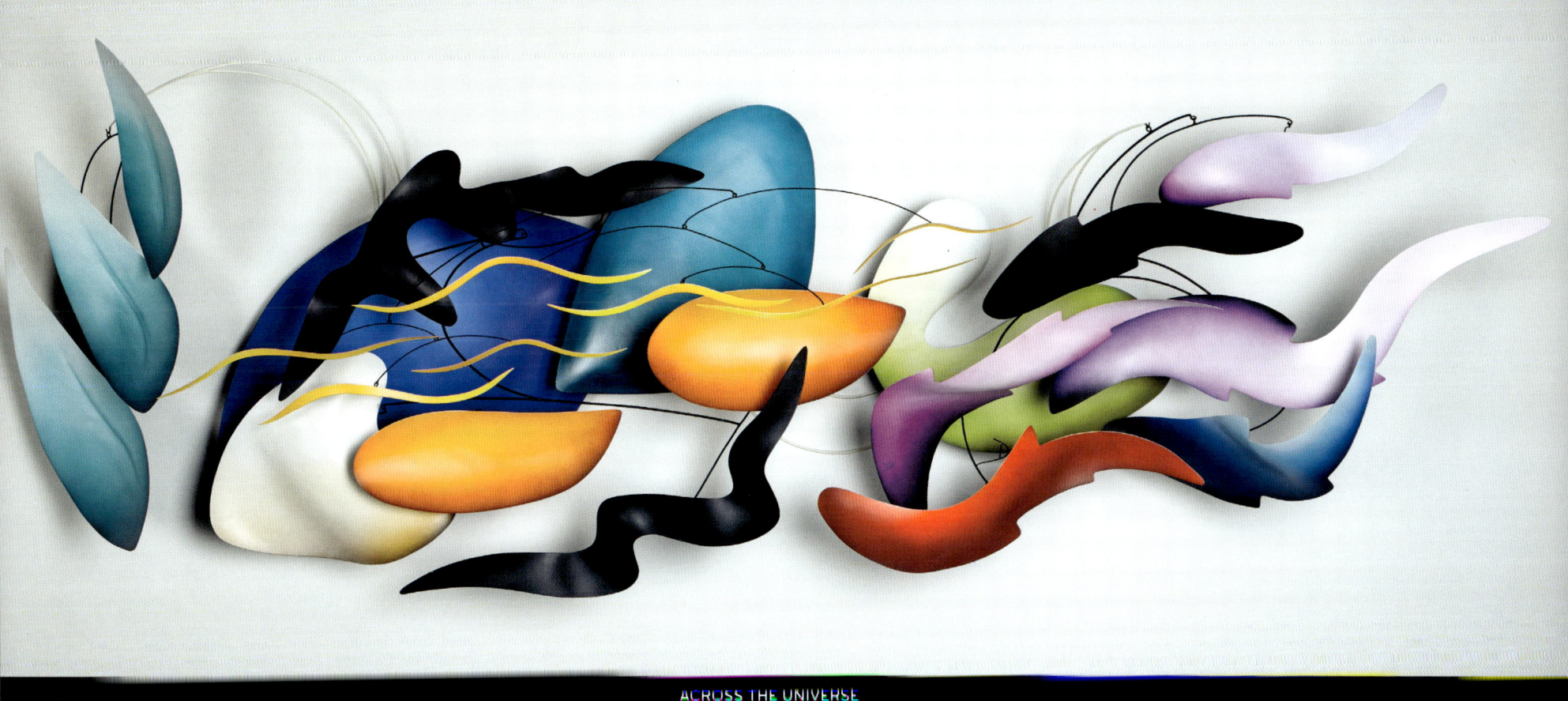

ACROSS THE UNIVERSE
Wall-mounted Mobile in brass and aluminum with steel wires, and oil and acrylic colors

MD710

NOCTURNE: BRIGHT LIGHT (FRONT)
Hanging room divider in aluminum
with steel wires, oil and acrylic colors,
and 23K gold leaf
87 x 45 x 1"
MD627

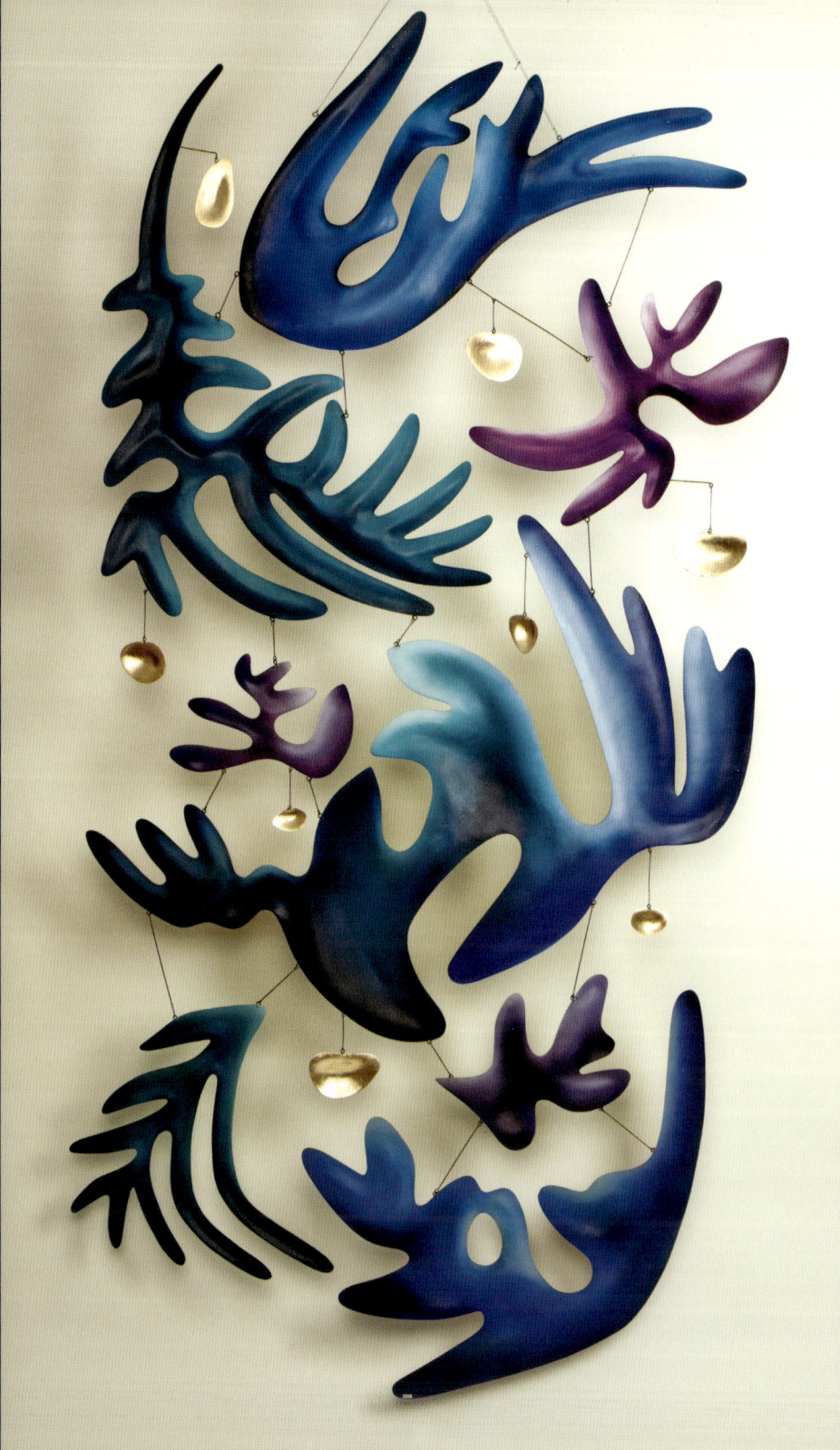

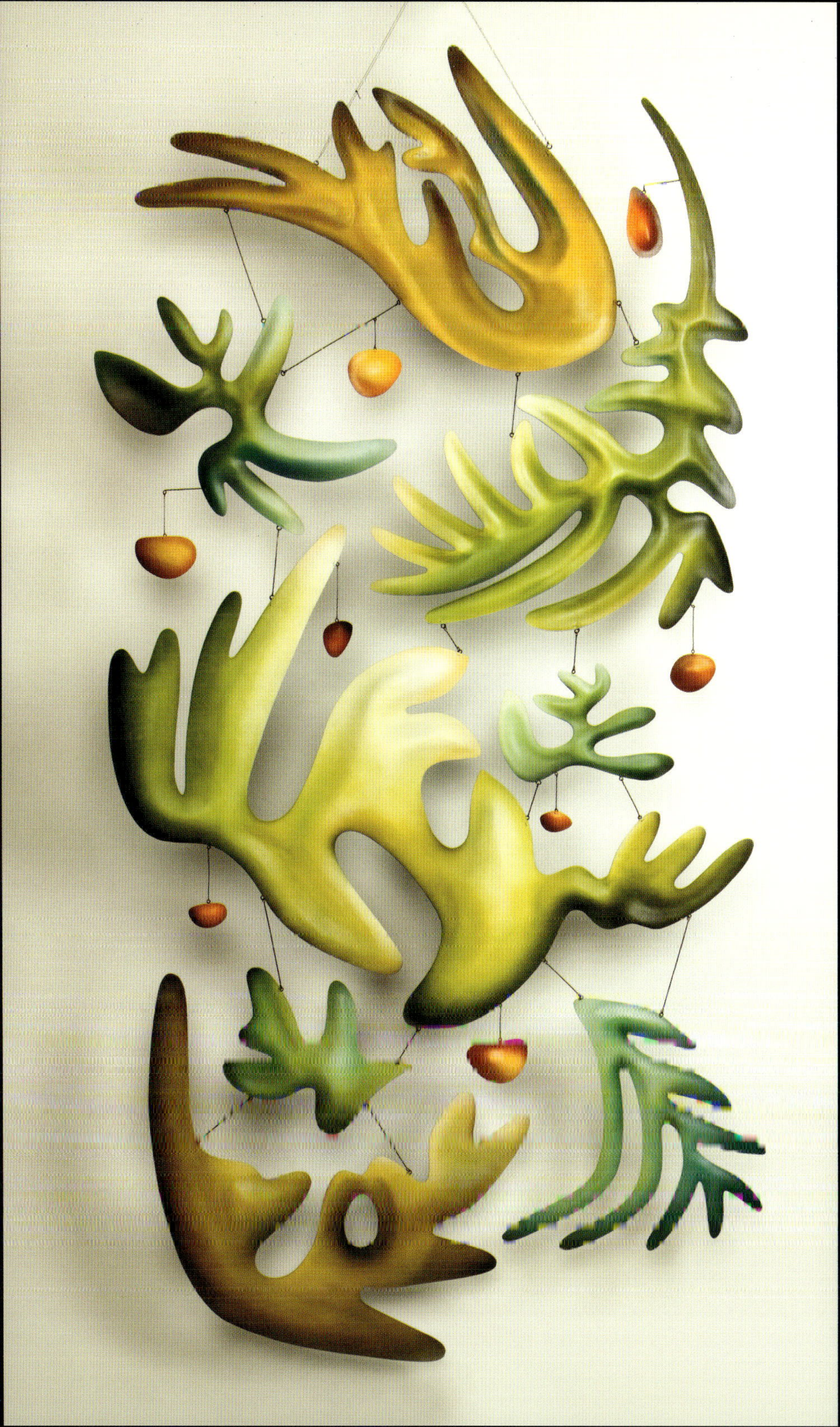

NOCTURNE: BRIGHT LIGHT (BACK)
Hanging room divider in aluminum
with steel wires, oil and acrylic colors,
and 23K gold leaf
87 x 45 x 1"
MD627

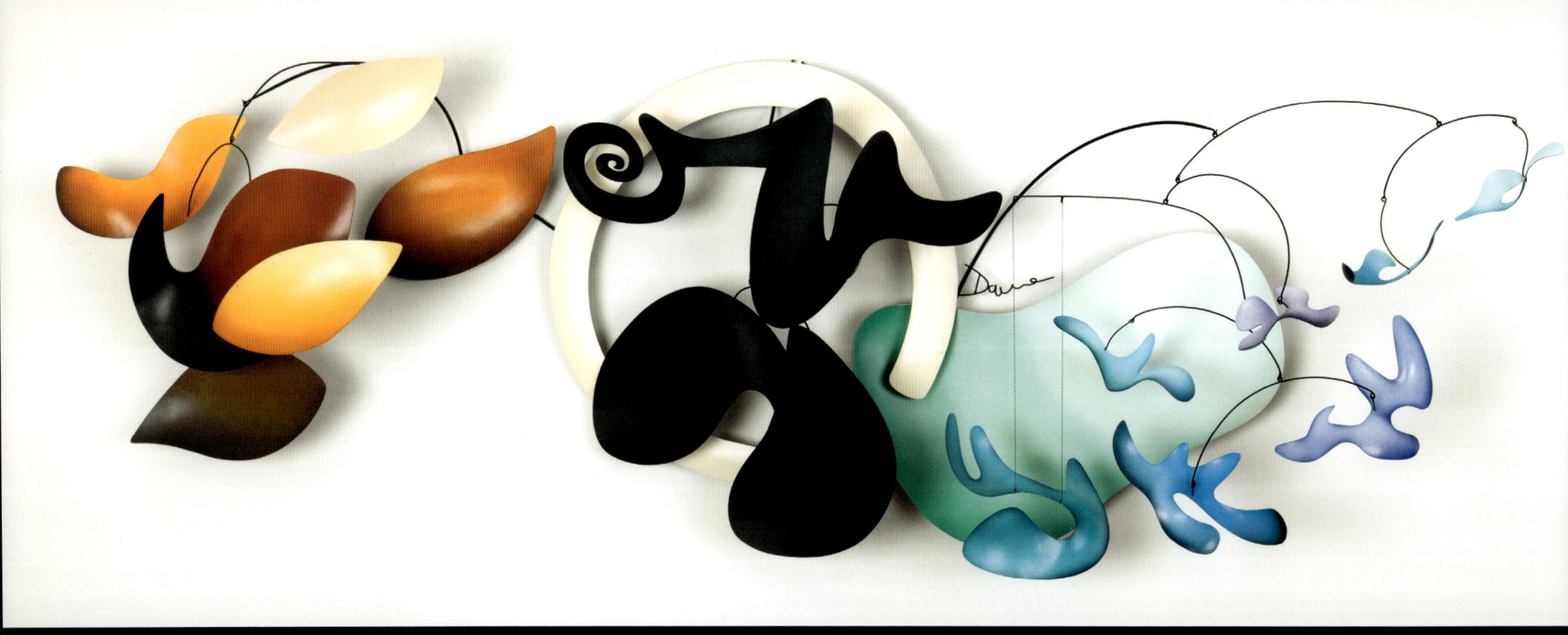

FAR AND AWAY
Wall-mounted mobile in brass and aluminum with steel wires, nylon cord, and oil and acrylic colors
21 x 66 x 14"
MD675

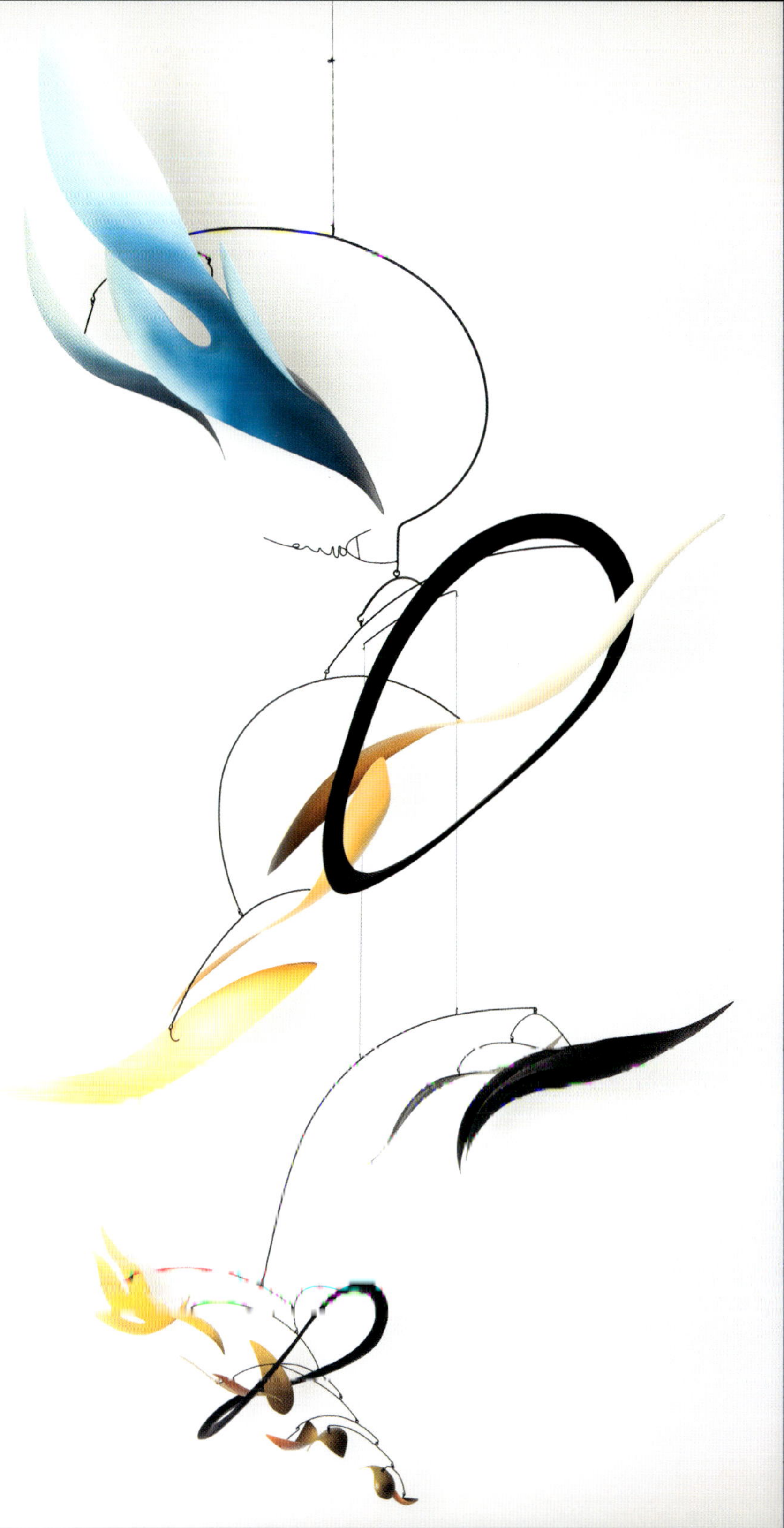

MAINTAINING CONTINUITY
Hanging mobile in brass and aluminum
with steel wires, and oil and acrylic colors
80 x 40 x 36"
MD574

RIVERBED
Wall-mounted mobile in brass
and aluminum with steel wires,
and oil and acrylic colors
32 x 25 x 19"
MD653

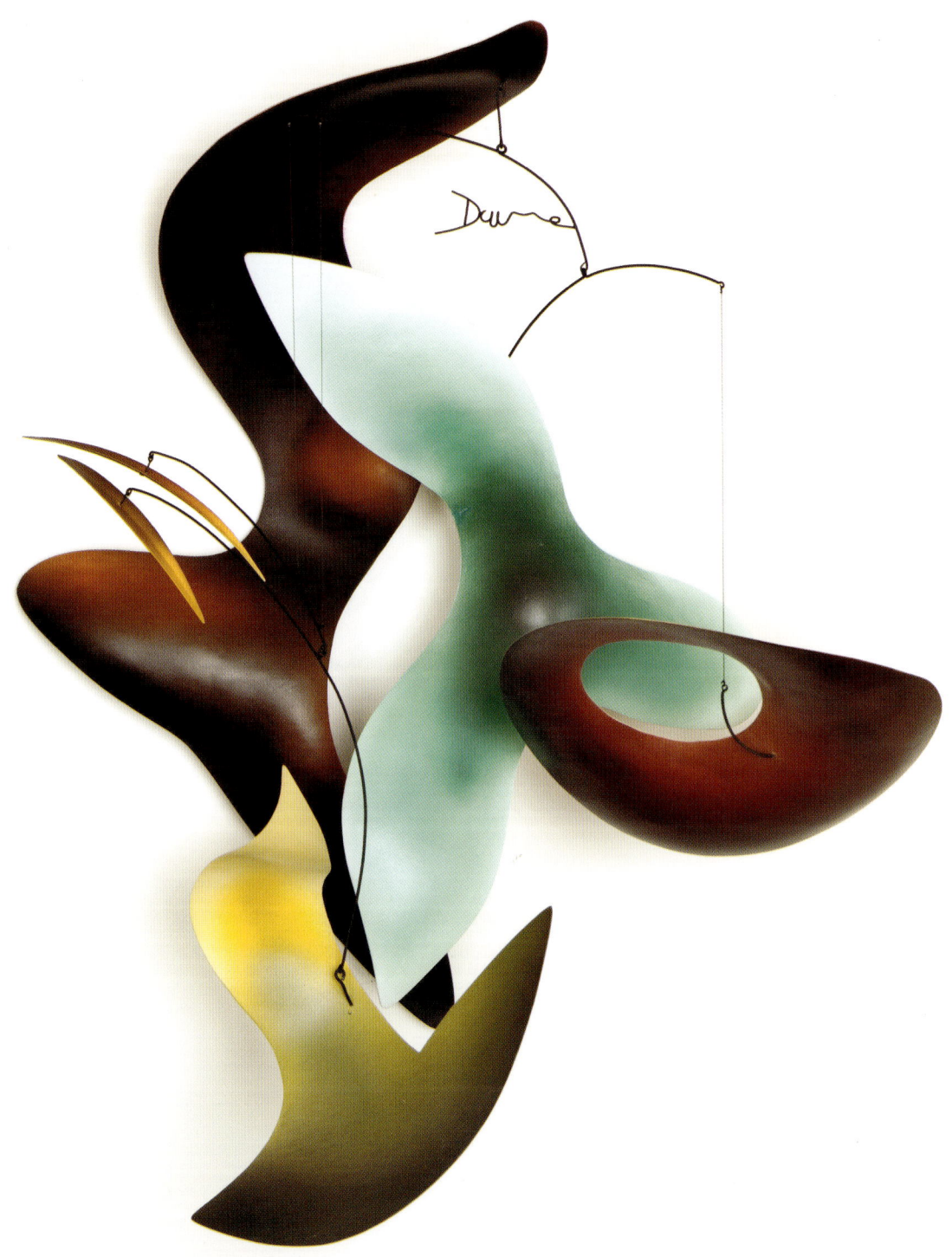

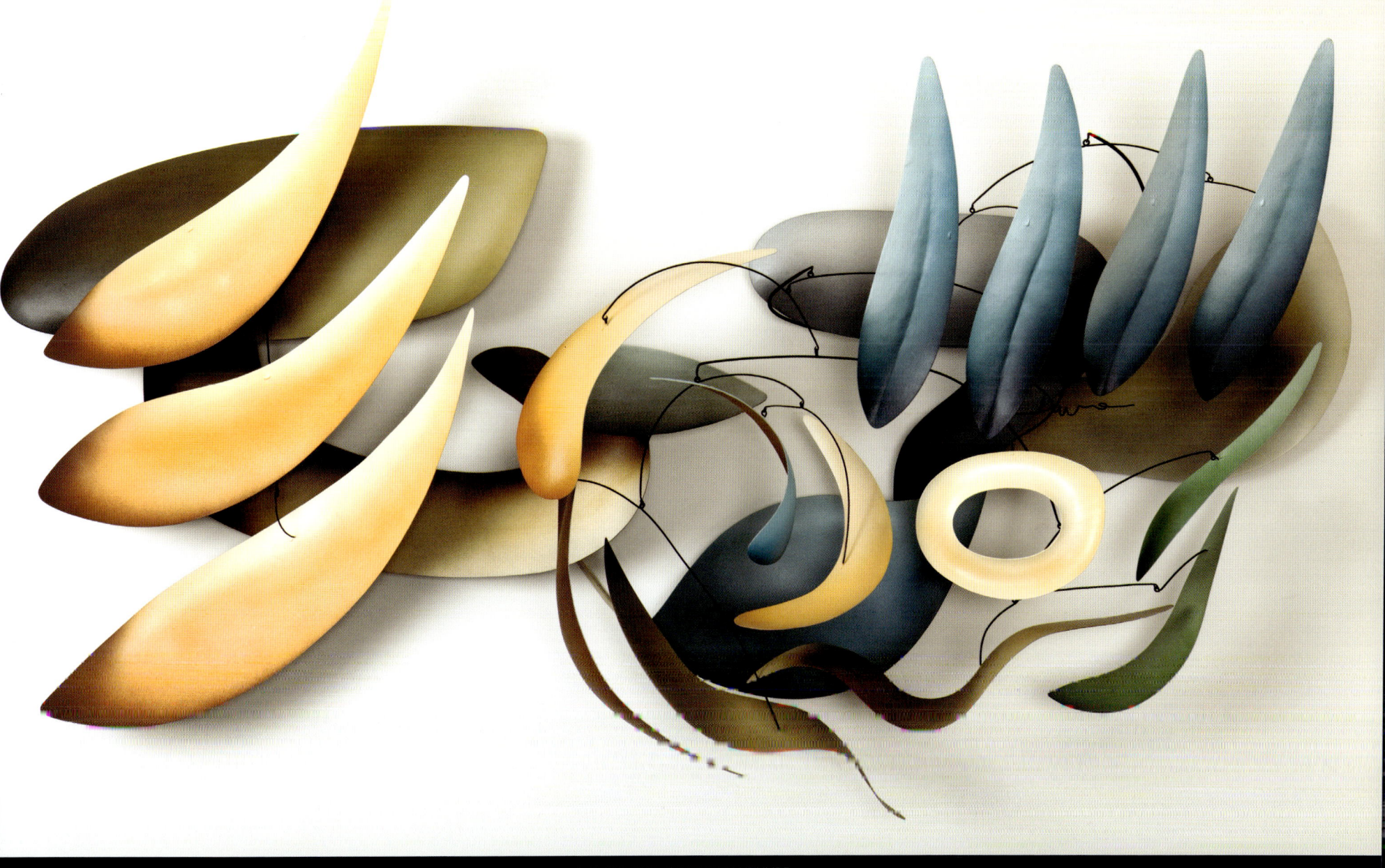

A SLOW AND SUBTLE MANEUVER
Wall-mounted mobile in brass and aluminum with steel wires, and oil and acrylic colors

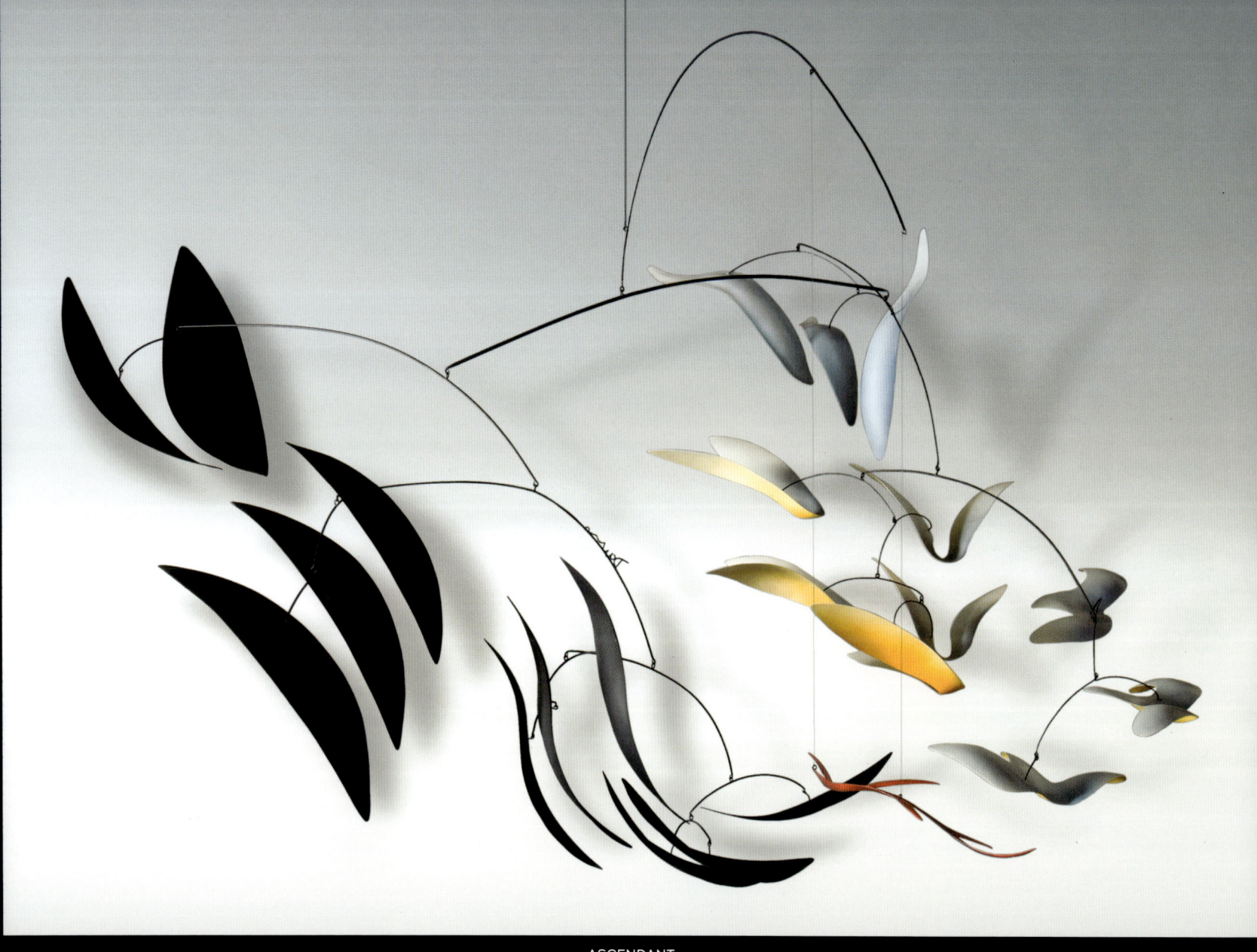

ASCENDANT
Hanging mobile in aluminum with steel wires, and oil and acrylic colors

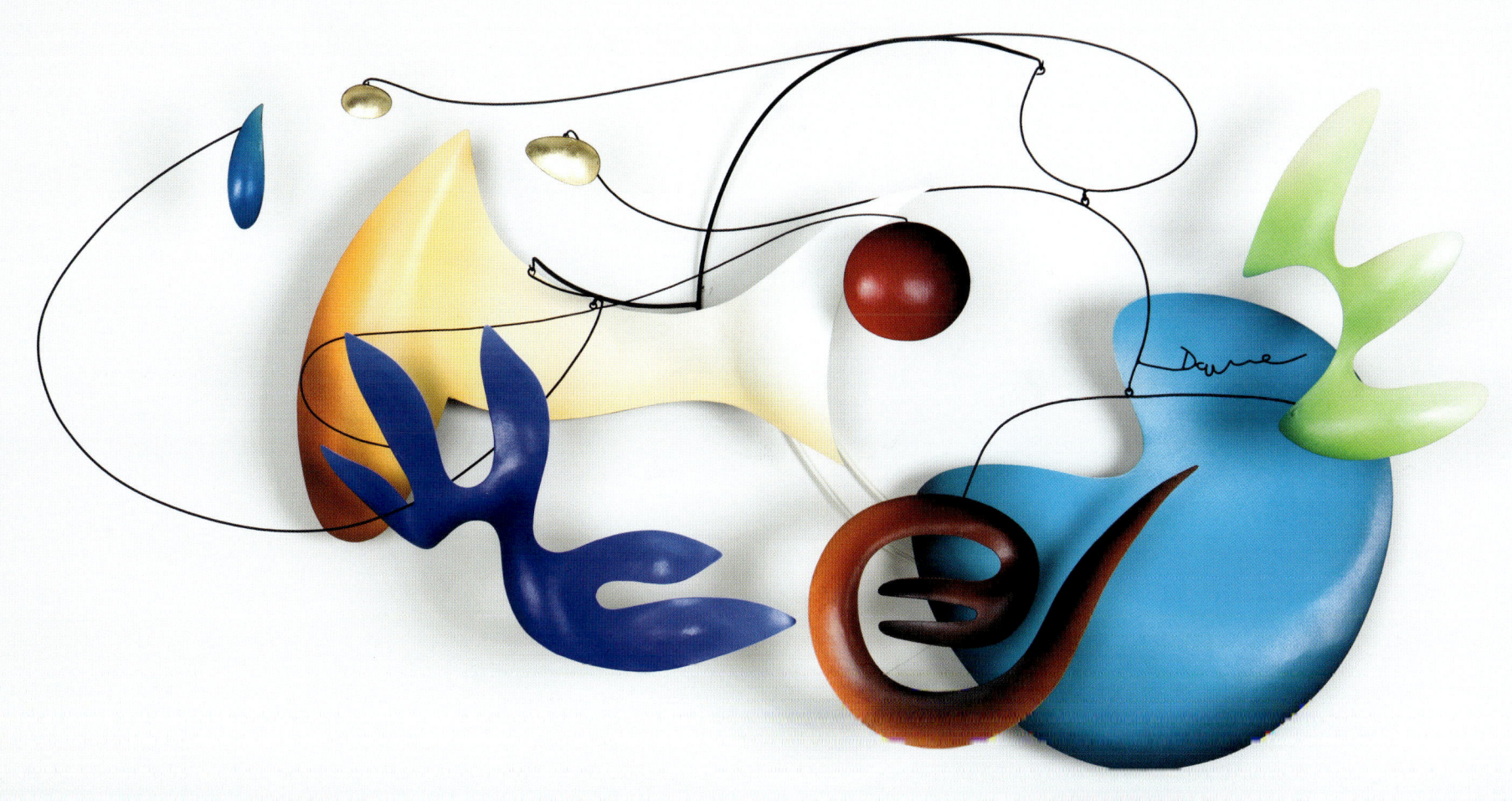

PRELUDE
Wall-mounted mobile in brass and aluminum with steel wires, oil and acrylic colors, and 23K gold leaf
21 x 40 x 10"
MD676

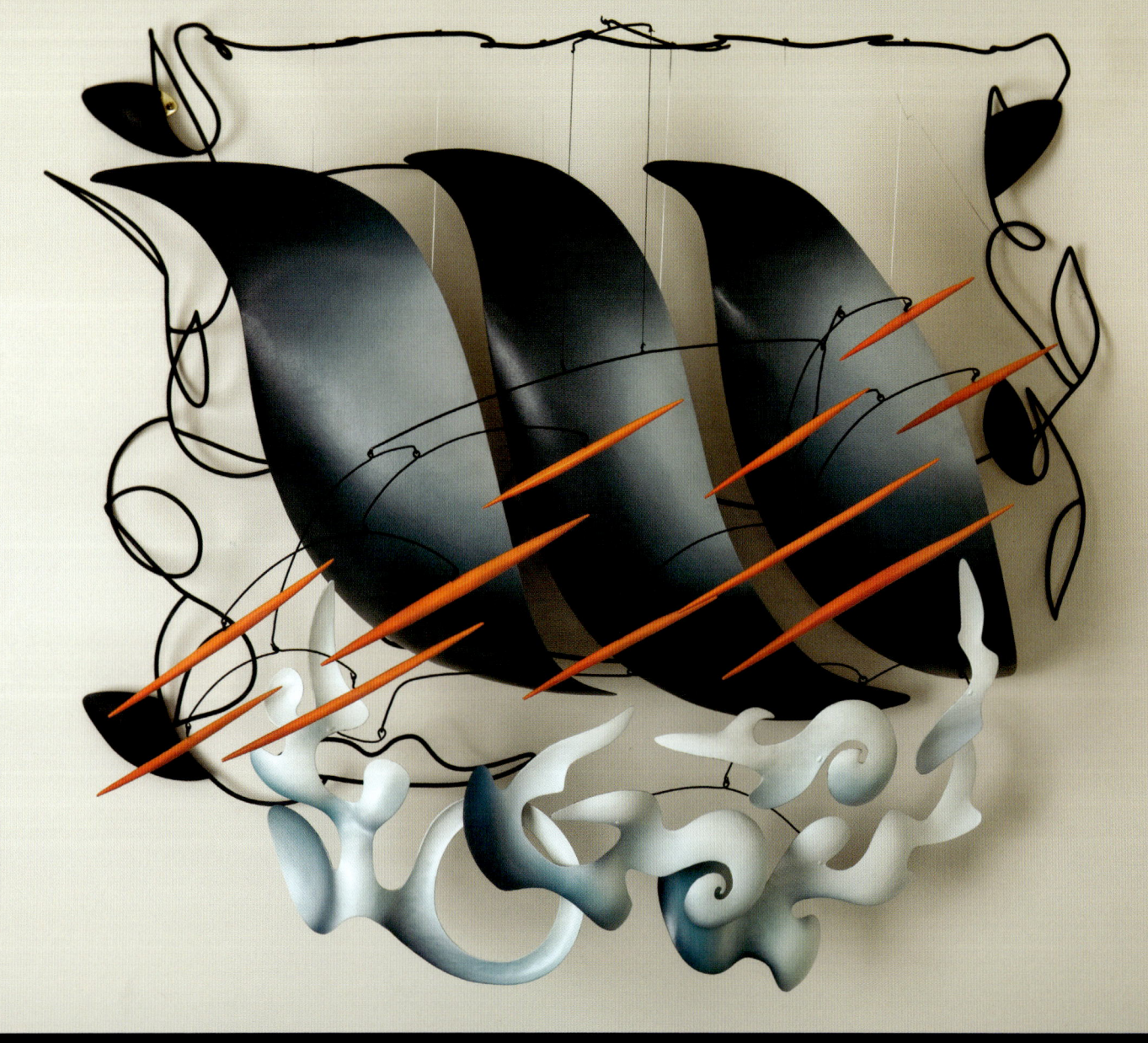

THE TEMPEST
Wall-mounted mobile in brass and aluminum with steel wires, and oil and acrylic colors

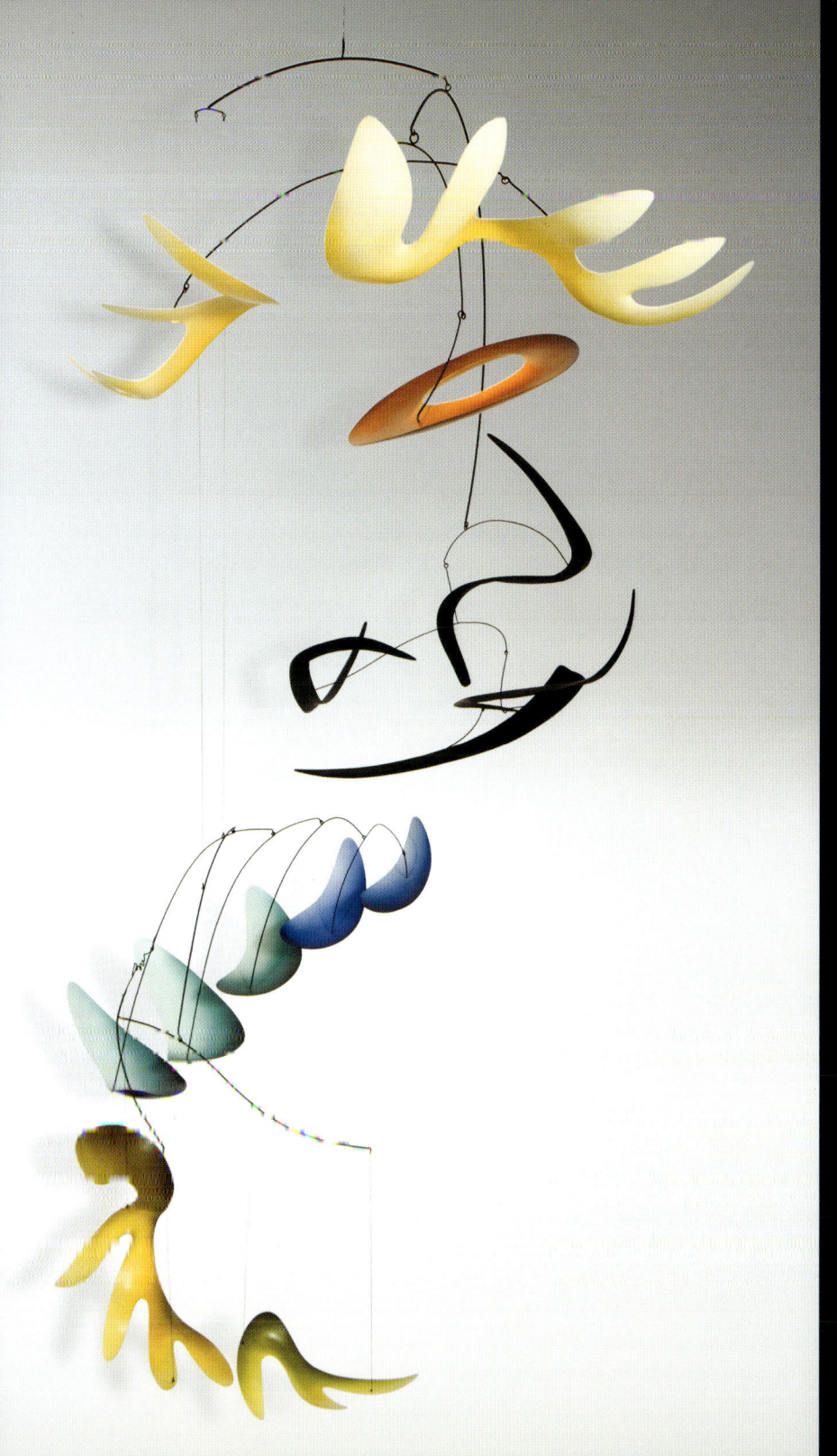

APOLLO AND DAPHNE
Hanging mobile in brass and
aluminum with steel wires,
and oil and acrylic colors
72 x 50 x 40"
MD489

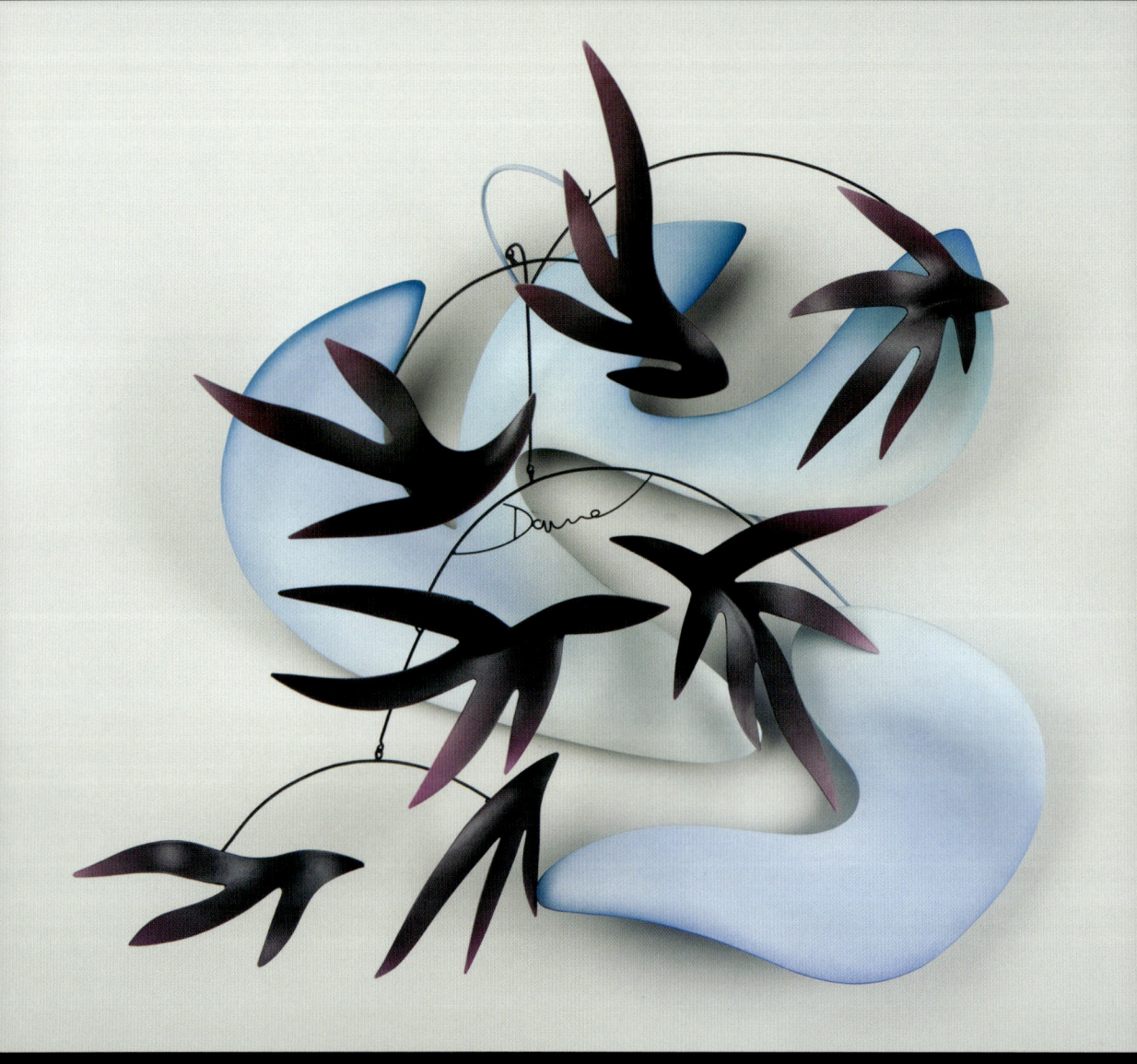

MAHOGANY AFTERNOON
Wall-mounted mobile in brass and aluminum with steel wires, and oil and acrylic colors
23 x 22 x 12"
MD723

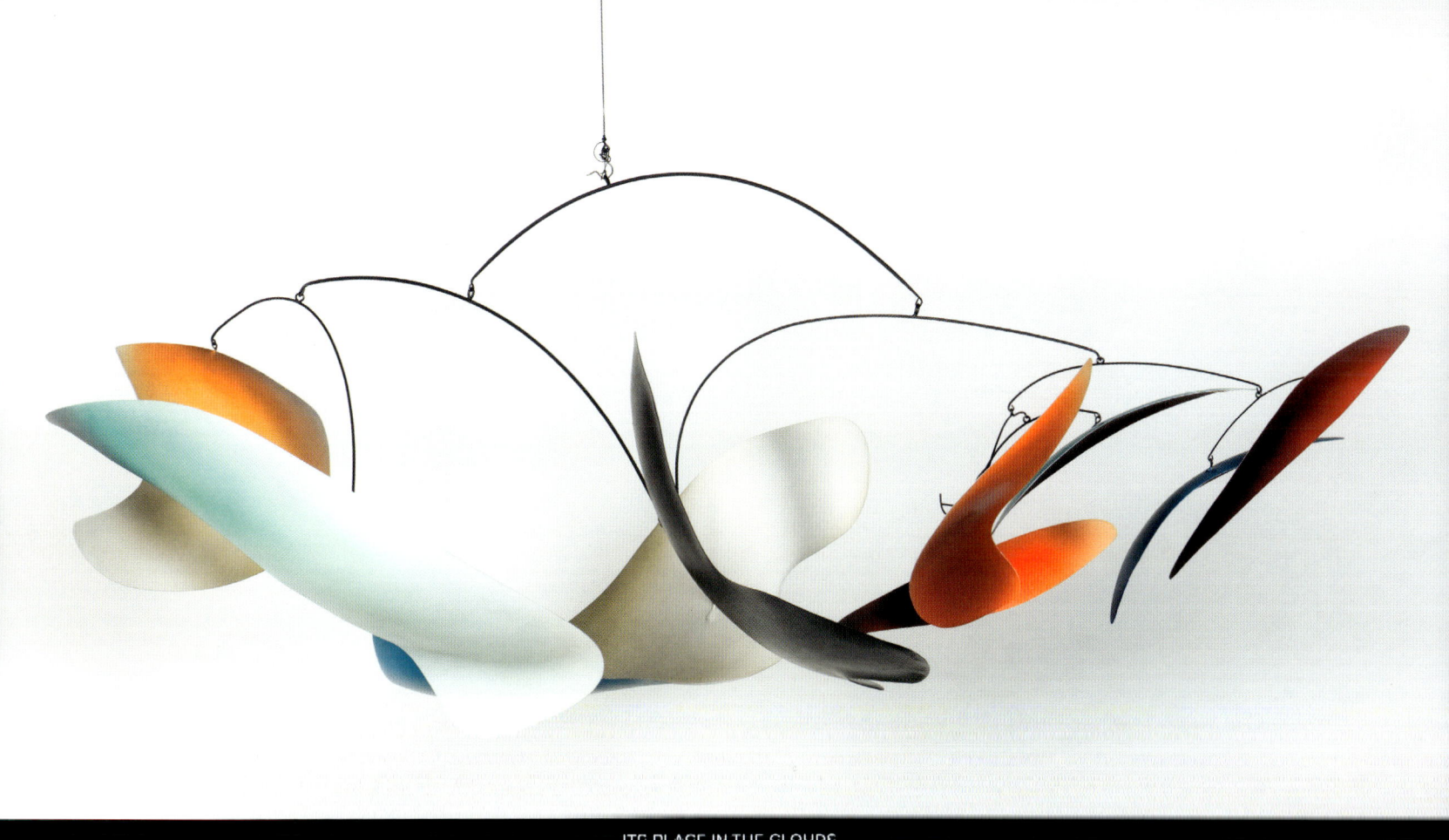

ITS PLACE IN THE CLOUDS
Hanging mobile in aluminum with steel wires, and oil and acrylic colors
20 x 50 x 20"
1975 1

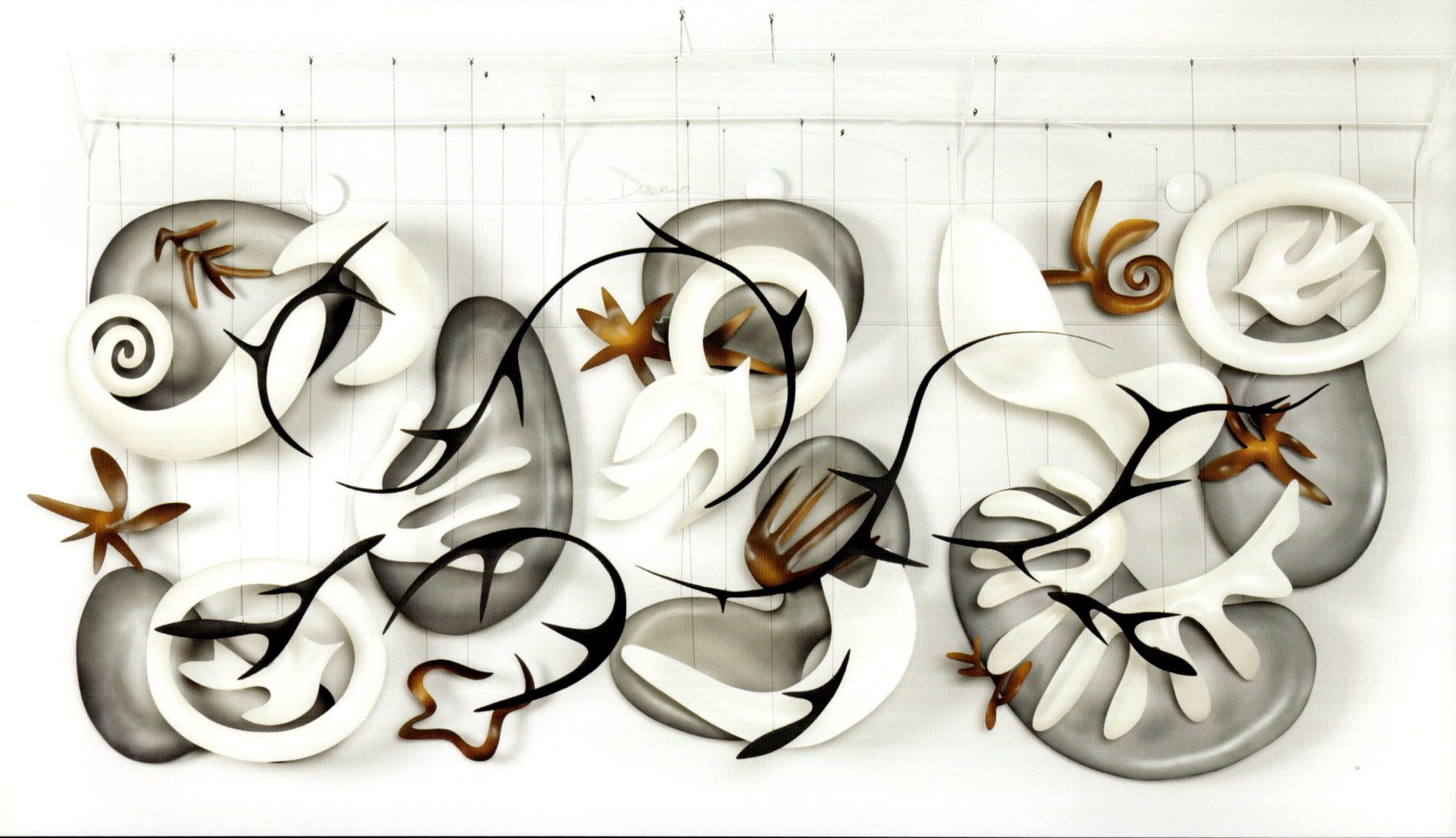

TEMPERED EXUBERANCE
Wall-mounted mobile in aluminum with steel wires, nylon cord, and oil and acrylic colors
55 x 108 x 19"
MD735

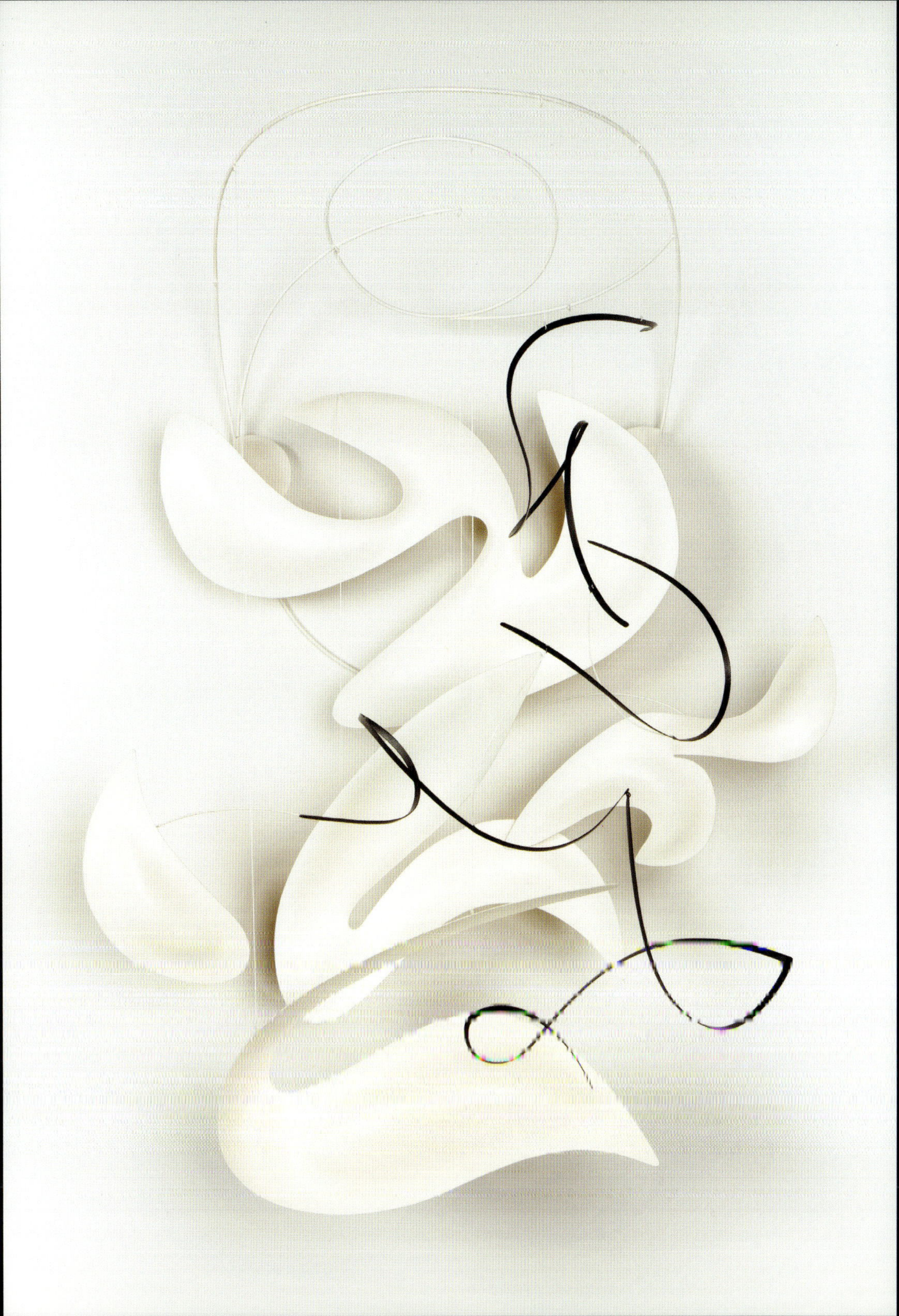

PURITY
Wall-mounted mobile in brass
and aluminum with steel wires,
and oil and acrylic colors
33 x 27 x 16"
MD722

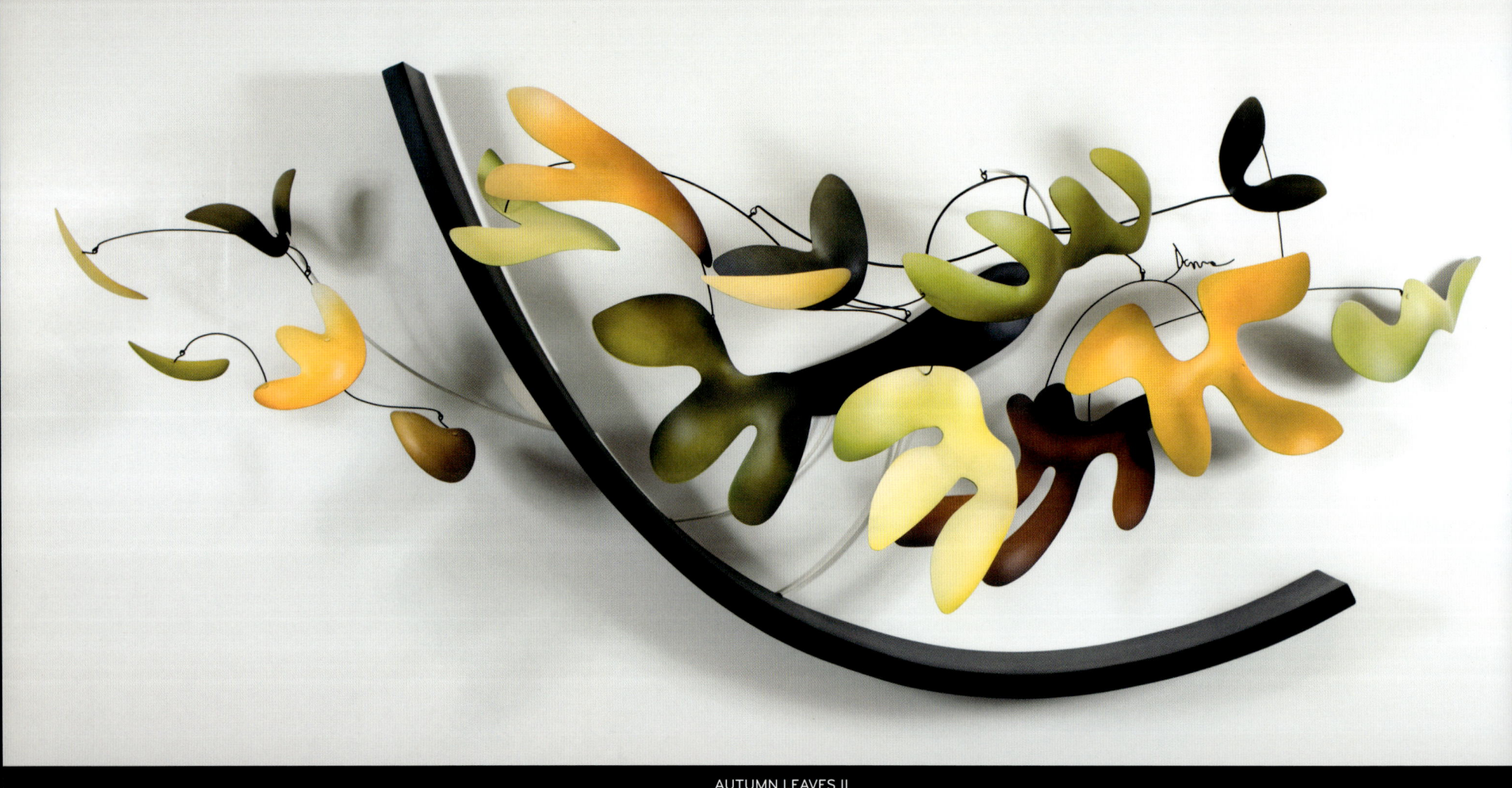

AUTUMN LEAVES II
Wall-mounted mobile in brass and aluminum with steel wires, and oil and acrylic colors
29 x 58 x 19"
MD480

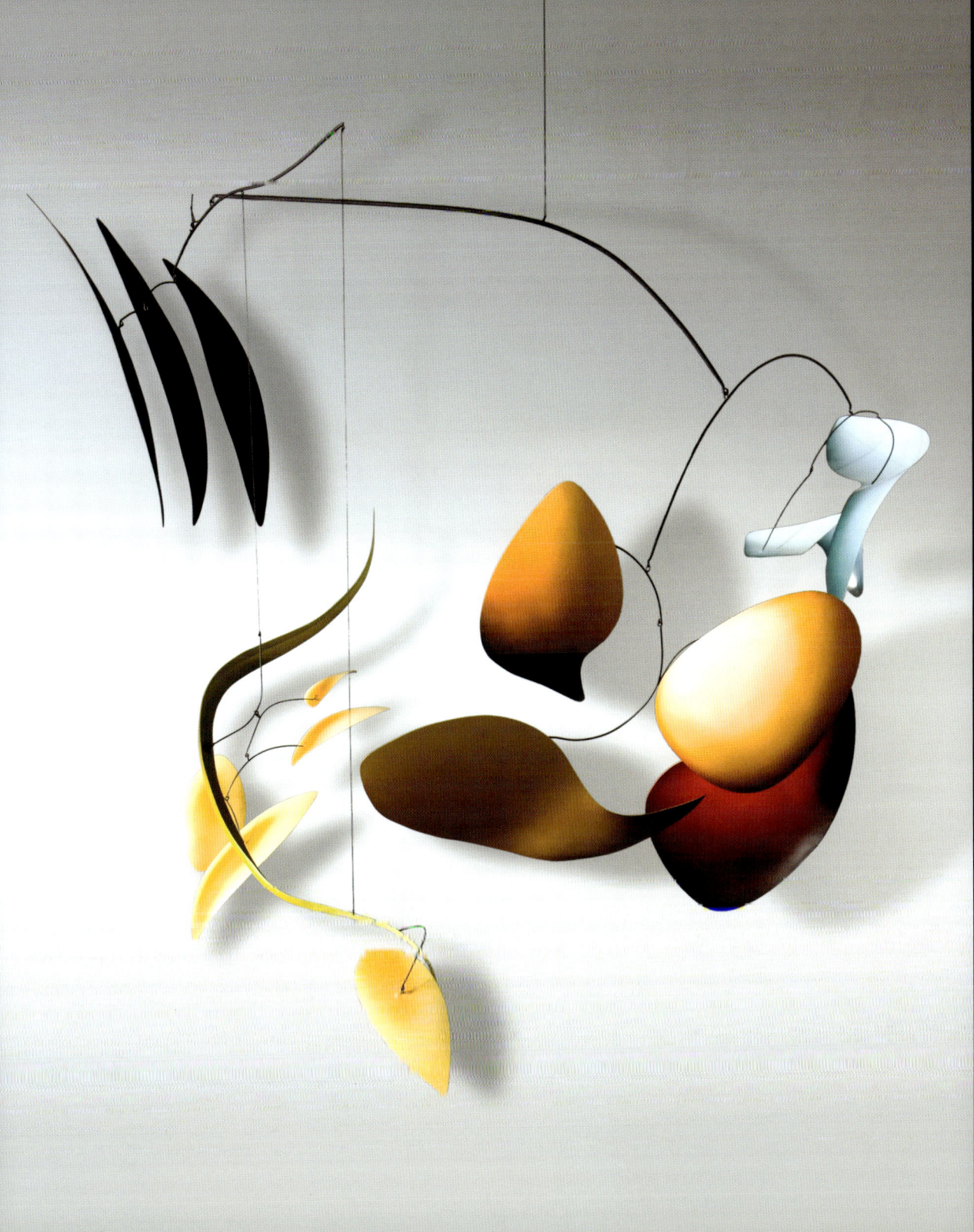

METAMORPHOSES
Hanging mobile in
aluminum with steel wires,
and oil and acrylic colors
60 x 40 x 36"
MD511

93

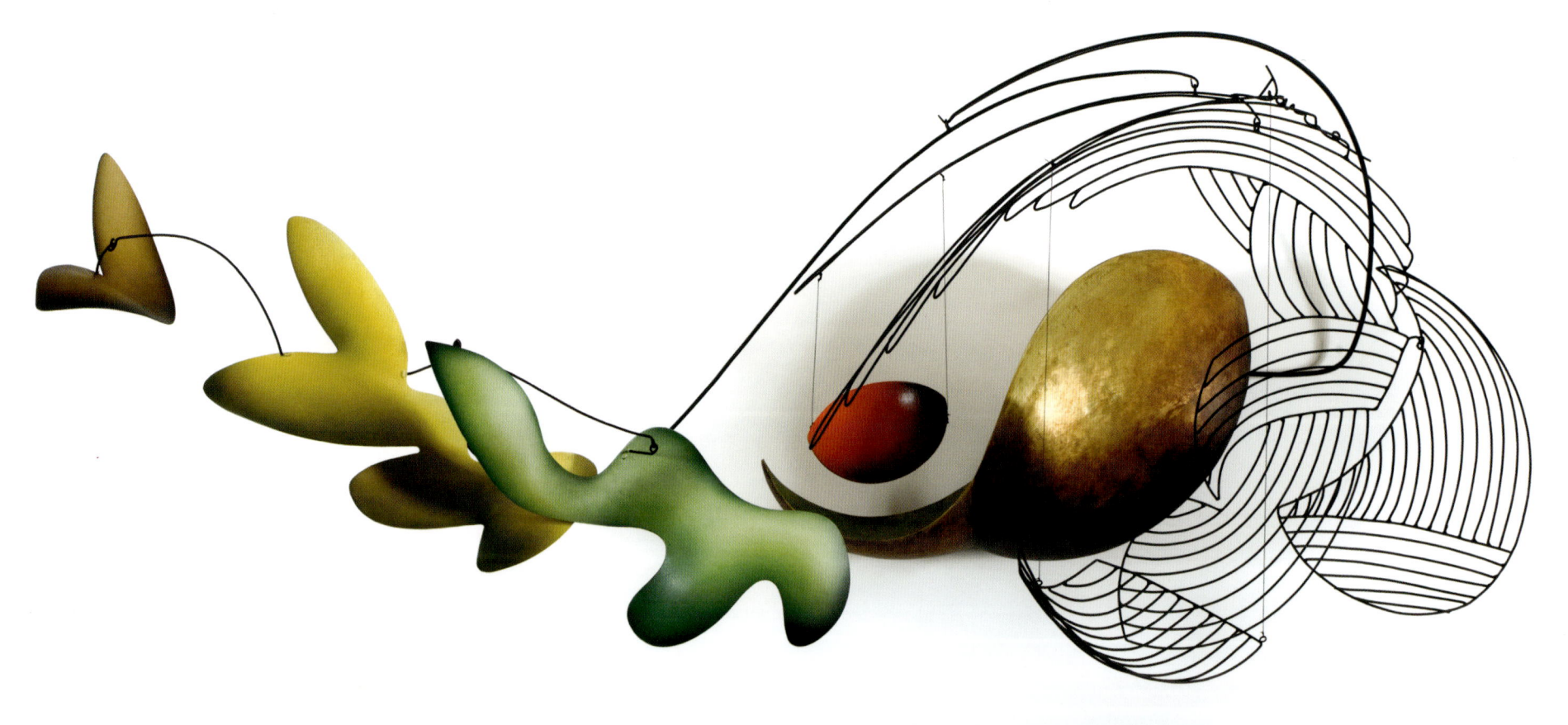

A GARDEN HERE ON EARTH
Wall-mounted mobile in brass and aluminum with steel wires, and oil and acrylic colors

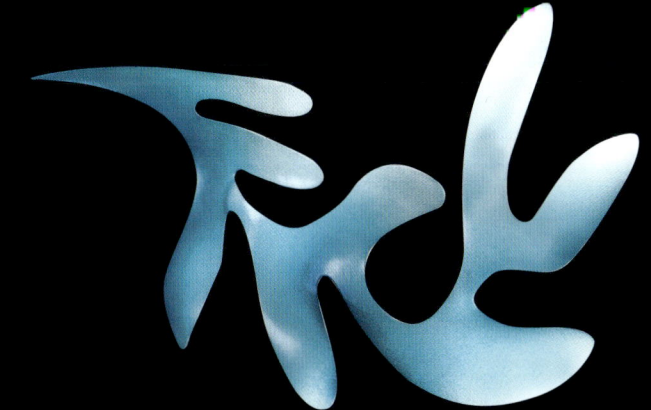

PUBLIC & PRIVATE COMMISSIONS

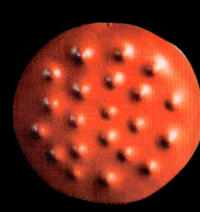

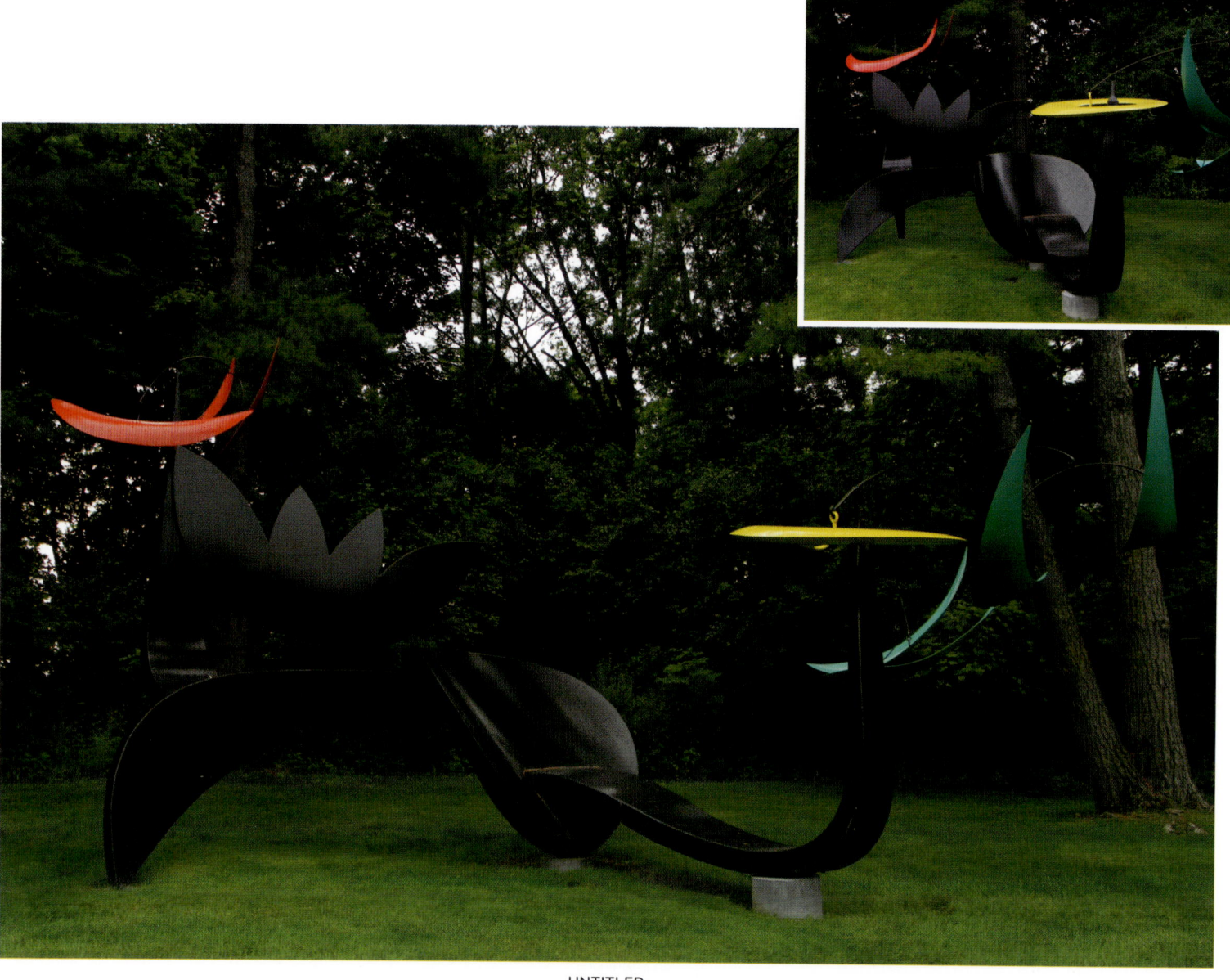

96

UNTITLED
Commission for private home
Standing mobile in brass, aluminum, and stainless steel, with oil colors and powder coating.
17 x 25 x 12'

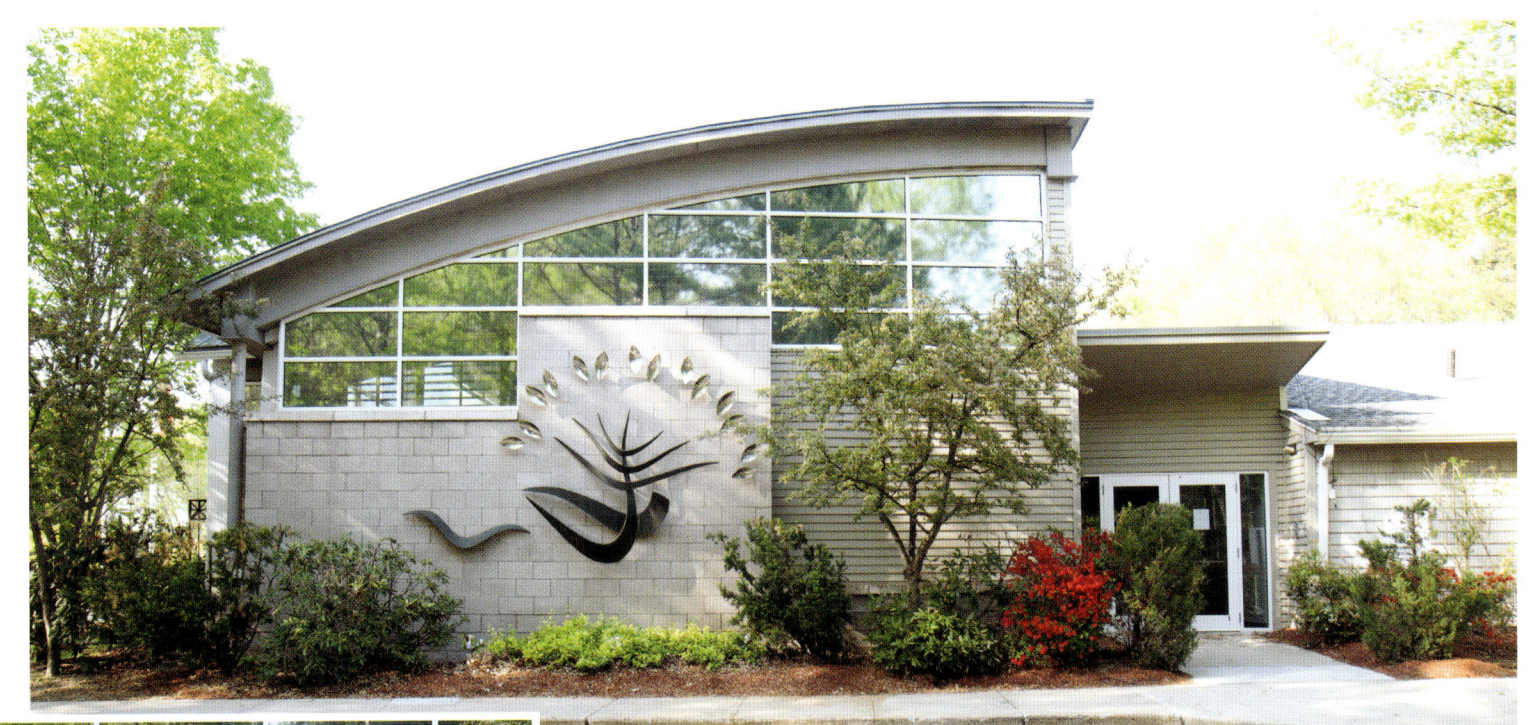

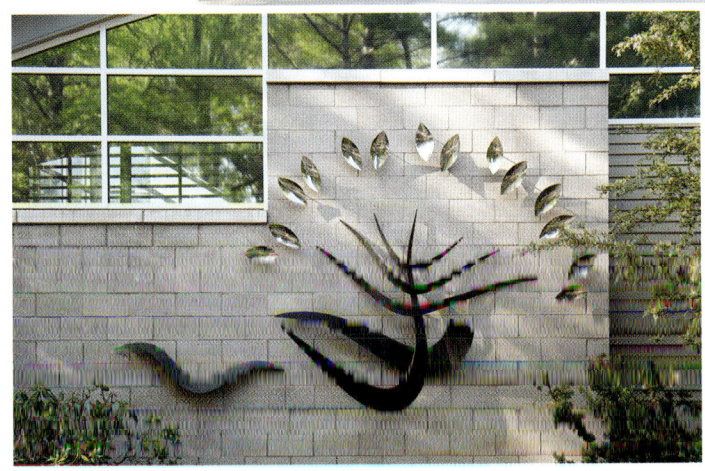

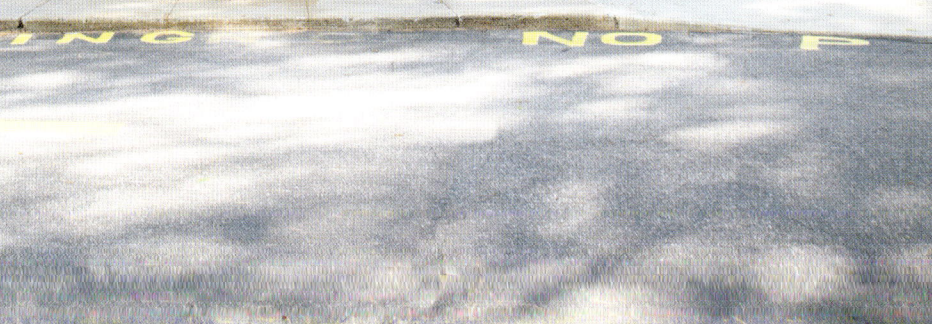

VOYAGE
Commission for Temple Emanuel, Andover, MA
Wall-mounted stabile in bronze and stainless steel
12" X 16' X 18"

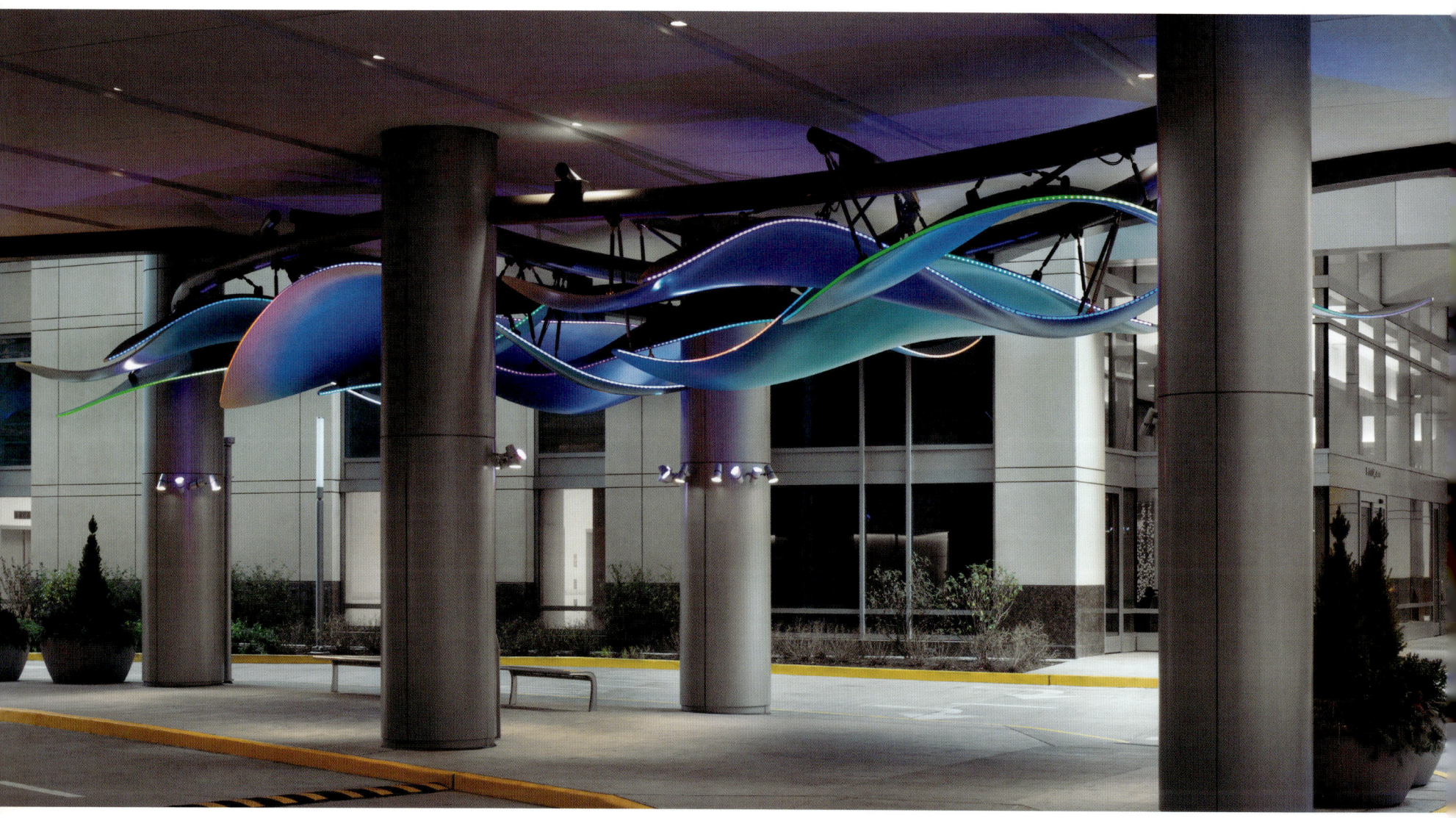

HEALING WATERS
Commission for Ann & Robert H. Lurie Children's Hospital, Chicago, IL
Suspended sculpture in carbon fiber polymer, acrylic colors, and powder coating, with steel support structure, and computerized LED light system
70 x 30 x 10'

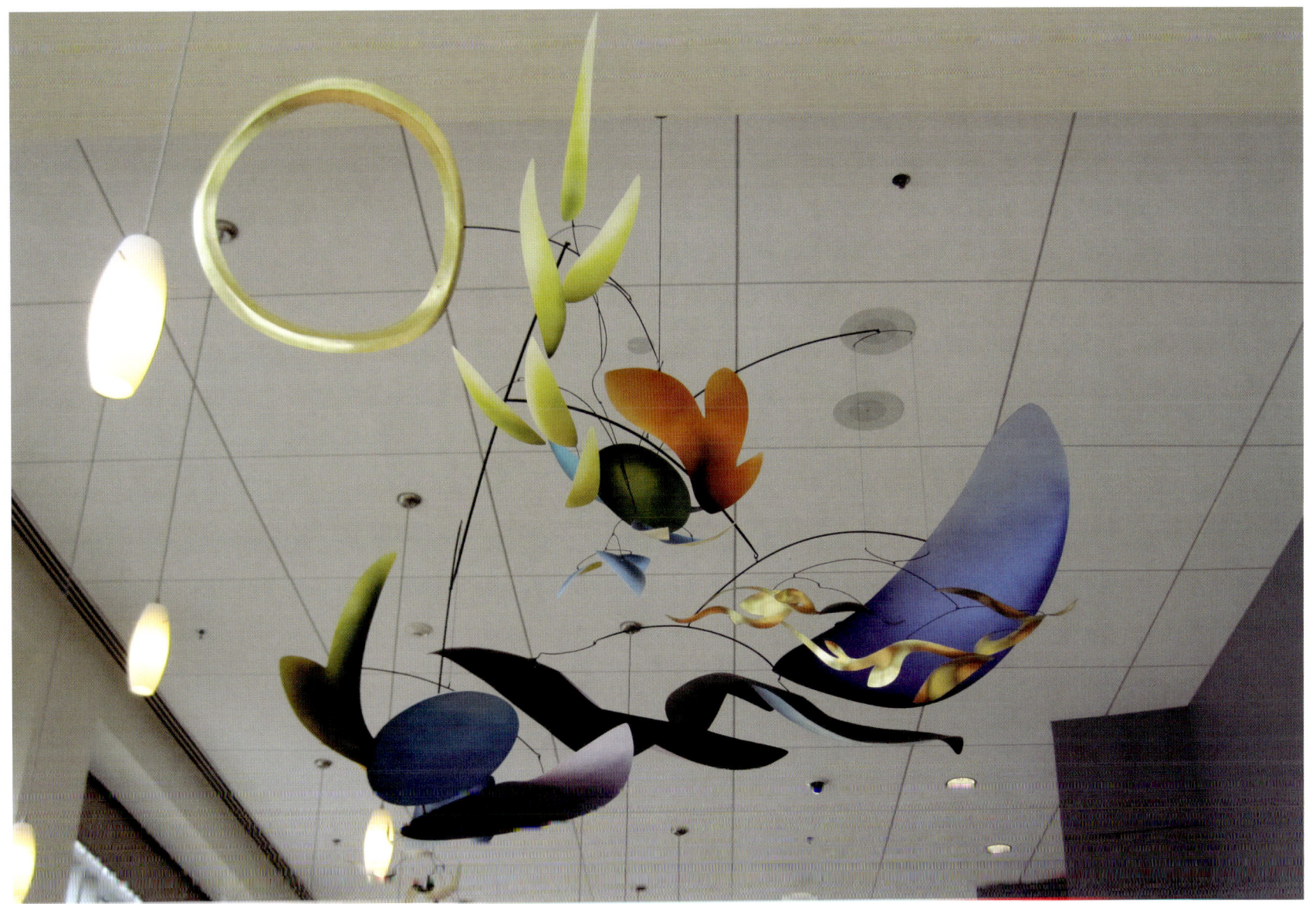

NATURAL ABUNDANCE
Commission for Good Samaritan Hospital, Brockton, MA
Hanging mobile in aluminum with steel wires, oil and acrylic colors, and 23K gold leaf
9' x 5' x 112"

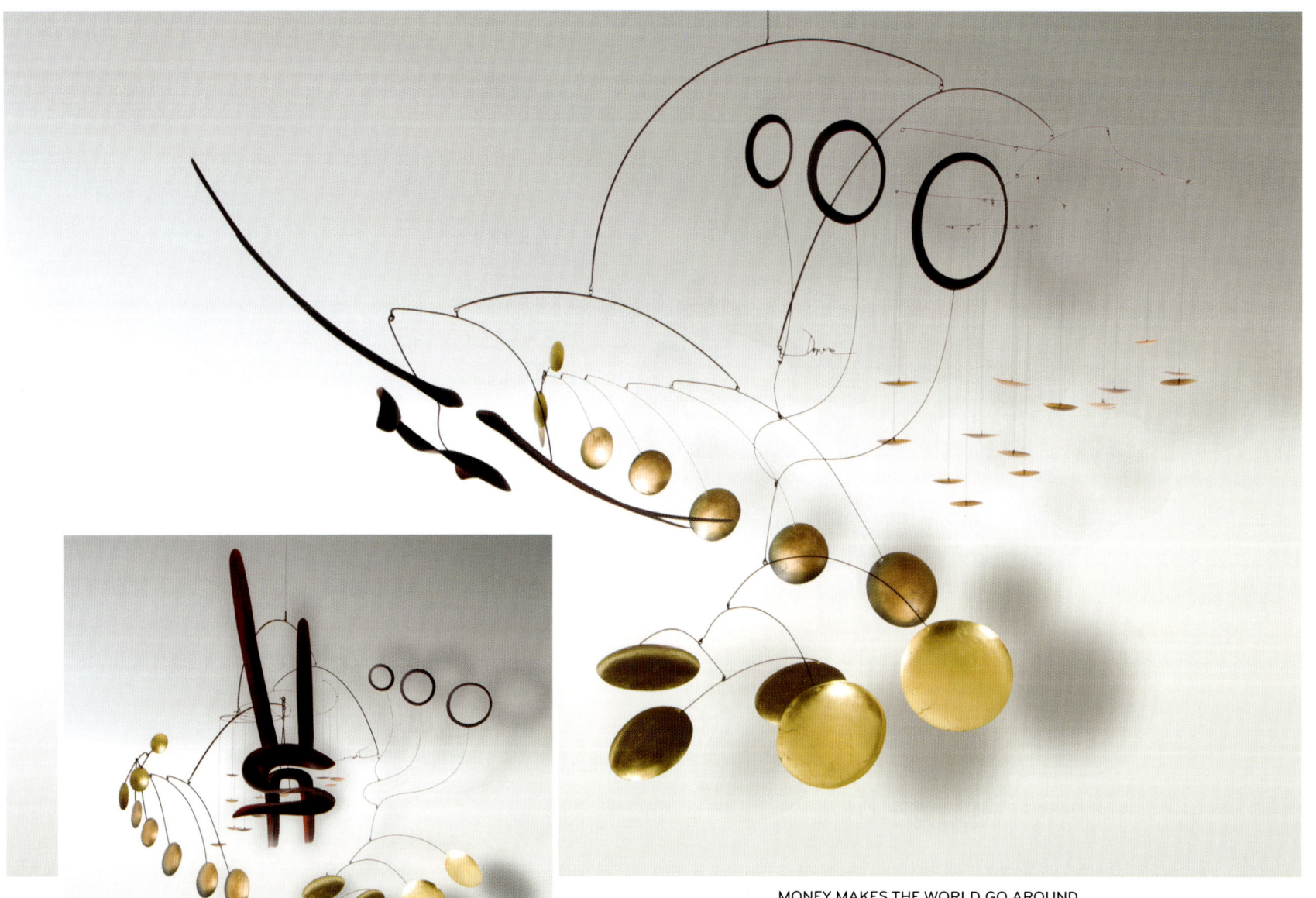

MONEY MAKES THE WORLD GO AROUND
Commission for Webster 5 Savings Bank, Worcester, MA
Hanging mobile in brass and aluminum with steel wires, oil colors, and gold, silver, and bronze leaf
4 x 5 x 4'

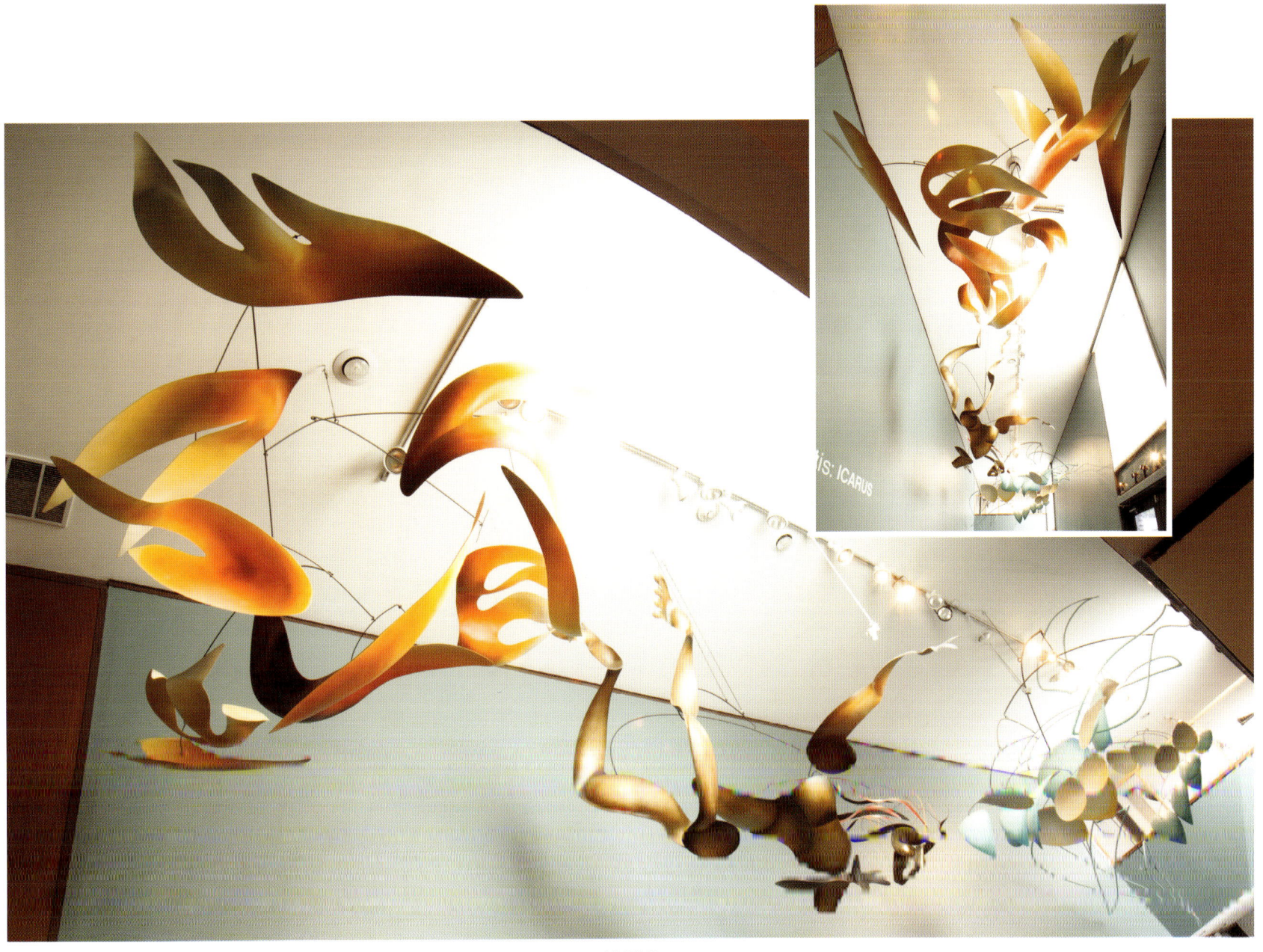

ICARUS
Commission for Fuller Craft Museum, Brockton, MA
Hanging mobile in brass and aluminum with steel wires, and oil and acrylic colors
10 x 38 x 10'

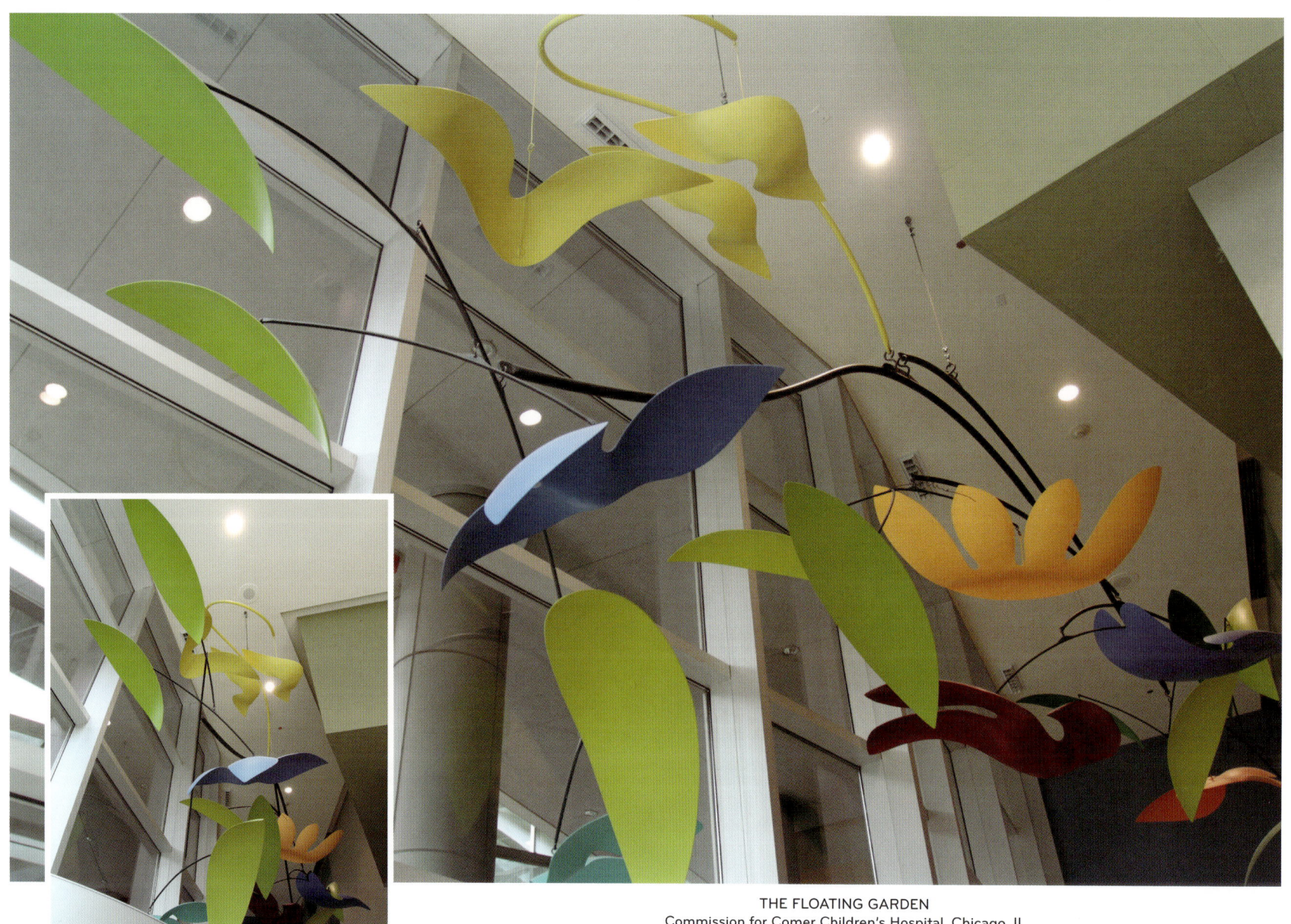

THE FLOATING GARDEN
Commission for Comer Children's Hospital, Chicago, IL
Hanging mobile in aluminum and steel with steel wires, and oil colors
13 x 30 x 9'

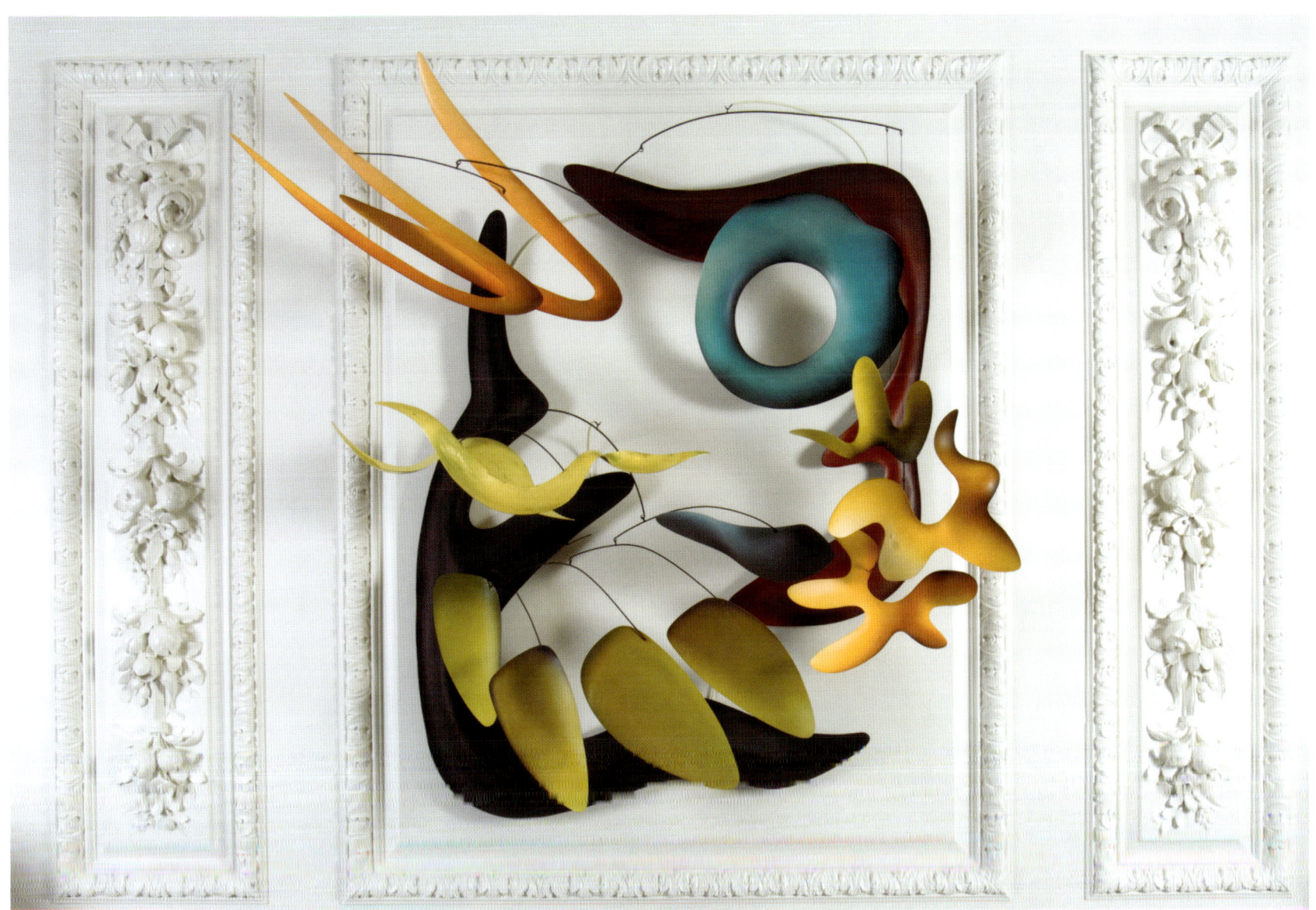

ISABELLA'S GARDEN
Commission for private home
Wall-mounted mobile in brass and aluminum with steel wires, and oil and acrylic colors
46 x 36.5 x 16"

FRATERNAL TOTEM
Commission for private home
Wall-mounted mobile in brass
and aluminum with steel wires,
and oil and acrylic colors
80 x 35 x 18"

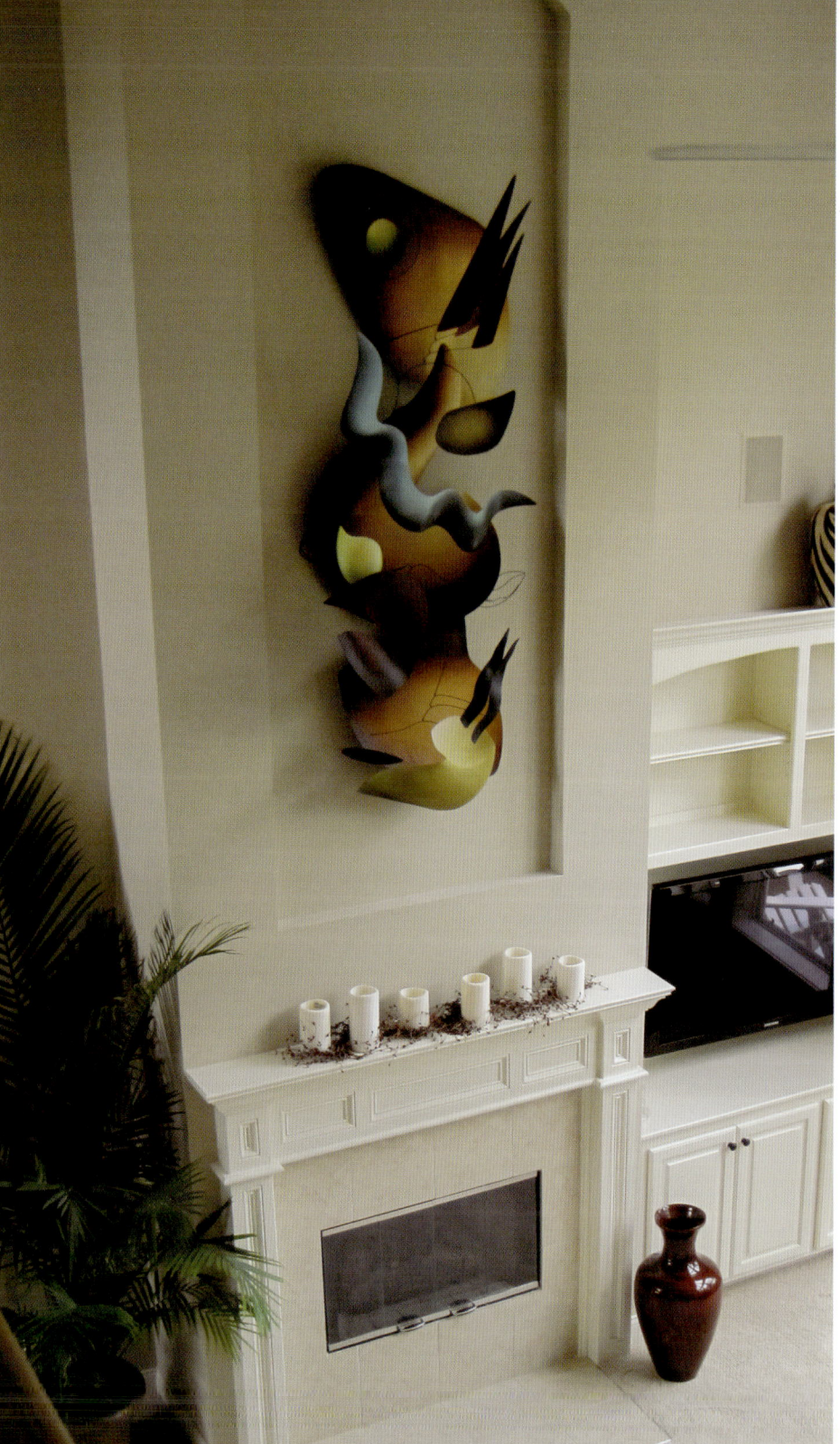

104

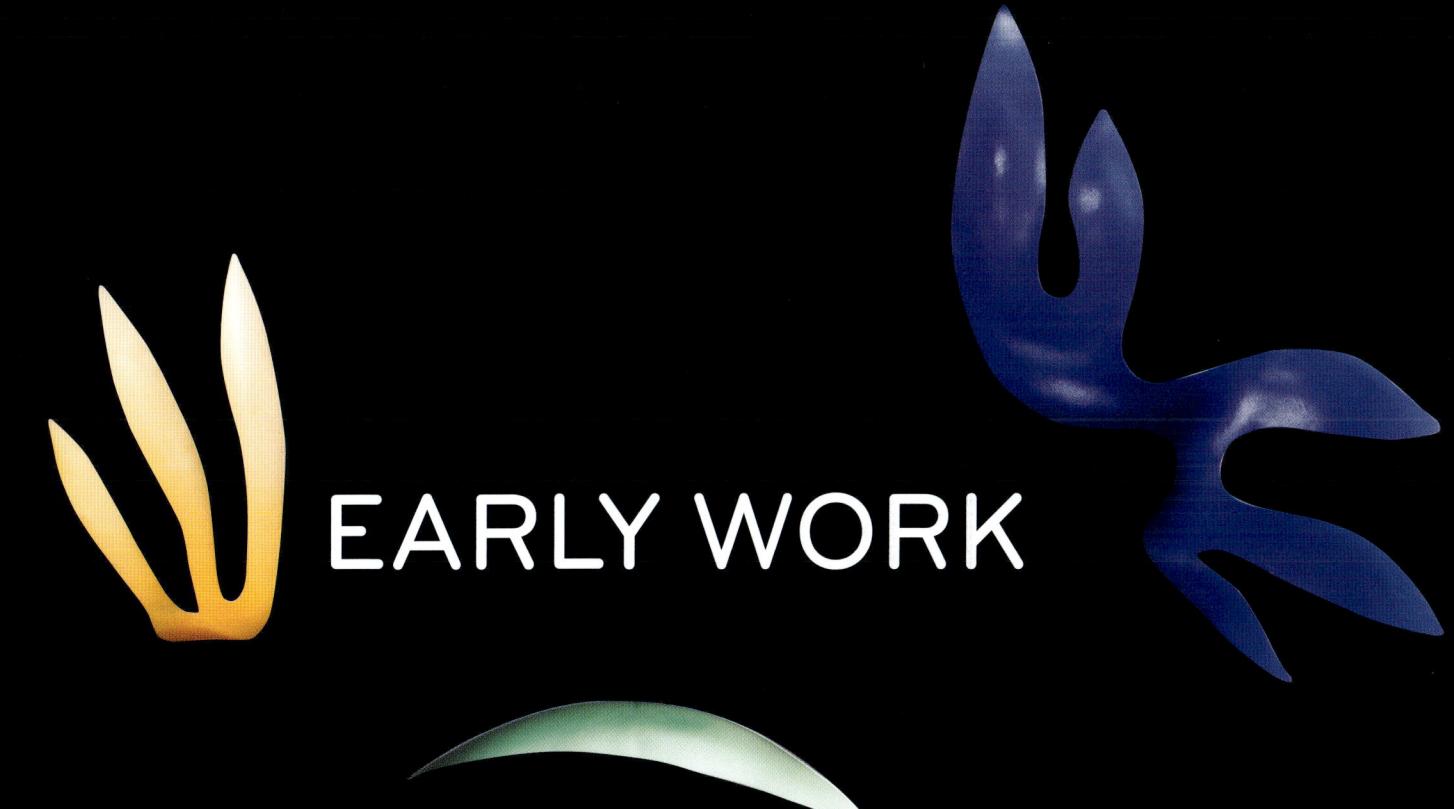

EARLY WORK

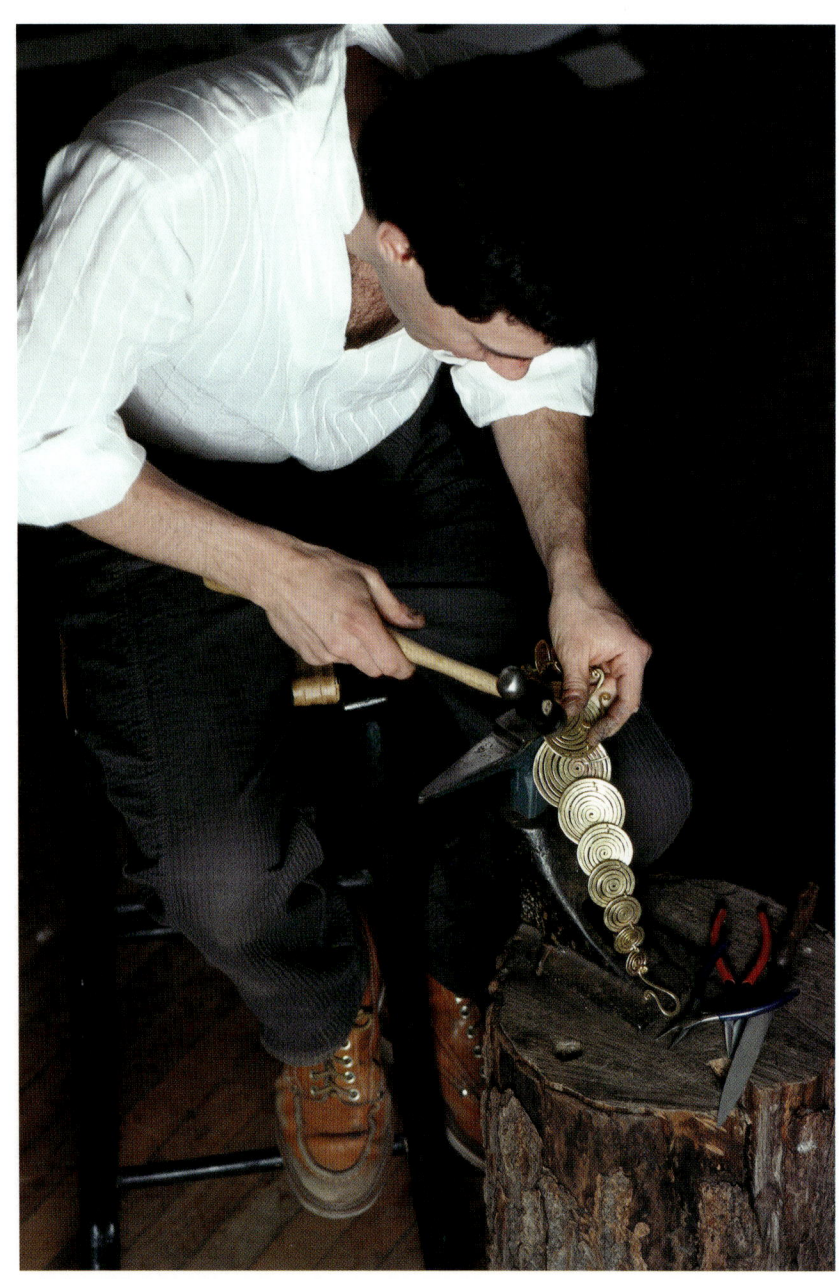

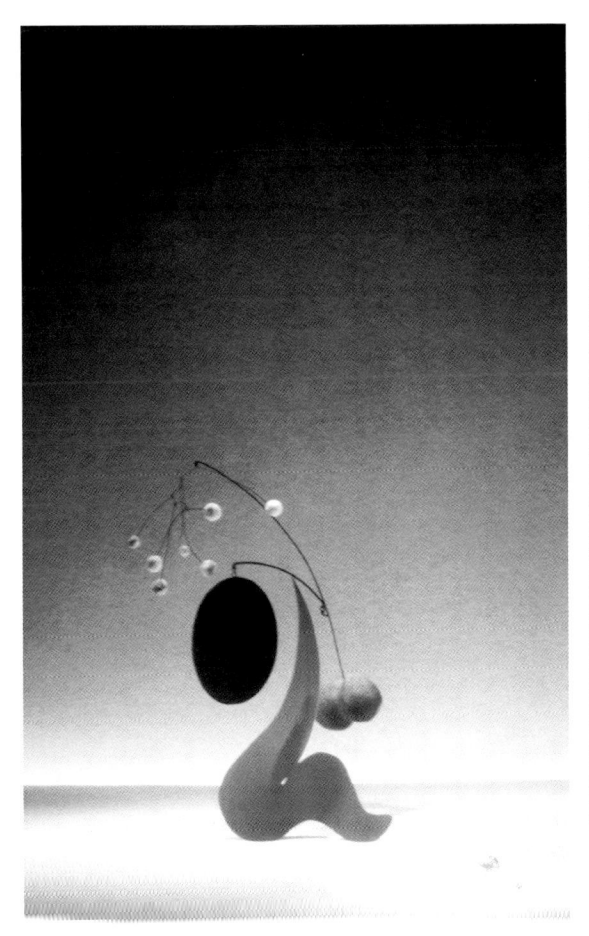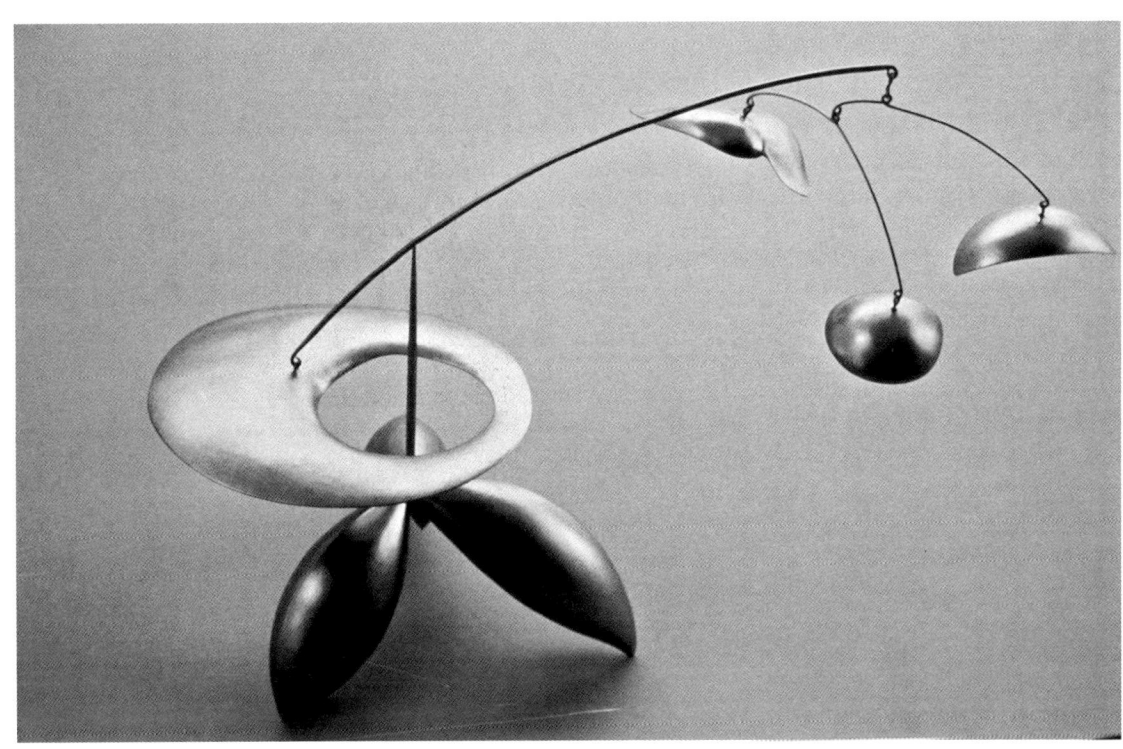

Window of Tiffany & Co., New York, NY, 1991

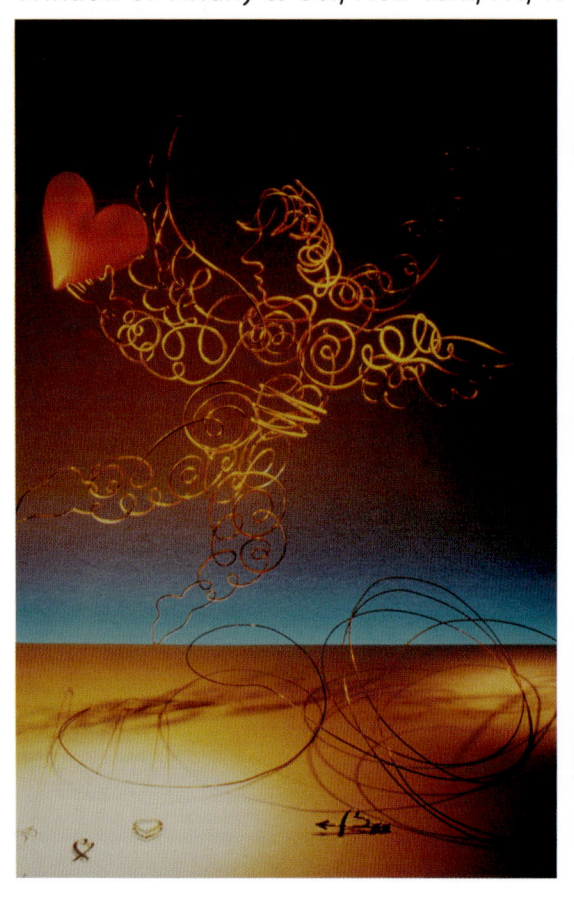
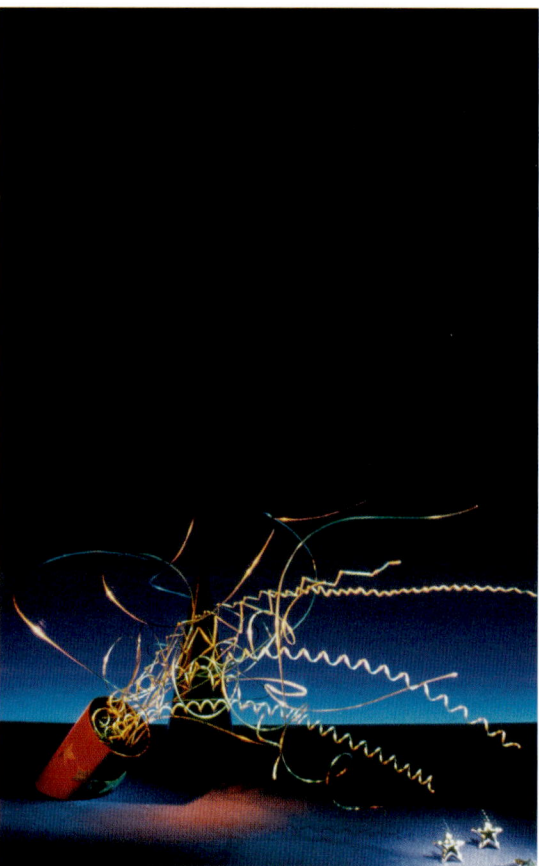
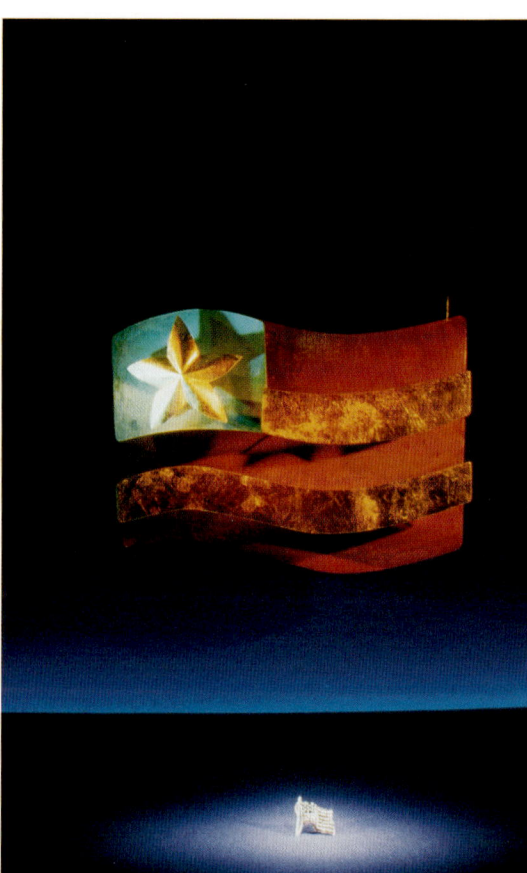

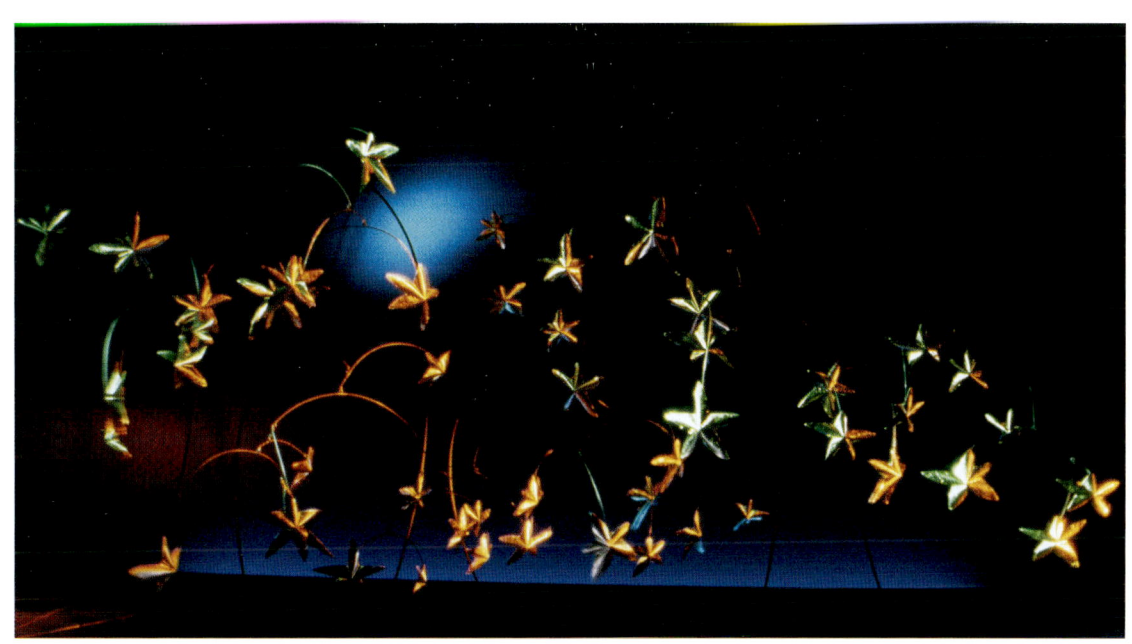

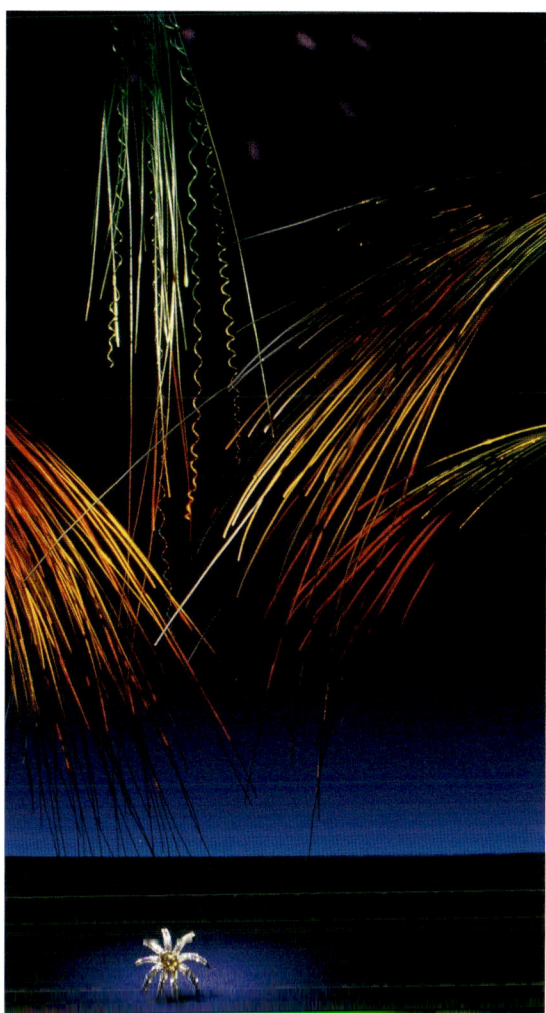

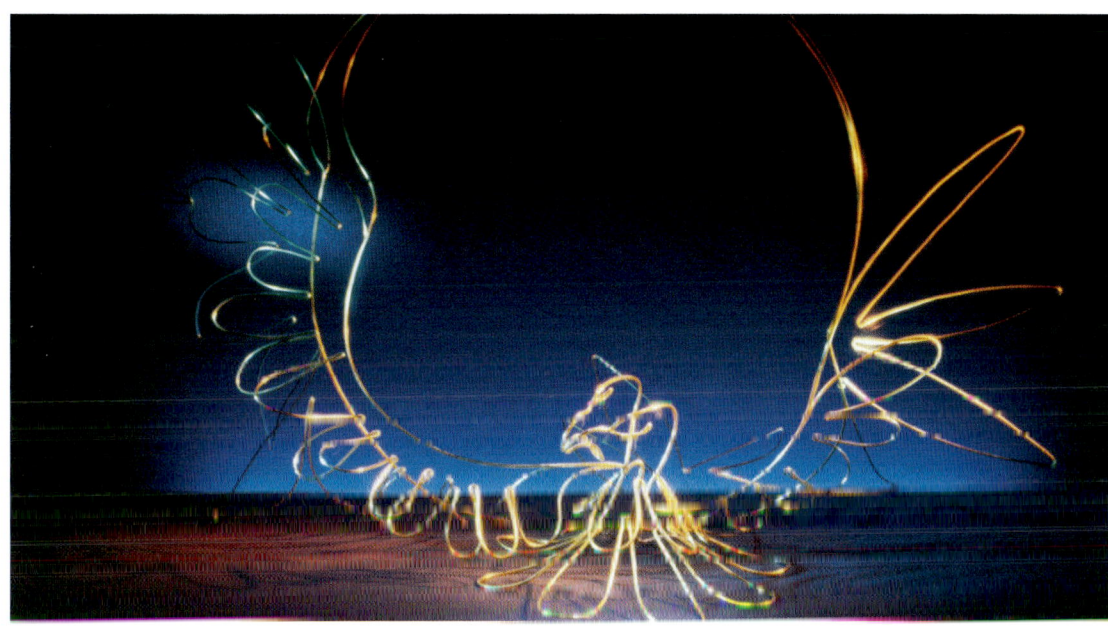

Selected jewelry pieces in brass, late 1980s

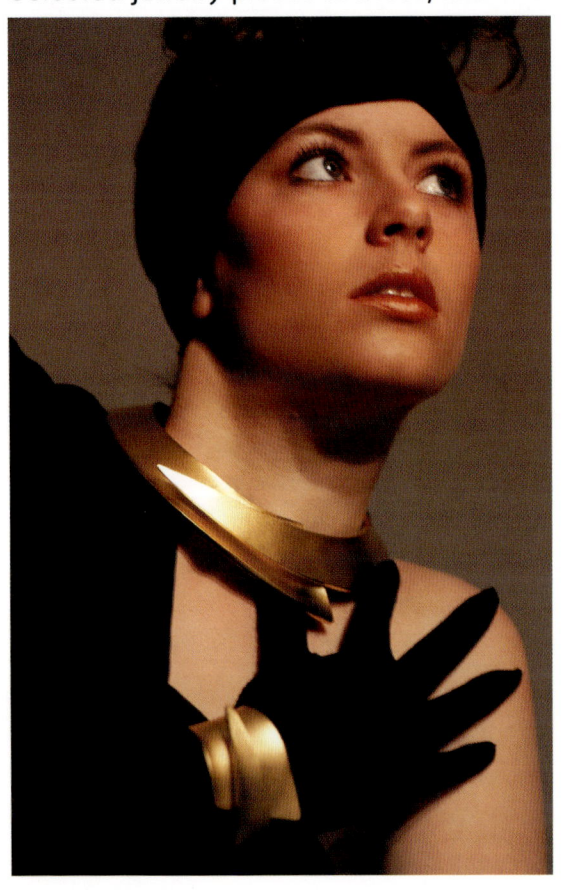
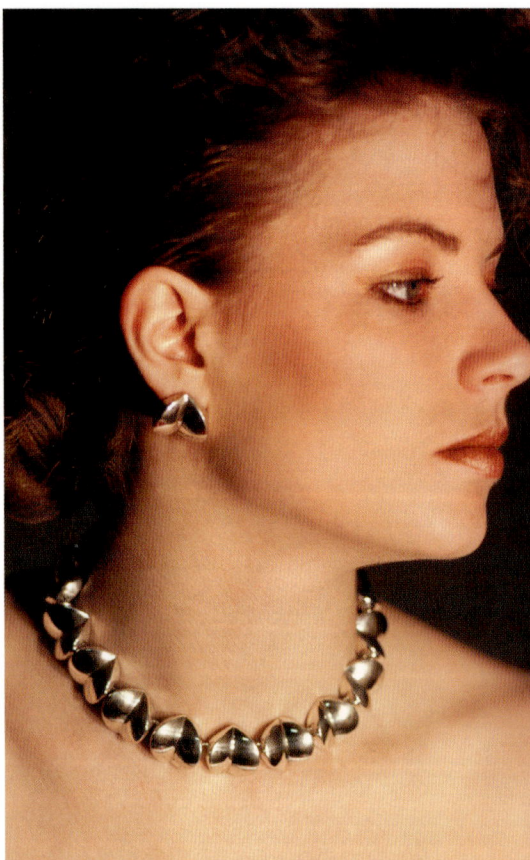
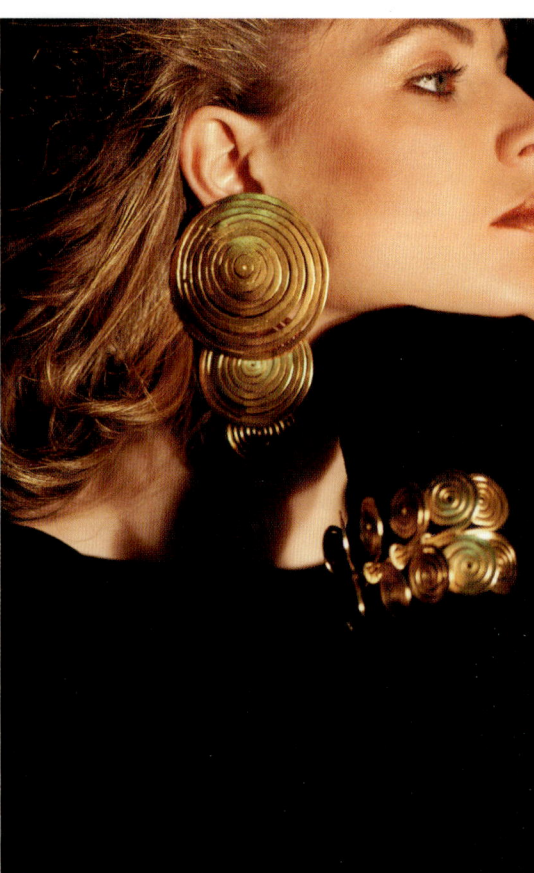

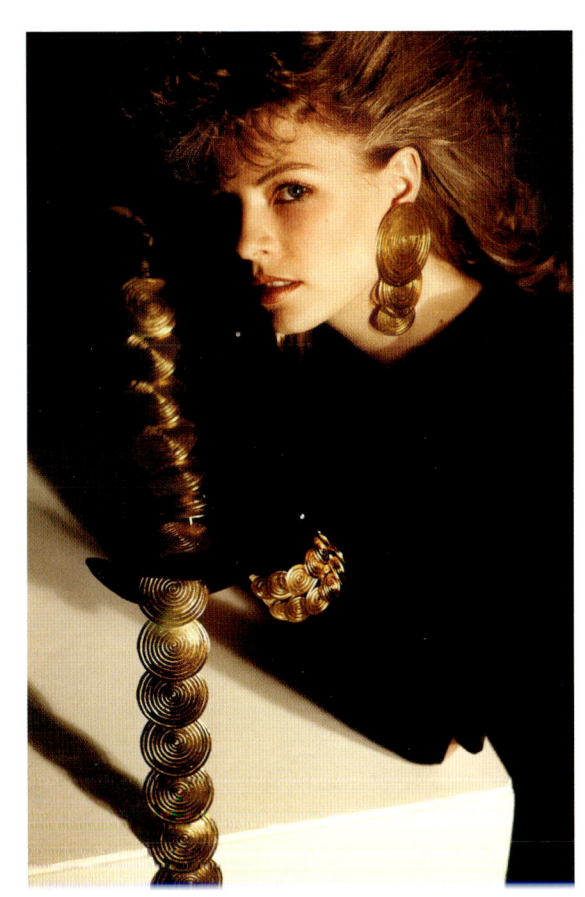 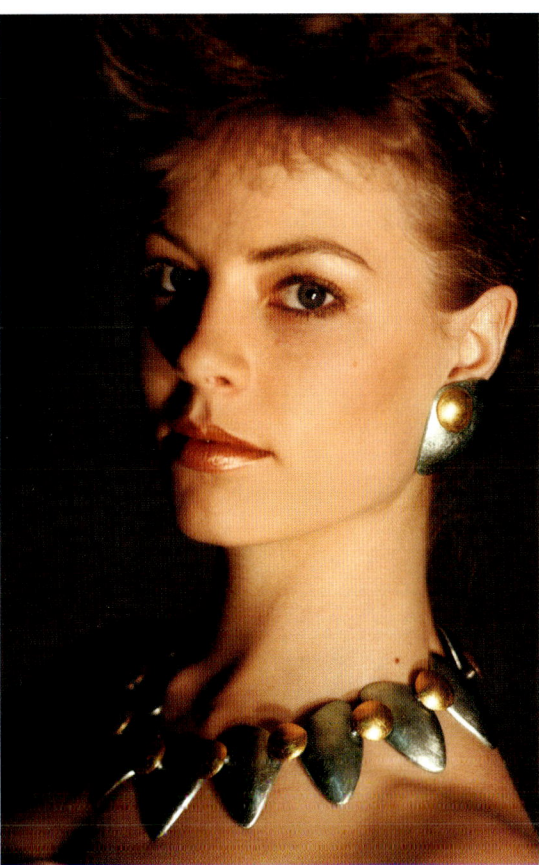 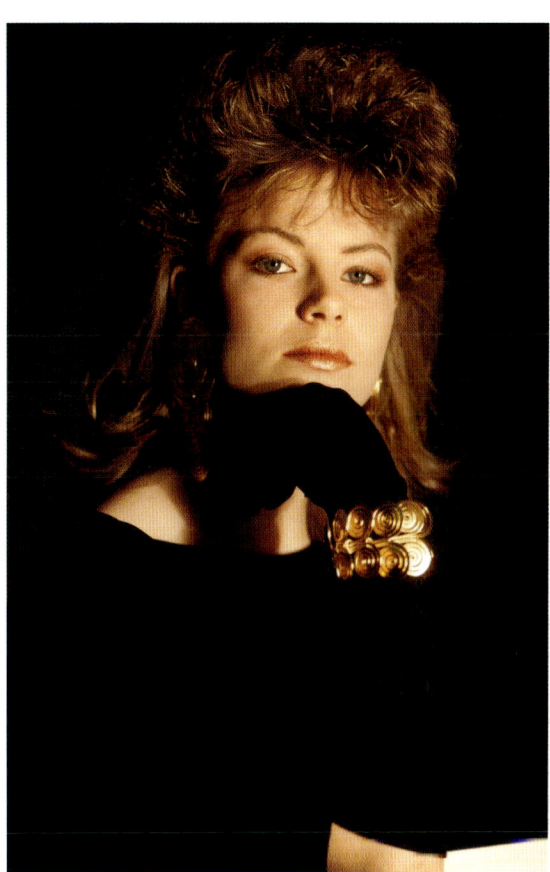

Selected jewelry pieces in mixed materials, late 1980s

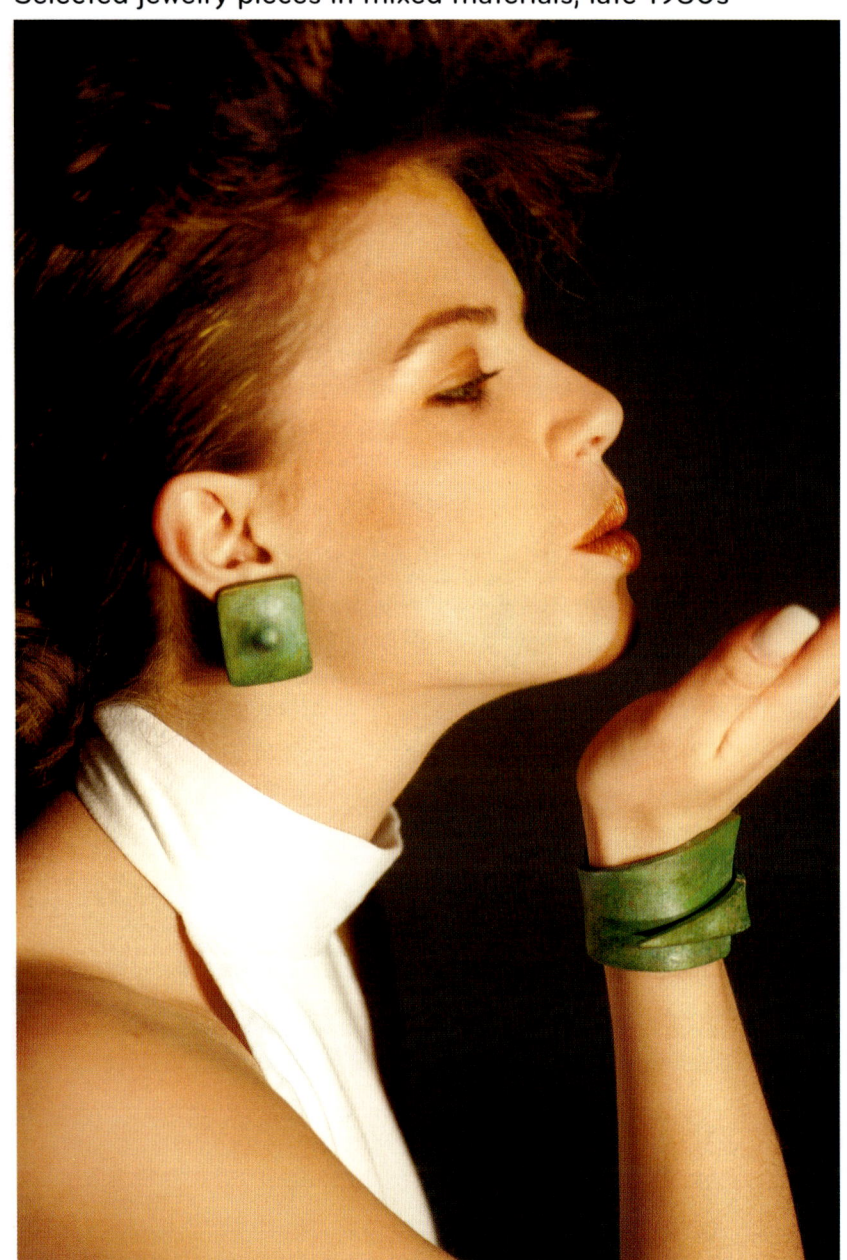

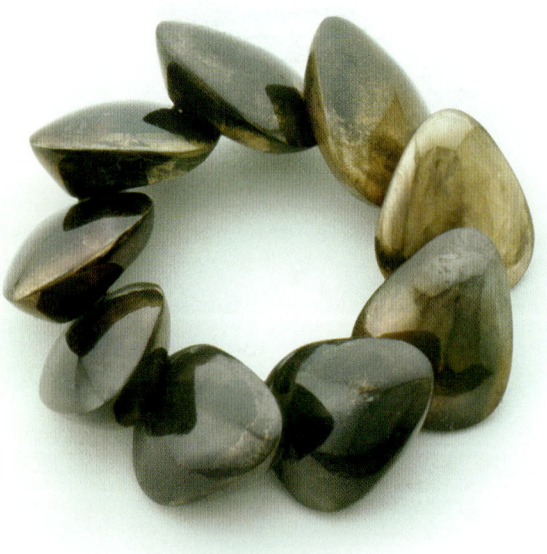

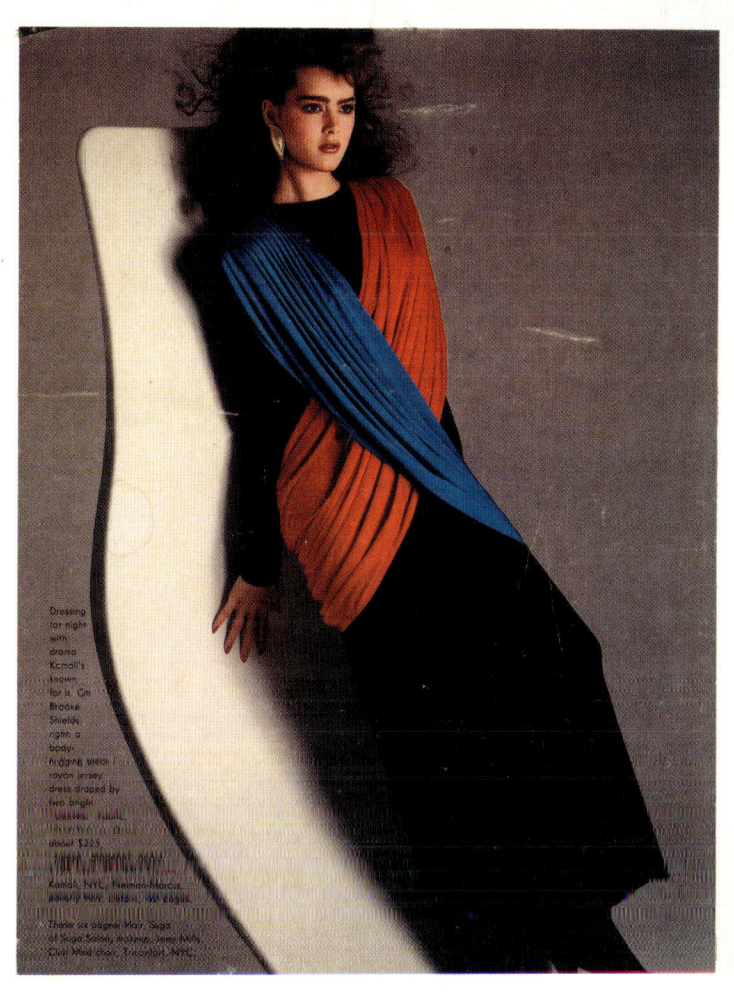

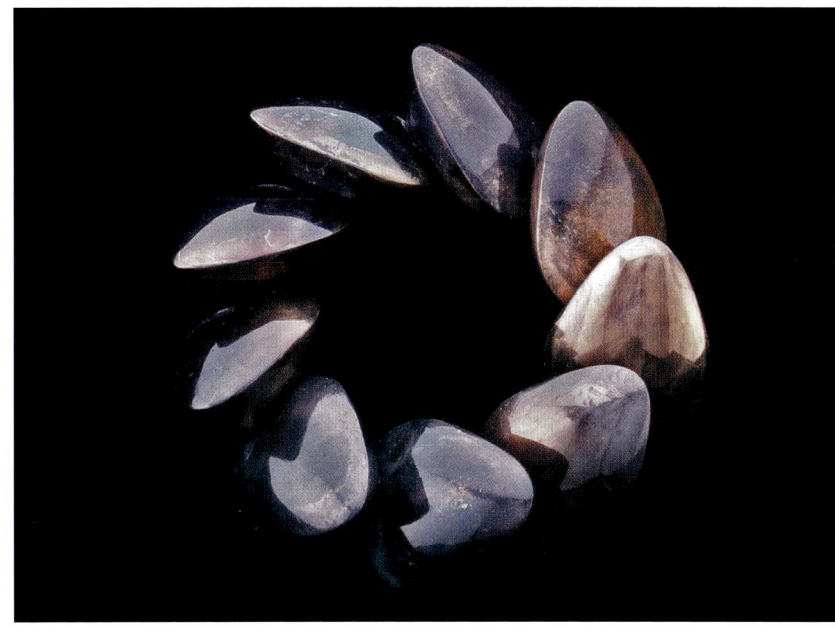

113

Selected jewelry pieces in sterling silver, late 1980s and early 1990s

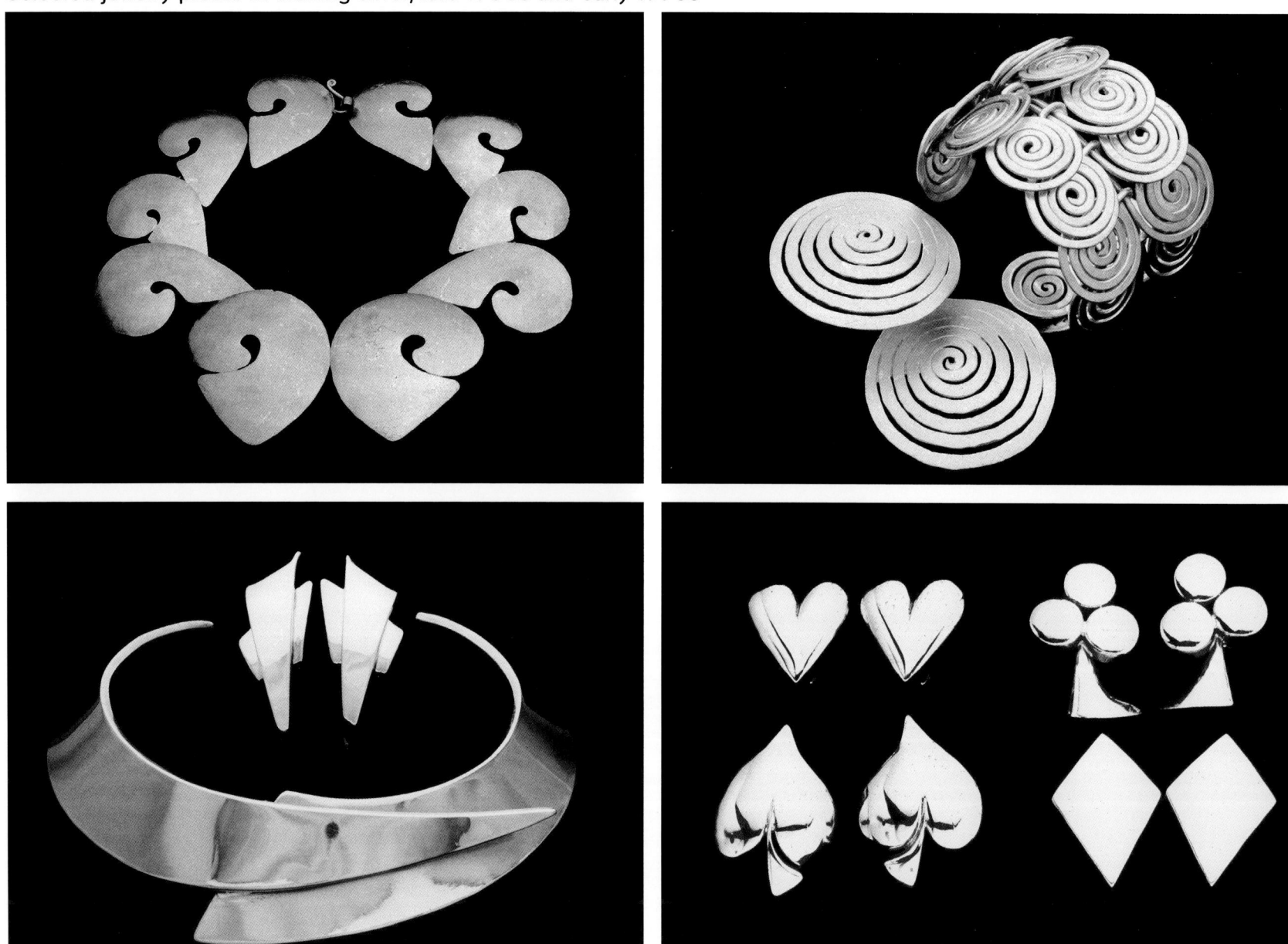

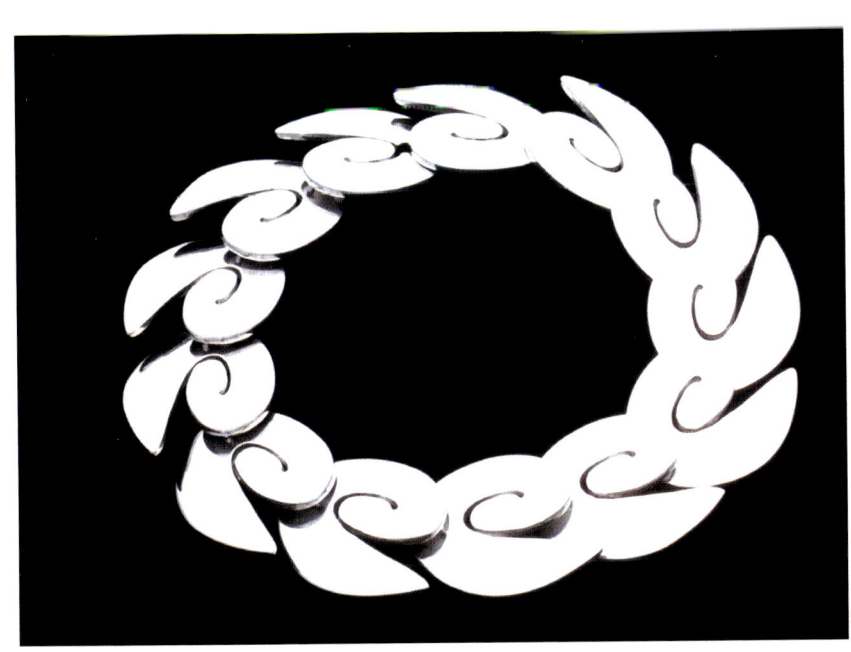

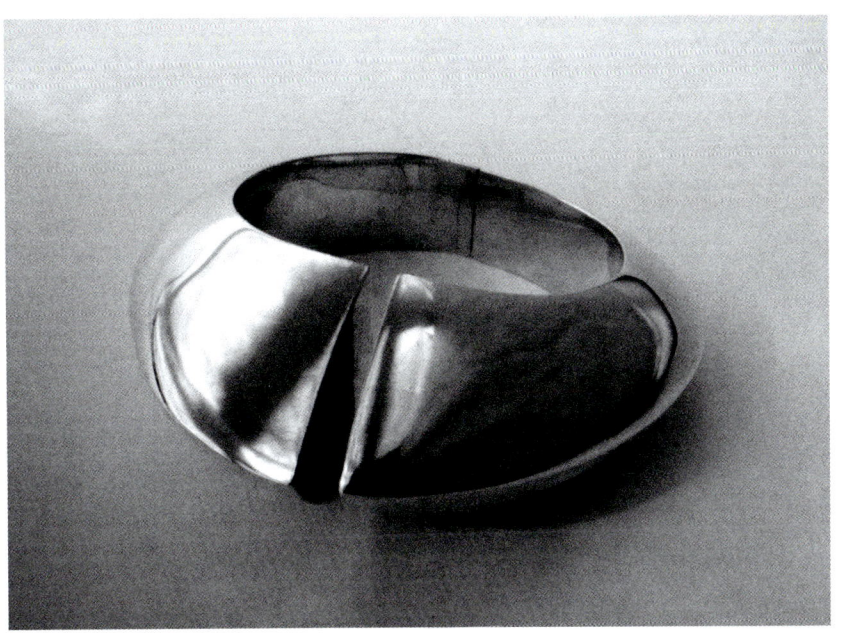

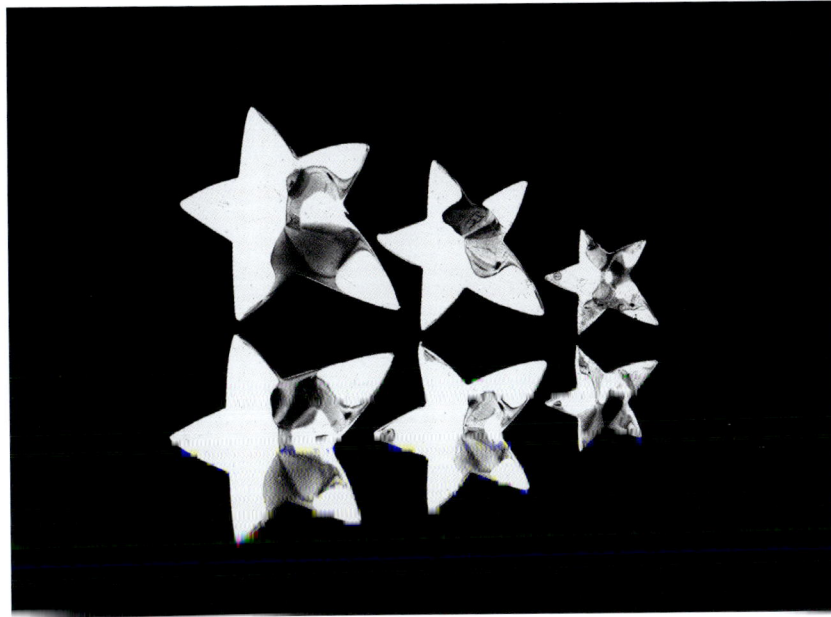

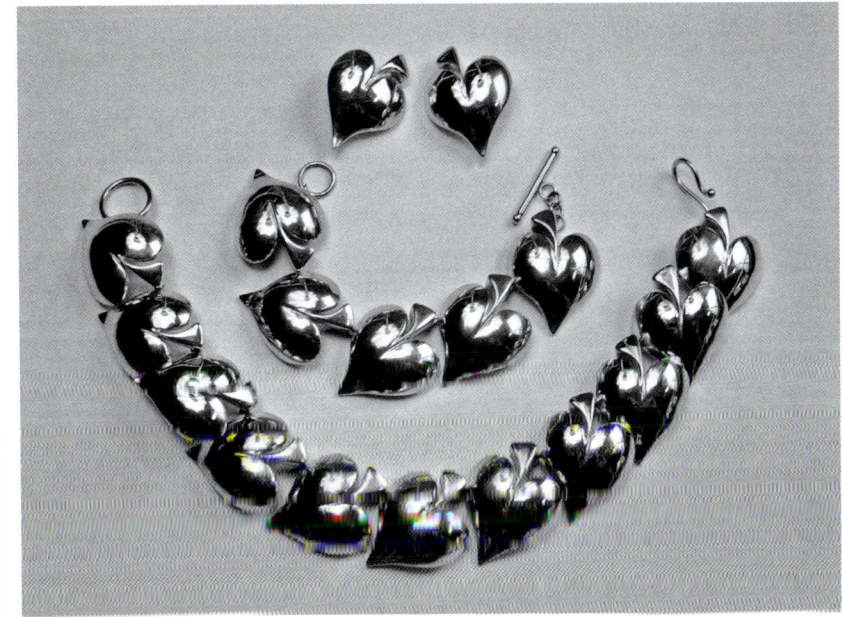

Selected jewelry pieces in mixed materials, late 1980s

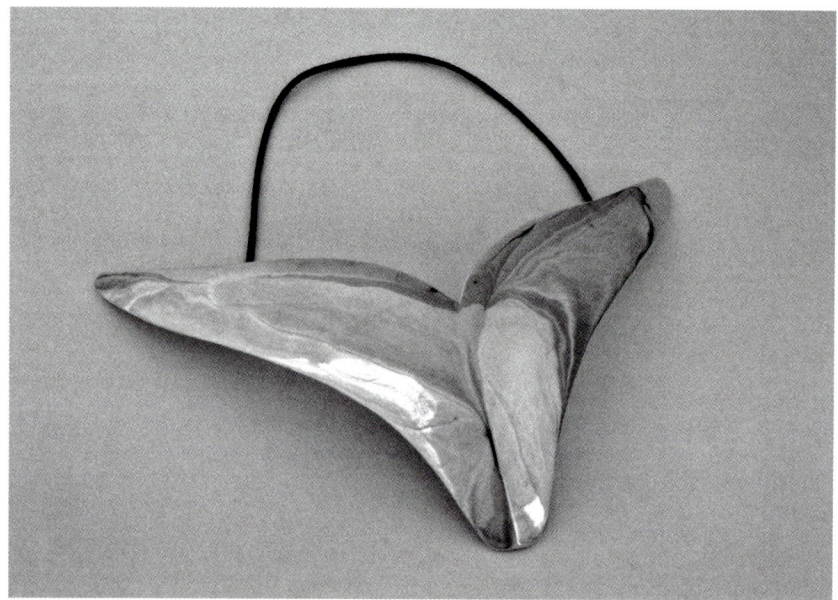

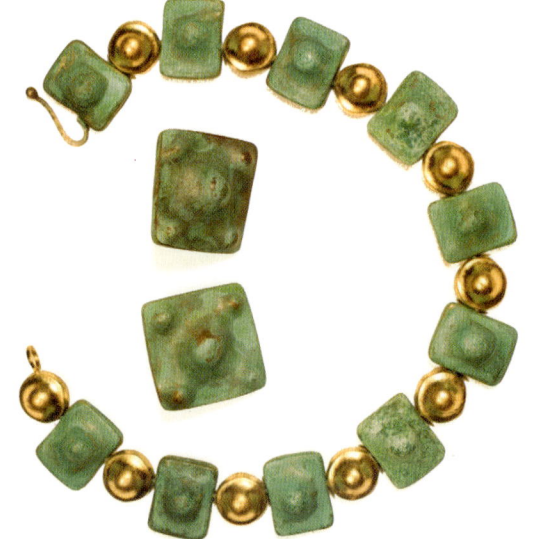

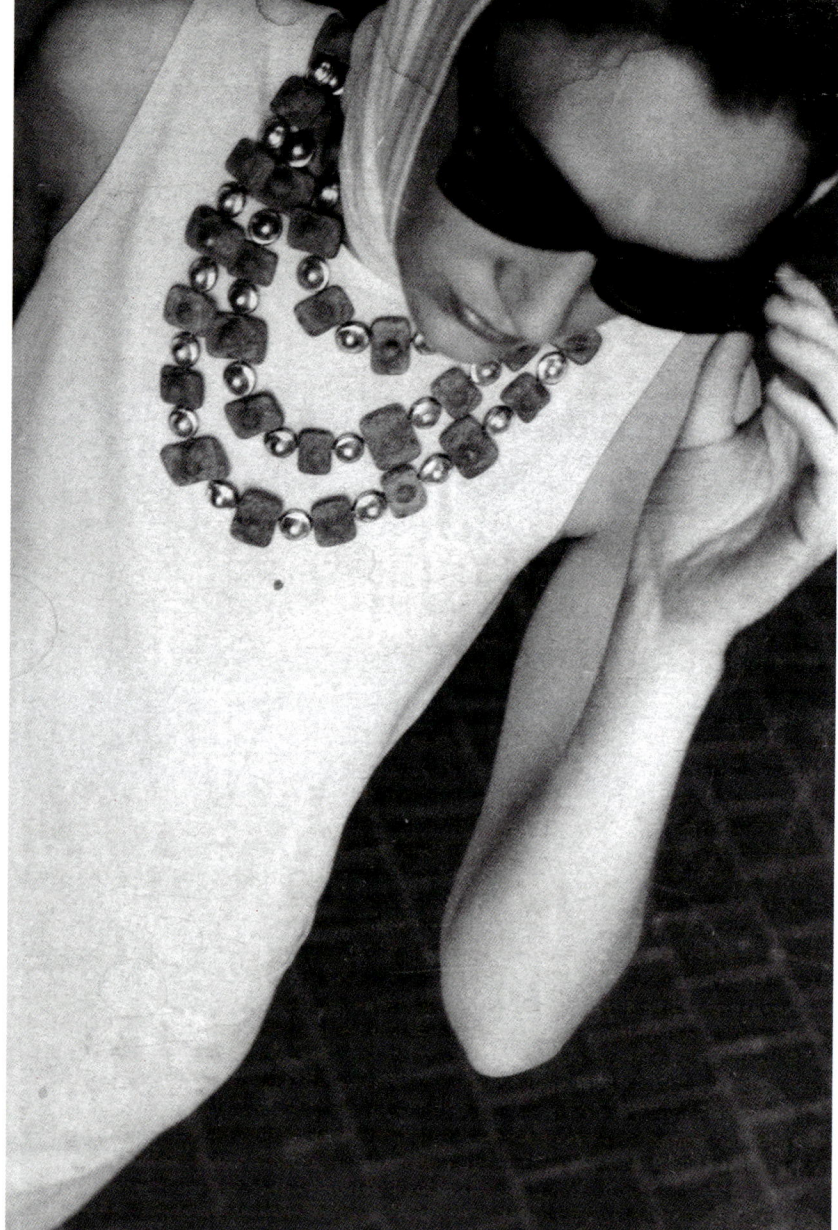

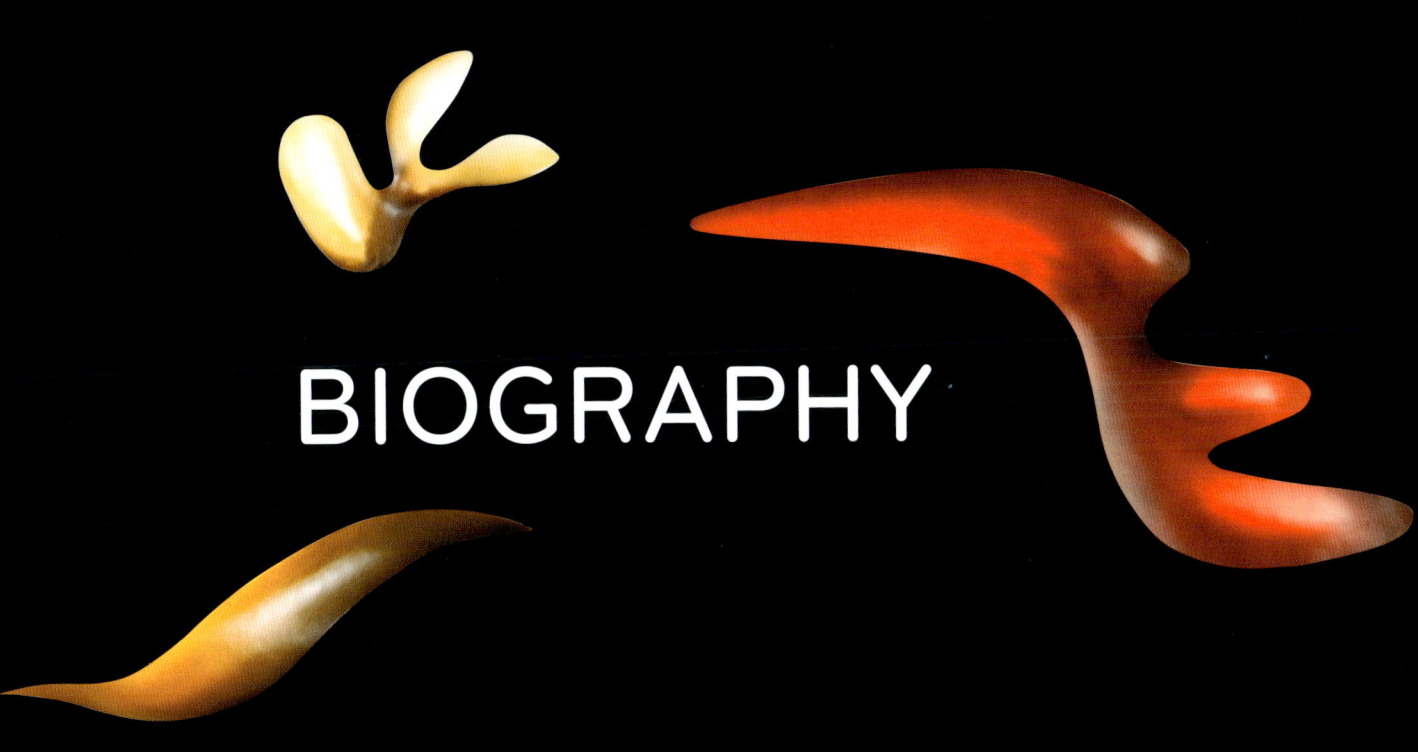

BIOGRAPHY AND EXHIBITIONS

1954
Born in New Haven, CT

1972
Attended Goddard College in Plainfield, VT

1980
Solo exhibition of sculptural jewelry and masks in sterling silver and brass at
Bloomingdale's at The Mall at Chestnut Hill, Chestnut Hill, MA

1982–1985
Sculptural jewelry exhibitions at Artwear, Bloomingdale's, Saks Fifth Avenue,
Macy's and Henri Bendel in New York City

Articles in *Vogue Magazine*, *New York Magazine* and others

1988
Tiffany & Co. of New York commissioned mobiles to be used as window displays

1989–1995
Bi-annual commissions of mobiles and sculptures for Tiffany & Co.
window displays

1991–1992
Solo exhibition of mobiles with Judith N. Wolov Gallery, Design Center, Boston, MA

1993–1996
In conjunction with Tiffany & Co. on Fifth Avenue, began creating small and medium
size mobiles for the L·S Collection on Madison Avenue and in Soho, New York City

1995
Featured in a group exhibition at Pucker Gallery, Boston, MA

1997
Exhibition, *Nature in Motion*, Pucker Gallery, Boston, MA

1997–2015
Created numerous significant commissions for public and private collections

1999
Exhibition, *Movement within Space*, Pucker Gallery, Boston, MA

2001
Exhibition, *Color and Form in Motion*, Pucker Gallery, Boston, MA

2003
Exhibition, *Boldly Balanced*, Pucker Gallery, Boston, MA

2005
Exhibition, *Energy in Motion*, Pucker Gallery, Boston, MA

2007
Exhibition, *Revisiting Nature*, Pucker Gallery, Boston, MA

Exhibition, Harrison Gallery, Williamstown, MA

2009
Exhibition, Harrison Gallery, Williamstown, MA

Exhibition, *Gathering Energy*, Pucker Gallery, Boston, MA

2011
Exhibition, *Icarus*, Fuller Craft Museum, Brockton, MA

Exhibition, *Phase Transformations*, Pucker Gallery, Boston, MA

2013
Exhibition, *Mark Davis*, Harrison Gallery, Boston, MA

Exhibition, *Form. Color. Balance: Recent Work by Mark Davis*, Pucker Gallery, Boston, MA

2015
Exhibition, *Reverberating Gravity: Mobiles by Mark Davis*, Pucker Gallery, Boston, MA

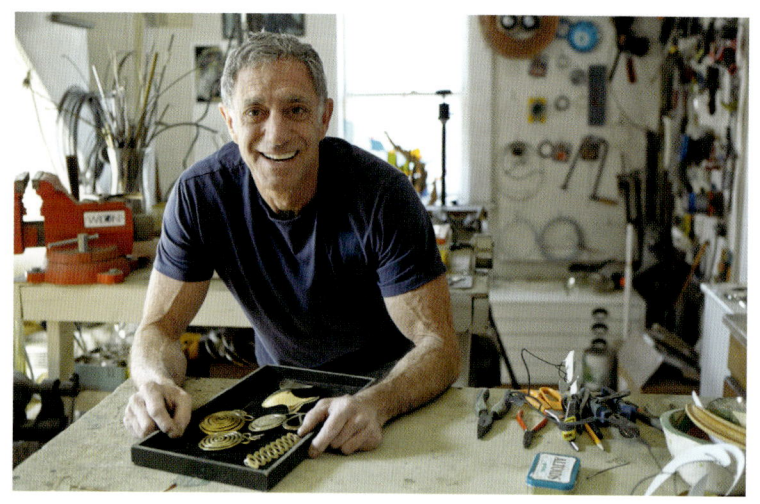

SELECTED PUBLIC AND PRIVATE COLLECTIONS

Congregation Kehillath Israel, Brookline, MA

Gary Trudeau, New York, NY

Healing Waters, Ann & Robert H. Lurie Children's Hospital, Chicago, IL

Howard Stern, New York, NY

Julie Andrews and Blake Edwards, Los Angeles, CA

Lexus Corporation, New York, NY

Liberty Mutual Corporation, Boston, MA

Richard Chamberlain, New York, NY

Rose Museum, Brandeis University, Waltham, MA

Temple Emmanuel, Andover, MA

The Farm, Libertyville, IL

University of Chicago Comer Children's Hospital, Chicago, IL

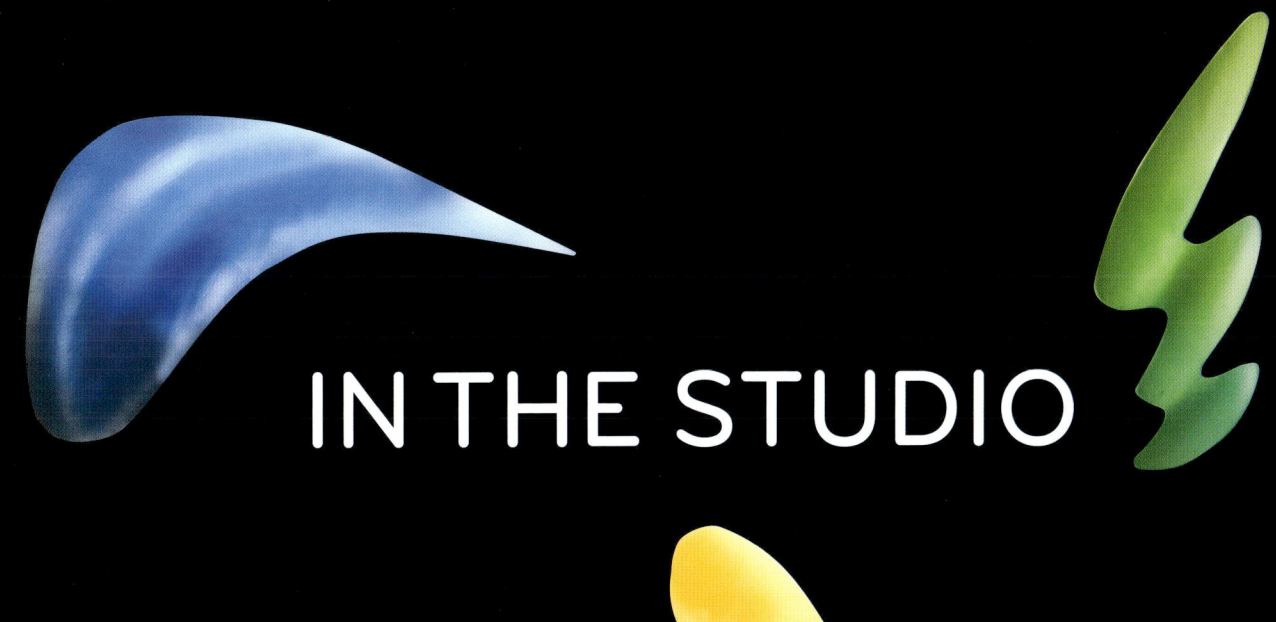

IN THE STUDIO

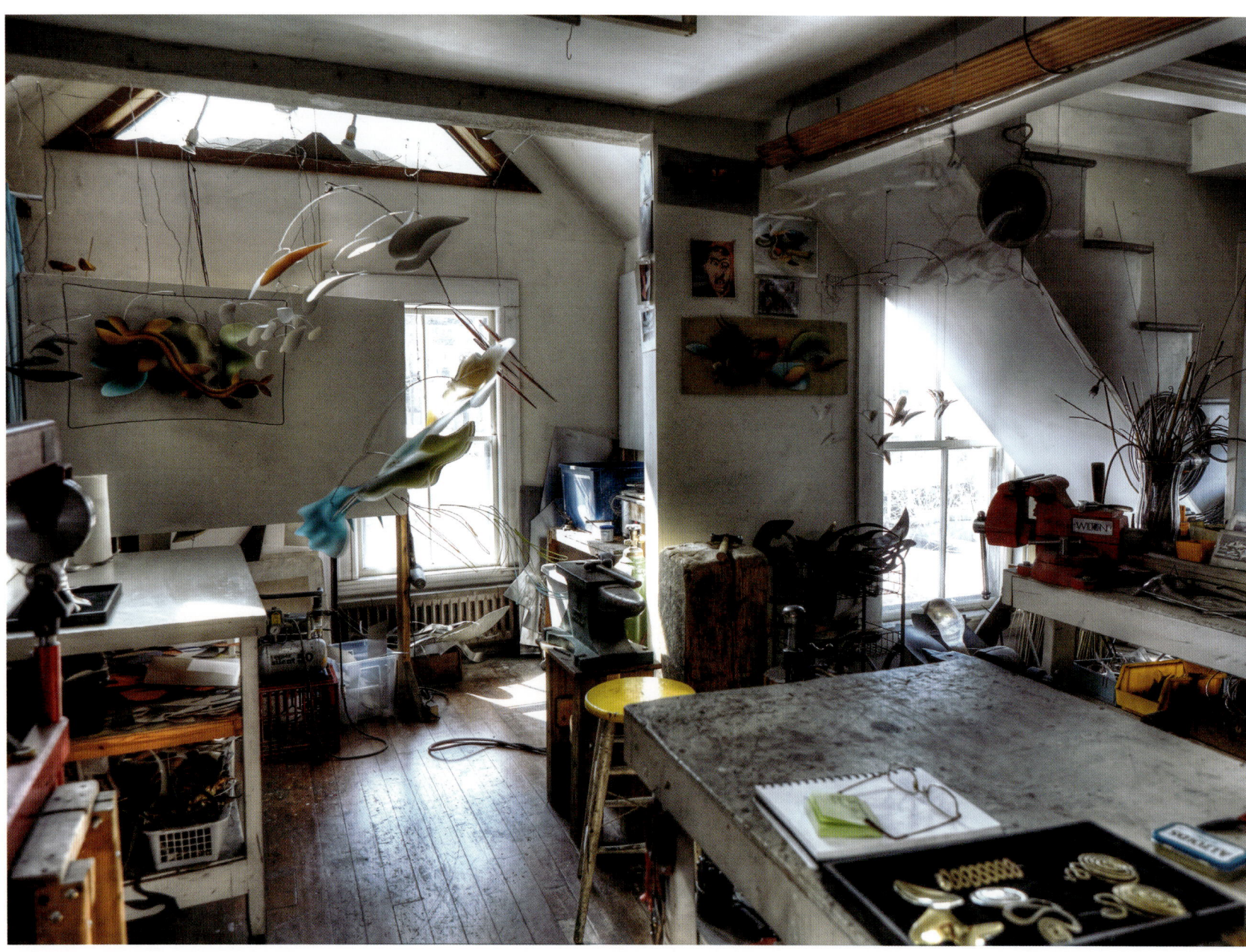

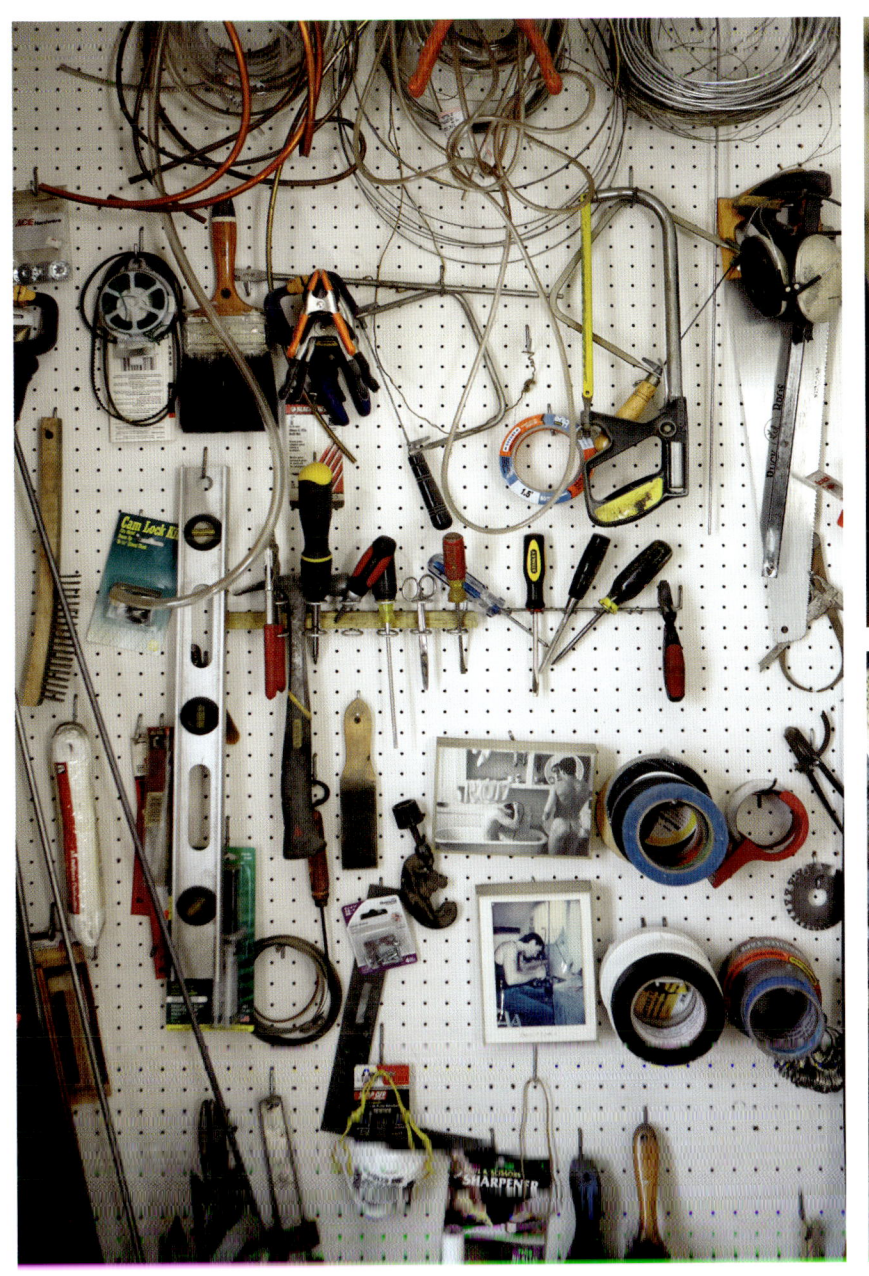

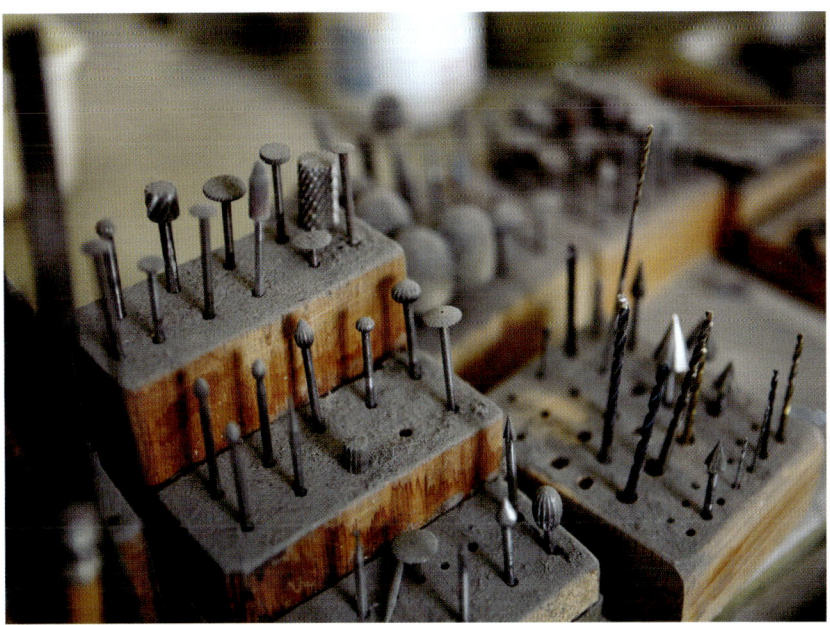

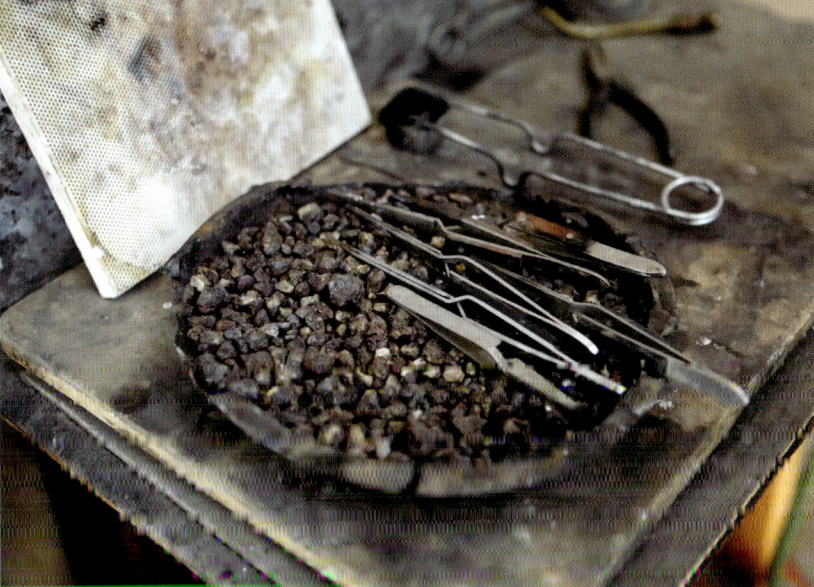

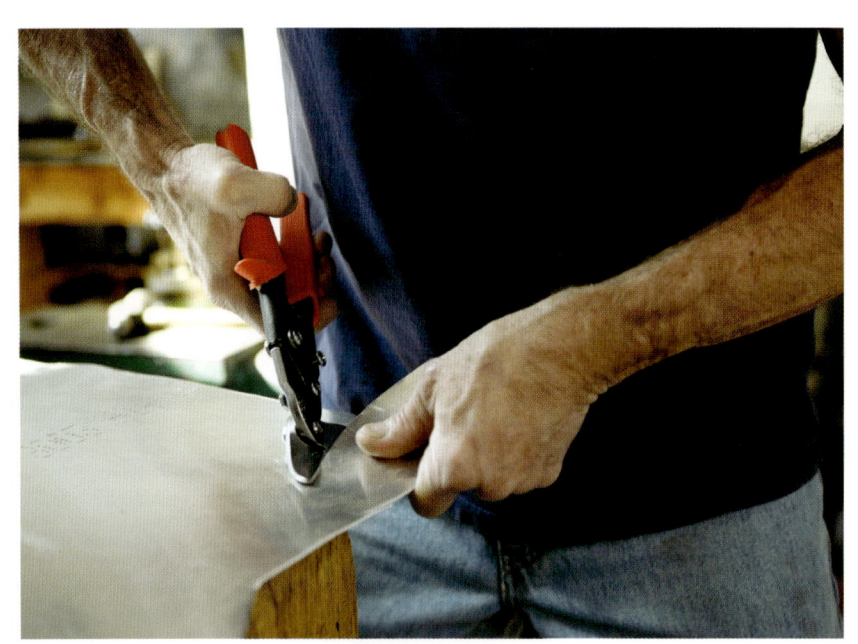
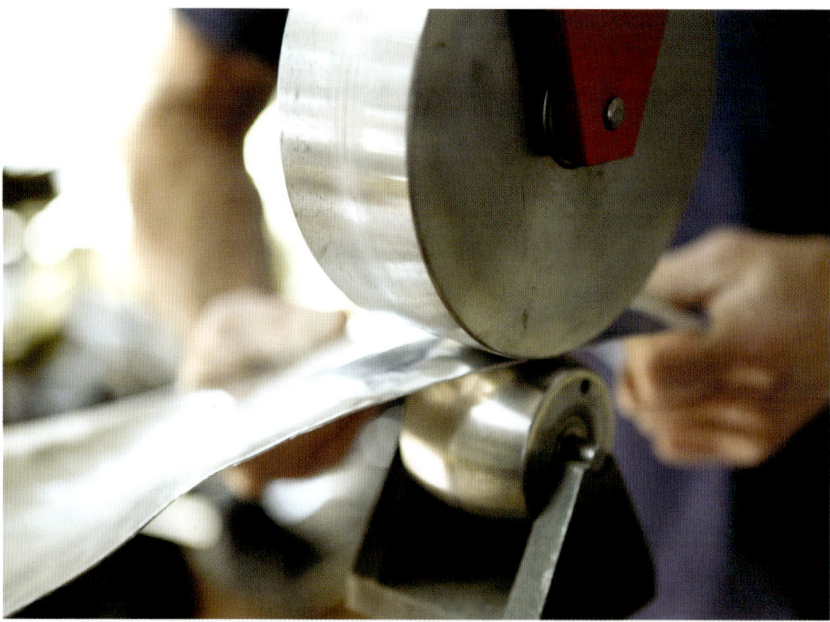

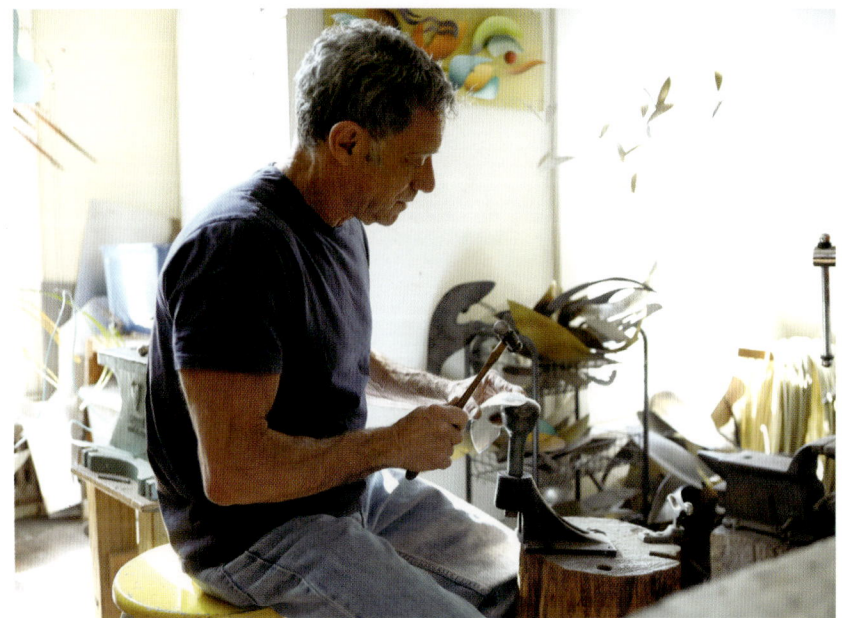
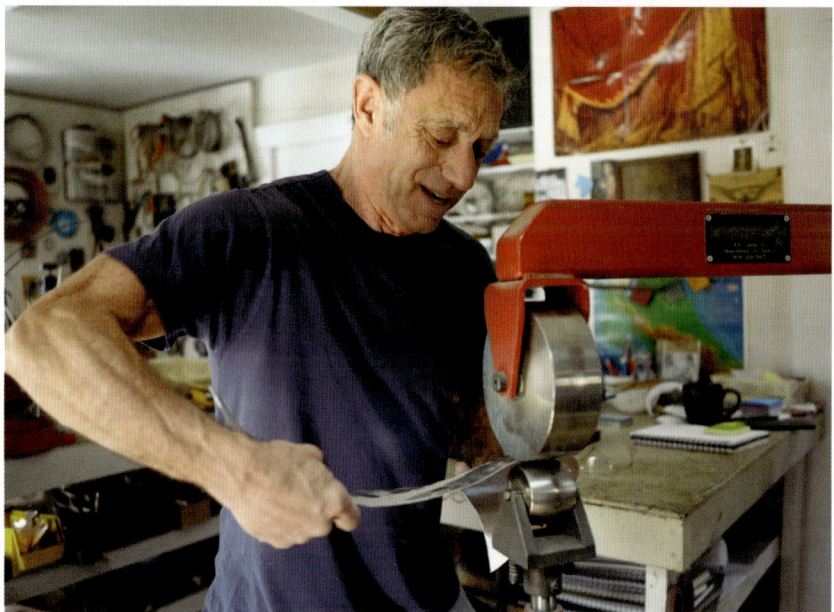

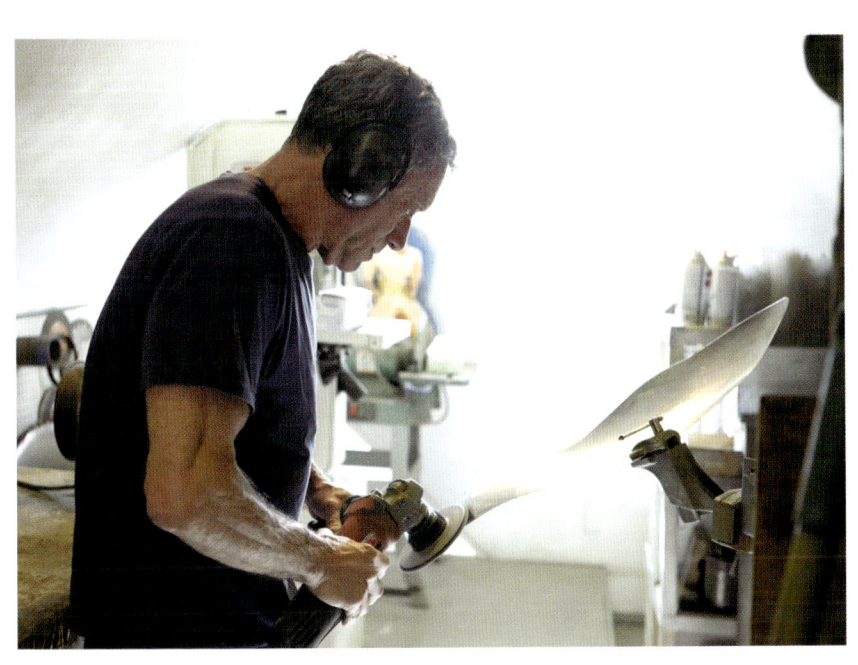
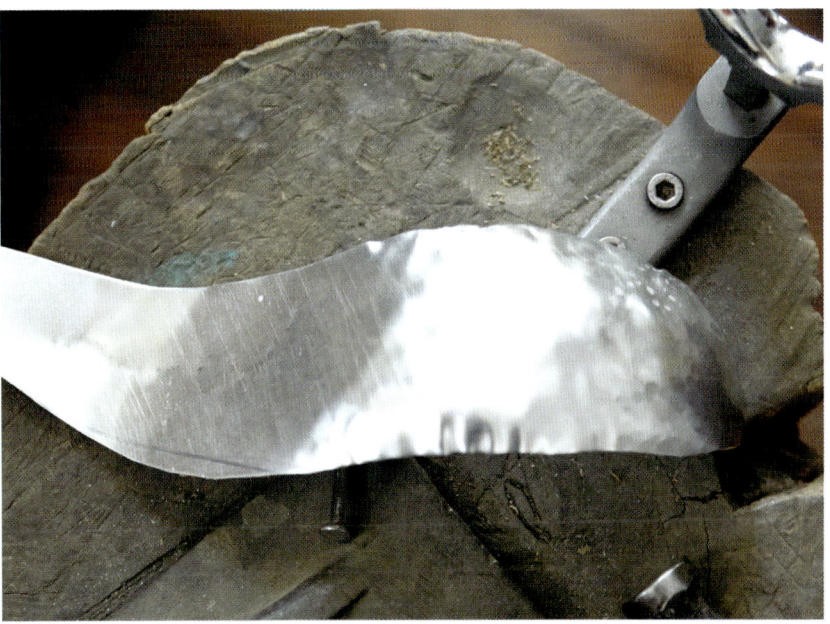

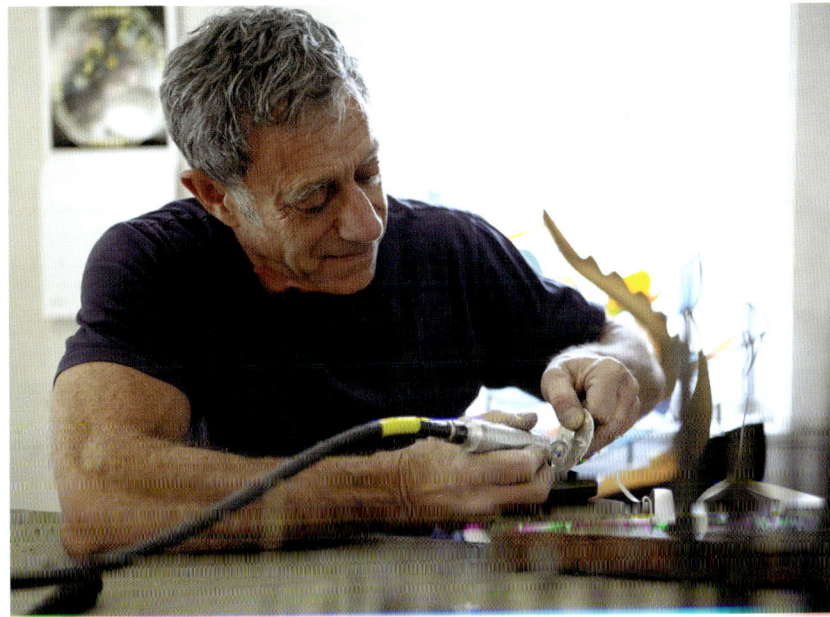
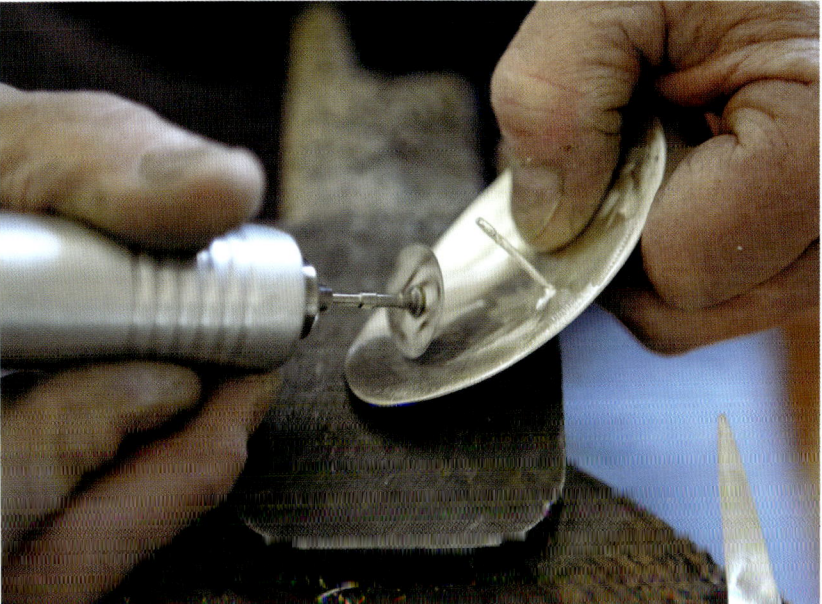

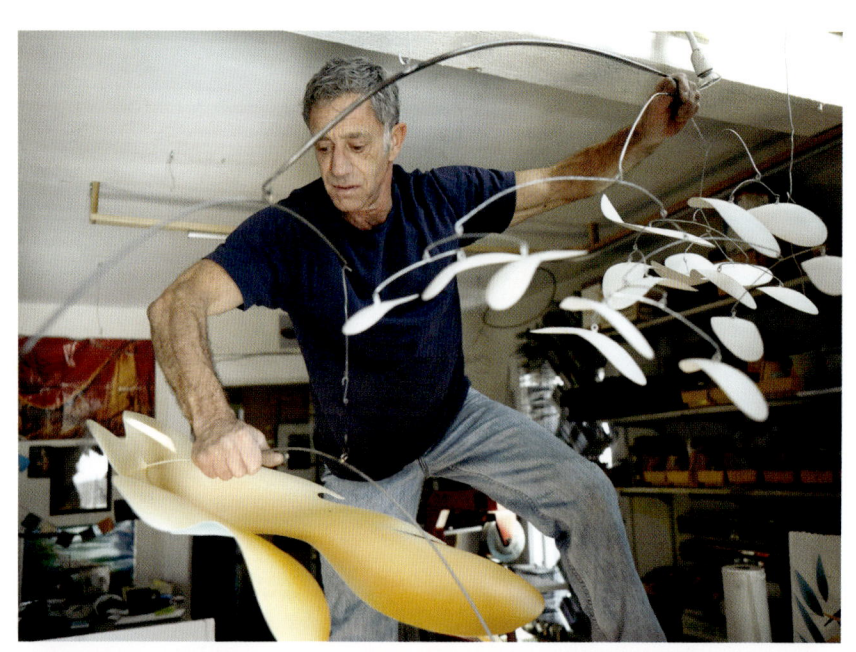

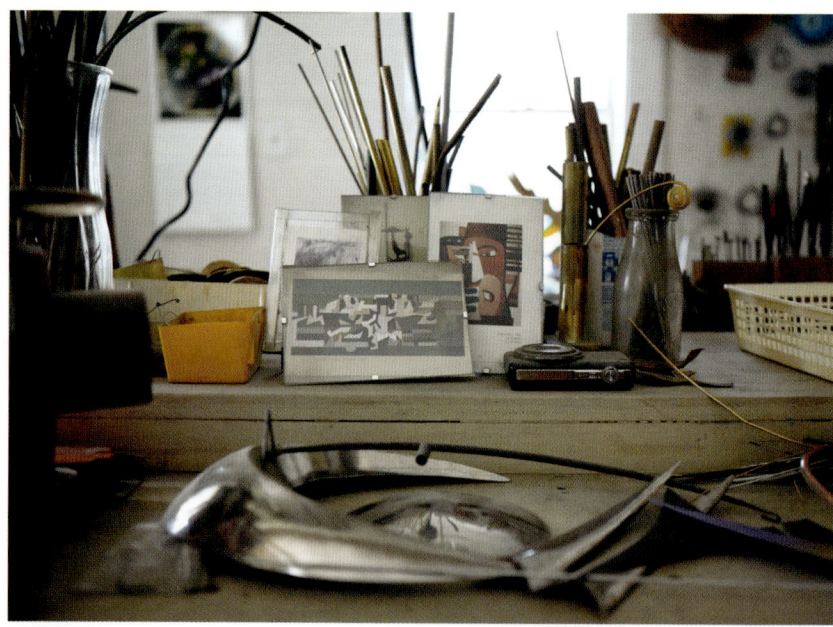

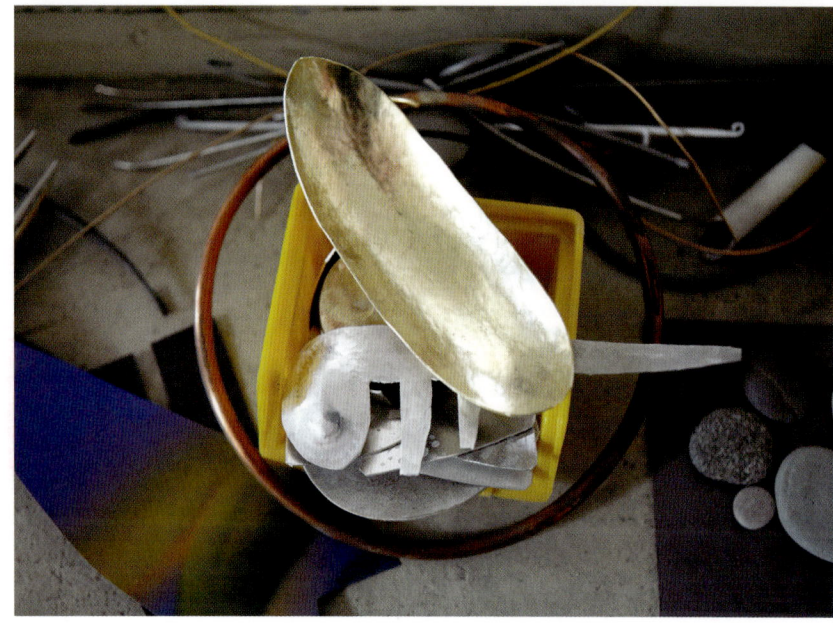

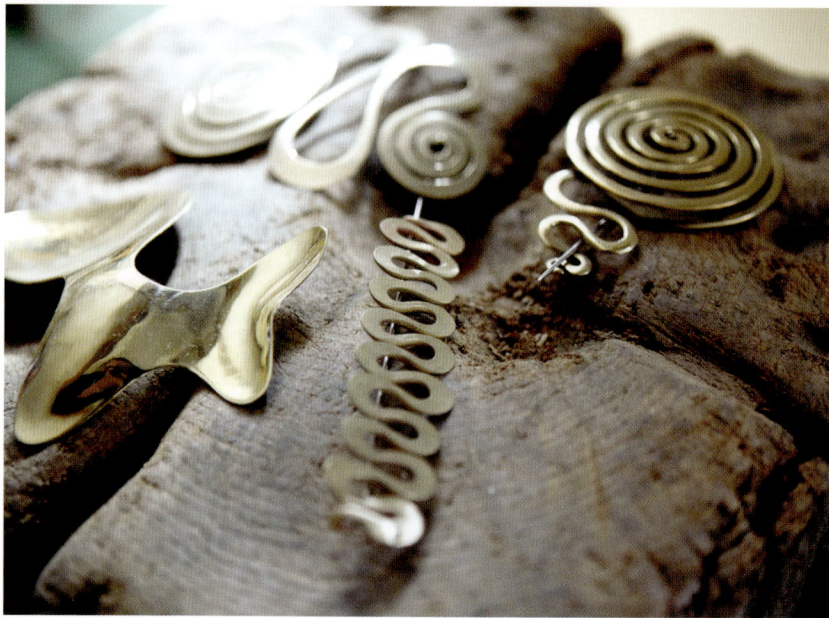

AFTERWORD

*"Whoever said, 'When you are doing what you love to do,
you never work a day in your life.' This is correct."*
— BROTHER THOMAS BEZANSON

Mark Davis's art embodies a great sense of joy and delight. He has created a personal universe of moving colors and forms that expresses positive energy and a life-affirming sensibility. For more than twenty years we have experienced, enjoyed, supported, and shared his ever-growing and changing art. From small, well-crafted mobiles to large, private and public works, Mark continues to fulfill his commitment to excellent artistry and unbounded joy!

He has worked masterfully on over forty commissions, creating a significant collection of *in situ* installations that enliven and enrich diverse public and private spaces and provide a remarkable sense of satisfaction for both the artist and patrons. Mark infuses each work—large or small—with his exceptional creativity and vibrant vision. What a gift his art is to us all!

We are grateful to the following patrons, whose commitment to Mark's art allowed the birth of this book.

- Charles Merrill and Julie Boudreaux
- Larry Singer and Morgan Beucler
- Frank and Jeanne Speizer
- Jonathan M. Zorn

We are also grateful to Destiny Barletta, Tess Mattern, and Leslie Feagley, who have been deeply involved in thoughtfully shaping this volume, and to Jeanne V. Koles for her essay with keen insight into an intense life molded by Mark's creativity and spirit. And especially to Mark we extend our great thanks for a life brimming with art that certainly is an ode to joy.

— BERNARD H. PUCKER
Boston, November 2016

127

The artist dedicates this book to the memory of his mother

YOLANDA ANITA LEISSIANO DAVIS

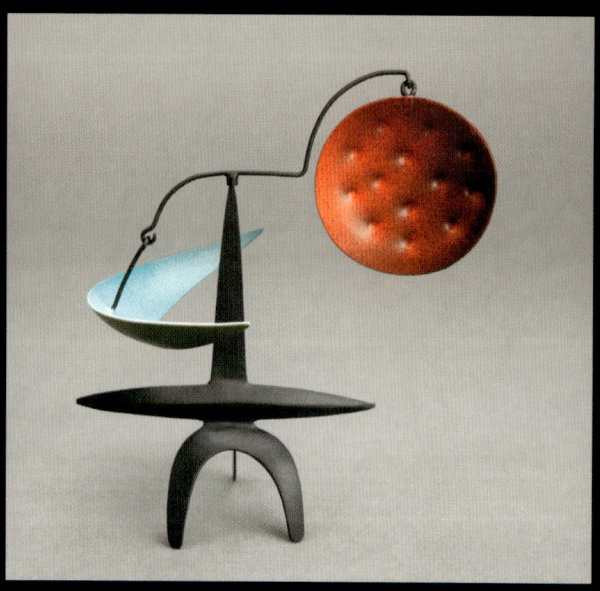

THE FIRST REVOLUTION
Standing mobile in brass and aluminum with steel wires,
and oil and acrylic colors
6.5 x 5.5 x 4"
MD707

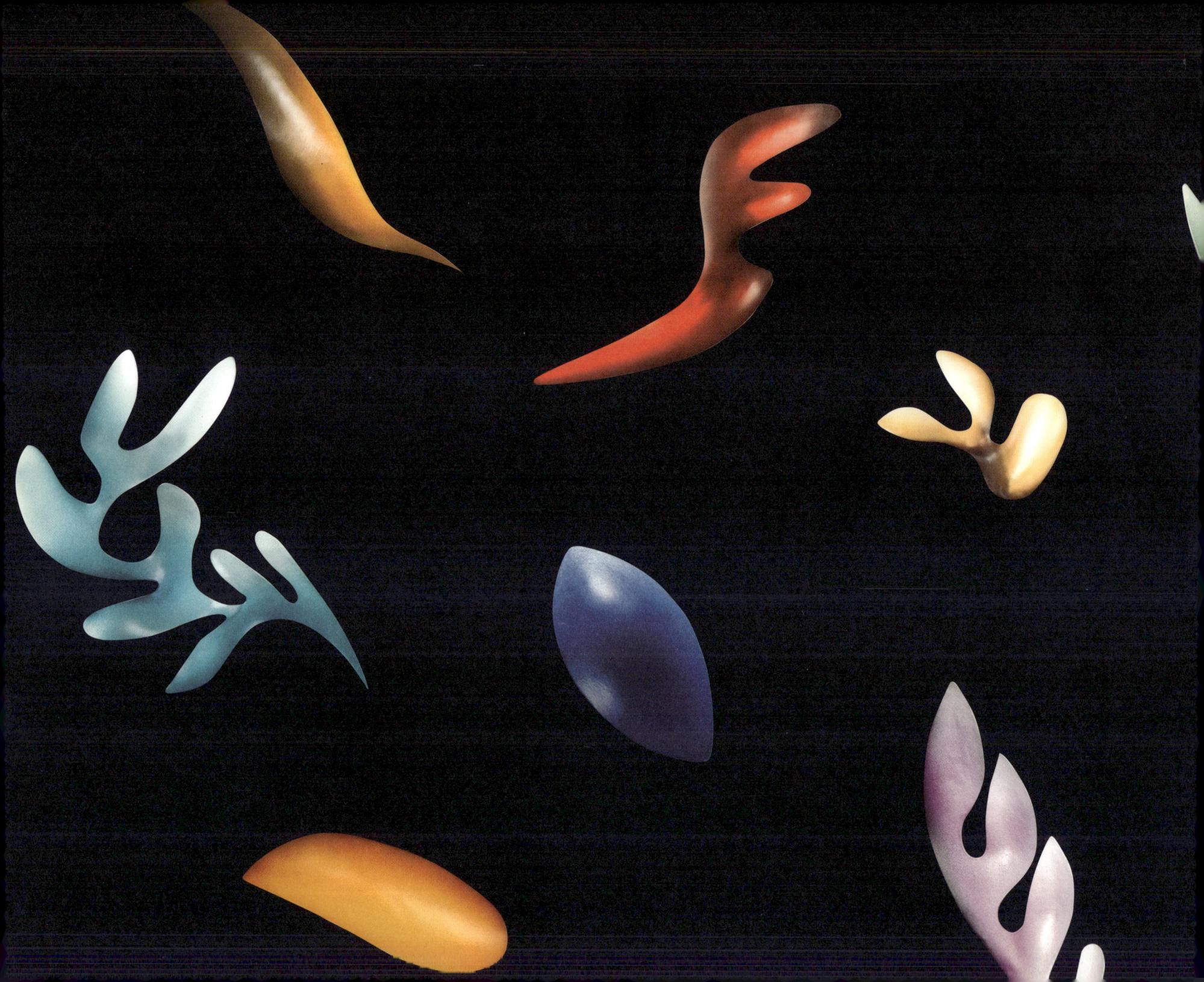